VANISHED

VANISHED

THE SIXTY-YEAR SEARCH FOR
THE MISSING MEN OF WORLD WAR II

———

WIL S. HYLTON

RIVERHEAD BOOKS
a member of Penguin Group (USA)
New York
2013

RIVERHEAD BOOKS
Published by the Penguin Group
Penguin Group (USA) LLC
375 Hudson Street
New York, New York 10014

USA · Canada · UK · Ireland · Australia
New Zealand · India · South Africa · China

penguin.com
A Penguin Random House Company

Library of Congress Cataloging-in-Publication Data
Hylton, Wil S.
Vanished : the sixty-year search for the missing men of World War II / by Wil S. Hylton.
p.   cm.
ISBN 978-1-59448-727-9
1. World War, 1939–1945—Aerial operations, American.   2. World War, 1939–1945—Campaigns—Palau.
3. World War, 1939–1945—Missing in action—United States.   4. World War, 1939–1945—Missing in
action—Palau.   5. Aircraft accidents—Investigation—Palau.   6. Airmen—United States—Biography.   I. Title.
D790.H95   2013   2013016759
940.54'26966—dc23

Printed in the United States of America
3   5   7   9   10   8   6   4   2

Cover photo by Tim Hetherington

Book design by Meighan Cavanaugh

For the missing

CONTENTS

Prologue   *1*

ONE: RUMORS   *7*

TWO: WRECKAGE   *17*

THREE: AIRMEN   *36*

FOUR: DISCOVERY   *51*

FIVE: LANDFALL   *65*

SIX: ARNETT   *79*

SEVEN: PLEDGE   *95*

EIGHT: COMBAT   *109*

NINE: CONTACT *123*

TEN: WASTELAND *138*

ELEVEN: SECRET POLICE *152*

TWELVE: LAST DAYS *164*

THIRTEEN: BREAKTHROUGH *180*

FOURTEEN: FALLOUT *197*

FIFTEEN: RECOVERY *205*

SIXTEEN: TRAPPED *223*

SEVENTEEN: CLOSURE *236*

Bibliography *241*

Notes *247*

Acknowledgments *267*

Image Credits *271*

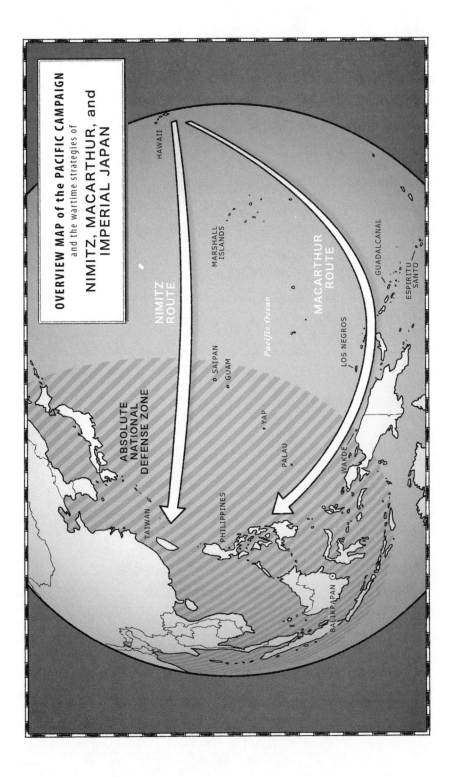

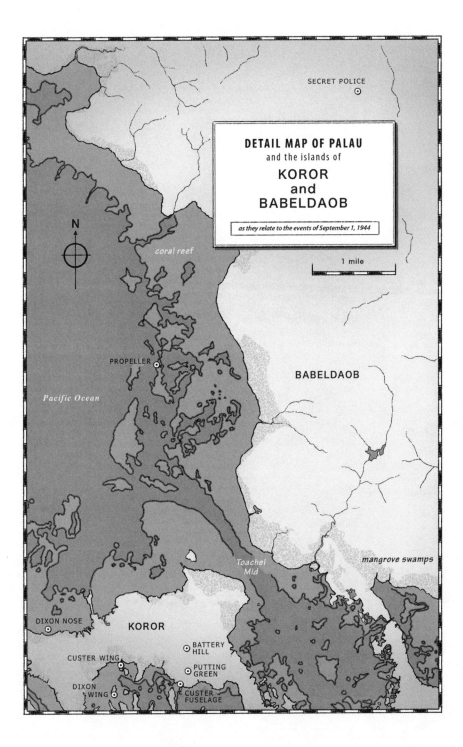

DETAIL MAP OF PALAU
and the islands of
KOROR
and
BABELDAOB

as they relate to the events of September 1, 1944

SECRET POLICE

1 mile

coral reef

PROPELLER

BABELDAOB

Pacific Ocean

Toachel Mid

mangrove swamps

DIXON NOSE

KOROR

BATTERY HILL

CUSTER WING

PUTTING GREEN

DIXON WING

CUSTER FUSELAGE

. . . when again bright morning dyes the sky
And waving fronds above shall touch the rain,
We give you this—that in those times
We will remember.

—HANDWRITTEN EPITAPH
BETIO ISLAND,
TARAWA

PROLOGUE

On a warm spring morning in 2008, a rumpled archaeologist named Eric Emery stood at the edge of a massive barge in the middle of the Pacific Ocean and glared down into the water.

All around him, the barge was a hive of activity. Two dozen young men scurried about the deck, preparing for the day's events. At one end, a small group huddled by a contraption made of two-by-fours, tugging at its joints and examining its design. At the other end, a long steel ramp descended to the water, with a speedboat parked at the bottom and a cluster of scuba divers on board. The rest of the barge was mostly filled with cargo-shipping containers, each one placed just far enough from the others to divide the deck into a series of hallways and rooms. One of the rooms was set up as a medical station, with an examination table in the middle and a stretcher propped against the wall. Another was arranged like a dive locker, with masks and fins and wetsuits hanging from a taut line. A third room functioned as a communications hub, with blinking machinery and streams of wire that converged on a small wooden desk, where a young man fiddled with the knobs of a yellow plastic box. The air all around was dank and heavy with morning rain and the sky was a gray camouflage of clouds and the tips of small islands peeked through a swarthy mist on the horizon, but standing at the edge of the barge Emery seemed oblivious to it all—the mist, the noise, the men, the islands— glaring down into the water as if daring it to a duel.

Even at a glance, it was obvious that Emery was unlike the other men on board. They were young and fit and clean-shaven, with tattoos of mermaids and dragons that snaked across long sinews of muscle. Emery was a dozen years older, stocky and grizzled, with deep lines etched around his eyes, his beard at least a week grown in, his hair an unruly explosion of wire, and his faded khaki T-shirt matted to his chest by a combination of rain and sweat. He smiled little and spoke less. From time to time, one of the other men would pause for a moment to study him, as if noticing their leader for the first time. Later, when they thought back on Emery, they would marvel at how little they knew him, how little he said or gave away, even at the end.

Most of the men also knew little about one another. Many had never met before and would never meet again. They had been pulled together from all four corners of the fighting forces—soldiers, sailors, airmen, and Marines—with each man chosen for his individual talent. There were deep-sea divers trained by the Navy's experimental school in Florida to endure underwater pressure so extreme that the depths were considered secret. There were bomb defusers just back from Iraq with tired eyes and easy smiles and the latest operational intelligence on IED design. There were Air Force historians trained to identify, from the smallest fragment of metal or plastic, the make and model of any US aircraft built since 1941. There were forensic scientists who could do the same with bones, studying a single sliver or shard to determine where it belonged in a human body, and the age of the body to which it belonged, and sometimes even the gender or ethnicity. There was a physician on board who specialized in the mystical healing properties of superoxygenated fields. There were fishermen equipped with massive spears to haul parrot fish and unicorn fish from the depths and grill them over an open flame on deck. Together, they would spend six weeks on the barge, and then they would disperse again: to the desert, to the jungle, to the rain forests of New Guinea or the airless peaks of the Himalayas. But here, now, in the deep cerulean nowhere of the Pacific Ocean, on a tiny archipelago more than a thousand miles from the mainland, they had come together for a single purpose: to bring up what they found below.

Of course, no one knew just what that was. That was the question; that was the mission. The coordinates of the barge had been guarded for years by the American and island governments. Only a few divers had ever been down, and those who had weren't sure what they'd seen. Or rather, they knew what they had seen, but they couldn't imagine what they hadn't. There were secrets still buried in the sand below, mysteries they had come to uncover. But the islands had a way of keeping their secrets. Sometimes they seemed to keep time itself.

On a clear day the islands appeared to sprinkle the water like a thousand emeralds on a plate of blue glass, each one glittering and distinct in the brilliant tropical sun, but from the sky you could see that it was an illusion: the islands were not islands at all. Beneath the surface, they were all fused together into a single underwater mesa, which rose ten thousand feet from the seafloor and leveled off just below the waterline. What seemed to be, from ship or shore, hundreds of individual islands were really just the slight hills and rises on the mesa top, bumps that rose a fraction too high and breached the open air, basking in the equatorial heat and decorating themselves with vines and flowers and carnivorous plants. In between those islands, the water remained shallow over the mesa, a pale blue expanse that shimmered like a ghost against the black ocean all around. The shallow water was warm, too, and brimming with ocean life—six-foot clams and sea snakes, octopodes and sharks, all taking refuge from the surrounding depths.

The people of the islands had also come for refuge. Anthropologists believed they were a mixture of races drawn from a thousand miles all around, lost sailors and adventurers, prospectors and rogues, converging over centuries on the coral shores to form a people in the jungle. The people did not have a creation story; they had many. One told of a girl who ate too much and grew enormous and toppled over in the water, the curves of her shoulders and breasts and knees forming the various islands. Another told of a young woman who offered food to the gods when they were hungry and was immortalized in death as the largest island, with her children arrayed around her. Many of the island myths featured women; women held special power on the islands. Women elected the tribal chiefs. Women controlled the tribal land. There were many princesses on the islands, each with a special necklace made of shells.

The anthropologist Emery knew the islands. He knew their history, their waters, their traditions, their stories. He had studied the islands with the singular zeal of a man who needs to understand. He had traveled to the southern end of the archipelago, across turbulent water in a small boat, to seek out the island of Peleliu (*pella'-loo*), still littered with the wreckage of war, with tanks and trucks racked on their sides from the aerial bomb blasts of World War II and the skeletons of Japanese soldiers lingering at the mouths of caves before a roiling cacophony of bats within. Emery had tasted the island delicacy of bat soup, a whole dead animal floating in broth, and he had made a pilgrimage to the marine lake at the center of another island, where a special breed of jellyfish evolved without stingers. He had stripped off his shirt at the edge of the water to dive in, his body suspended in a haze of gelatinous yellow orbs, a strange euphoria washing over him as vivid as a fever dream. He had studied the islands' colonial history, stories of mineral exploitation and plunder, and he knew in some private place that what he needed from the islands was more precious than any stone. What he needed, he could not find anywhere else. What he needed, no one else could find.

Eric Emery's journey to the islands marked the end of a personal quest. It was a journey that began a decade earlier, ten thousand miles away, on a small helicopter crossing an alpine lake in the treeless *páramo* of the Andes, with a terrifying shriek as the chopper fell from the sky, its blades colliding with the water, his lungs filling as his mind went dark. Or maybe it began even before that, at the old gas station on Lake Champlain, filling up scuba tanks with his father and casting off in the ragged sailboat, the one rule etched forever in his mind: *Never stop breathing.* It was a rule that Emery had only broken once, and had been trying to mend ever since. In a sense, he had spent his whole life preparing for this mission. In another sense, he'd already died for it.

In that, he knew he was not alone. All across the American landscape, men and women were waiting for him to return from the islands with answers. Some had been waiting all their lives; some felt they were waiting for their lives to begin. When Emery stood on the barge in the din and clatter of men at work, in the warm, wet air, under the scent of the shallow sea, he was forever conscious of those men and women and all that they had lost. He thought of the young soldiers who vanished on these islands six decades earlier, and of the haunting stories their families passed down through generations. He thought of the first military team that came to find them in 1945. He thought of the strange, pale doctor from California who had taken up the search, returning to the islands year after year for reasons Emery could only imagine. He thought of the retired colonel in Hawaii who had built a special Army unit to find the lost men, hiring hundreds of scientists and explorers who were trained as Emery had been. Few of those scientists, officers, explorers, and family members had ever met. Few of them even knew the others existed. They were all separated by time and distance, by fate and grief and chance, yet he knew that, like the islands themselves, their separateness was an illusion. Beneath the surface, they were all fused together; together they formed an archipelago of grief rooted in this forgotten place. Now the islands called them back.

RUMORS

When Tommy Doyle's mom died, in 1992, Tommy inherited a big wooden trunk. It was about four feet long and two feet wide, and sitting on the floor of his ranch house in West Texas, it came up to his knee. Tommy could remember seeing that trunk all his life, tucked at the foot of his mother's bed with books and blankets piled on top, but he'd never looked inside. There was always something private in the way his mom regarded the trunk, so for a while, Tommy left it shut.

His wife, Nancy, was more curious, but she didn't want to seem nosy. "I decided to let him open it in his own time," she said later. "But it seemed like he never would." Nancy was patient. She waited weeks, then months, then a year. Tommy never opened the trunk. He dragged it to a back room, shut the door, and walked away.

Nancy knew enough about Tommy to guess what bothered him. There

were painful rumors in his past, stories that cast a shadow over his life—
over who he was, who his daddy had been, and why Tommy never knew
him. Those were things that Tommy and his mom never discussed. There
might be clues inside the trunk, and he wasn't about to start looking for
them now.

Tommy had been just fifteen months old when his dad shipped off to
war in 1944, and Jimmie Doyle never came back. Or anyway, that was the
official story. That's the story his mother told him: His daddy's plane
went down in the Pacific Ocean, some patch of islands called Palau. The
crew was never found.

But Tommy heard another story growing up, one he wasn't supposed
to hear. As a kid, he heard his uncles whispering. Jimmie was still alive,
they said. He'd survived the crash. He'd come back from the war. He was
living in California with a new wife and two daughters. He just didn't care
about Tommy anymore.

Tommy never believed that story. Mostly, he didn't. But he wondered.
In time, he grew into a powerful kid, tall and fast, played basketball on
the state championship team, starred in high school football. In one
game, he scored off two interceptions and kicked the winning field goal.
But underneath, the hurt and suspicion coursed through Tommy's life.

Nothing about the family stories made sense. If his dad was dead, then
why did the military send his mom letters that said they were looking for
him? Why did the Army say that some of the men on his plane escaped,
but they never said which ones? And why didn't Tommy's mom remarry,
when at least two good men had asked? She and Tommy scraped by on
nothing. For a while, they lived in an apartment with no front door. But
she never told Tommy that she missed his dad, or loved him, or hoped he
would come back. She rarely mentioned Jimmie at all: never told Tommy
what his father did or loved, never described his voice or his laugh. She
kept Jimmie close, like she couldn't stand to share what little she had left,
not with anyone, not even Tommy.

Football was supposed to be Tommy's ticket. He got a full ride to Texas Tech in 1961 and joined the Air Force ROTC to earn money on the side. For the first time in Tommy's life, he had a future and not just a past. If he played hard, he might go pro; if not, he'd stick with the Air Force and follow his dad into the sky.

From the first day of practice, Tommy took off. By junior year, he was on the starting lineup alongside future pros like Donny Anderson and Dave Parks; by the end of that year, when Parks was chosen as the first pick in the NFL draft, Tommy was tied with him for the most touchdown receptions, and he'd set a school record for the most in a single game. "He had great hands," Donny Anderson said. "We called him 'Touchdown Tommy.'" Anderson got the call in 1965, drafted by the Packers in the first round for more money than anyone in history. A lot of people thought Tommy Doyle would be next. A lot of people still think he might have been, if things had broken differently. Or if they hadn't broken at all.

It started with his shoulders in spring practice. They felt loose, wobbly, sore. He'd go to make a play and his arms just wouldn't do it. He put his joints on ice and slept in the locker room all summer to stay close to the rehab weights. When that didn't work, he moved to defensive end—but the play was rough and Tommy was lean. He kept taking hard hits. In one game, he came down wrong on a jump and both of his legs got crushed. By the middle of the season, between his shoulders and his knees, he knew his game was over. He lost his spot on the starting lineup, then his place on the team. Then he had to give up his position in ROTC, and with it, his last hope for the future.

Tommy was working in a windowless room at an airplane factory in North Texas when a friend introduced him to Nancy. She came from a prominent family near Dallas, but after she and Tommy got together, she followed him back to West Texas. They got married, bought a ramshackle house in the town of Snyder, and Tommy took a job coaching football at the local school. While Dave Parks roared through a decade in the NFL and Donny Anderson won two Super Bowls, Tommy was on the fields of West Texas shouting for teenagers to hustle. Then a new head coach came in and fired everybody, including Tommy.

A friend was starting an oil company and Tommy went all in. He poured his retirement money into the business, and he poured in Nancy's, too. Then the oil market bottomed out, and Tommy lost it all again.

Now he was in his late thirties with no job, no savings, no plan, no dreams, and two young kids, one of whom was sick. "I was just born crooked," his son, Casey Doyle, said. One day it was asthma wracking Casey's lungs; another day, he was coughing up blood. His little legs were so weak he had to wear metal braces. The medical bills were crushing. One morning, Tommy took Casey to a new doctor and spent the whole day waiting to be seen. At five o'clock the doctor came out to explain that Tommy's name was on a list of people who couldn't pay.

Tommy took any job he could find. He mowed lawns. He patched leaky plumbing. He re-grouted tile. He took a job at the local bank, but the oil crash was hurting banks, too. When one of Tommy's friends got laid off, she went home and shot herself. When the bank called in a loan on another guy, he threatened to blow up the branch—and the whole town came out at three o'clock to see if it would happen. In a good week, Tommy might catch a job building a shed in someone's yard. In a bad one, he turned to his friends in the church for help.

When another coaching job came up, Tommy Doyle grabbed it. It was only junior high, but he figured that was a blessing in disguise. This was West Texas, after all. A varsity coach was never safe. A few bad seasons and he'd be packing. Tommy had been down that road before. He promised himself that he'd never put ambition over his kids. When the high school offered him a varsity coaching position, he took a JV spot instead. When another school offered to make him head coach, Tommy thanked them anyway. For twenty-five years, he stayed under the radar, mostly running the JV team and helping with varsity on the side. "He did that for us," Casey said. "He did that for his family and he never said a word."

But inside, Tommy always wondered. Not about coaching, about everything else. He wondered what else might have been. What would have been, if his dad had come home. He wondered who he might have become, and what he could have given his own kids. He wondered if there was anything to those old family stories. Was it possible that his dad survived? If so, how long? Did he really come back? Why would he refuse to see Tommy? Was there any explanation that could make it all okay?

Tommy pushed the questions down, but they were always there. The slightest mention of his dad would bring the old coach to tears. The doubt lingered inside Tommy like a weight. It was there when he drove to work in the morning, and when he came home at night, unfolding his long, sore body to watch a game tape. It was there when he called out drills on the football field, and when his kids opened their presents on Christmas morning. Sometimes it seemed to Tommy as though he'd spent his whole life waiting for something. Waiting for a future that never came. Waiting for answers to make sense of the past. Waiting for a sign of that twenty-five-year-old kid with the cocky grin and jaunty hat, the rascal eyes that stared back at Tommy from the one good portrait he'd ever seen. On weekends, his mother came to the house and played with the kids and helped in the kitchen, but she never mentioned Tommy's dad. She never asked Tommy what he heard, or believed, never told him what she knew. Everything stayed packed up and locked away, pushed out of view like the trunk.

FOR NANCY, walking past the trunk was a kind of test. It was Tommy's past and Tommy's choice and she wanted to let him make it, but it wasn't like Nancy to leave a closed door shut. She loved Tommy all the way through, but they were as different as they were in love. When something bothered Tommy, his voice would fade to a whisper and his whole laconic frame would settle into a cryogenic stillness. Not Nancy. She was just about half his size, but she seemed to occupy twice the space, with a high clear voice and biting wit that called out what she saw. When Nancy walked into a room, the lights got a little brighter. When something in the room upset her, the lights got brighter still.

Nancy came from a conservative family, devout in the Church of Christ. Growing up, she'd always kept her faith, but she wore it her own way. She was the daughter who might turn up in town wearing a short skirt and go-go boots, the one who might miss curfew by a lot. When Nancy announced that she was heading off to study at Abilene Christian College, her parents prayed that she'd come home on the arm of a handsome preacher. Instead, she came home with Tommy—a Methodist, a football player, a kid from the West Texas nowhere. "It didn't go over so well at first," Casey Doyle said with a chuckle. But Nancy's family knew better than to try to talk her out of something. They welcomed Tommy and watched him closely, and soon enough they loved him, too.

Back in Snyder, Nancy set about sanding Tommy's edges. They left his family church to attend the local Church of Christ three times a week. At home, there wasn't any drinking or smoking or dancing or cursing, except that one time Tommy said, "Crap," and if little Casey or his sister, Brandi, forgot the rules, well, Nancy helped them remember.

But walking past the trunk involved a different kind of faith for Nancy. It meant leaving things in Tommy's hands, and doing things Tommy's way. For two years, Nancy followed that path. For two years, she walked past the trunk. Then two years began to seem like enough.

One night after supper, they were settling into the living room and Nancy brought it up.

"Tommy," she said quietly, "is it okay if I open your mother's trunk?"

Tommy hesitated, then he whispered, "Sure."

So Nancy did.

SHE WAITED UNTIL he was out of the house, then she cleared off the top of the box and pried open the lid, embarrassed by her own racing heart.

There was an old blanket on top, and she set it aside, then another blanket, some sweaters, a photo album, and a handmade coat. But near the bottom of the trunk, Nancy spotted an old shoe box. It was worn and separating at the seams, and somehow she knew instantly that she'd found what she wanted. She raised it gingerly to her lap, and lifted the cover.

The envelopes were stacked in tidy rows and Nancy felt her hands trembling as she pulled them out, one by one, the airmail paper as thin as tissue, with red and blue checks around the edges and Jimmie's loose cursive spilled across the pages inside. Line after line of his thoughts and dreams, all written to Tommy's mom.

"My Dearest," he wrote in one of the first, from May 1944. "At last I can write a few lines, but of course there isn't so very much I can tell you except I'm okay and a long ways from home. I'm in the South Pacific, but can't say just where. It's a pretty place, but Lord, it sure is hot. There are worlds of vegetation that I have never seen before, and I would be as well satisfied if I never had. But the nights are really beautiful. We are south of the equator and there are thousands of new stars, and they seem to be a lot closer. There is a lot to do tomorrow, so I will have to stop for now, but I'll write again soon. Tell the folks hello, and kiss Tommy for me. Keep our home and our baby safe, and maybe in the not too distant future, we can be together again. Write as often as possible, and remember I love you very, very much. Forever, Jimmie."

A few days later, he wrote again: "My Precious, sure am ready for bed tonight. Have been swimming in the ocean today, and eating coconuts, and trying to find some ripe bananas. Sure wish you could be with me, what a lot of fun we could have, finding all these new things together. Gee, I sure do miss you, and of course you know you are the sweetest wife in the world. I am sending you a necklace and bracelet, made from shells from the sea. I hope you like them, and later on, maybe I can send one to Mother. As I can, I will try to send you different things from this part of the world. Take care of yourself and Tommy, and write often, and know I love you with all my heart. Forever, Jimmie."

Nancy stopped reading and stared forward, trying to grasp what it meant. There seemed to be a new letter almost every day, most of them several pages long, but Tommy's mom had never shown them to anyone or even hinted that she had them. When Tommy got home, Nancy found herself crying as she said, "Oh, Tommy, just look," but Tommy turned away, his eyes welling up and his big hands shaking. So Nancy came back to the box for a few hours each night, curled up on the sofa to drift through Jimmie's words. She read V-mail cards from training in Nevada, and eight-page descriptions of the islands and the ocean, and long professions of his love signed with that word, *Forever.*

"Darling," he wrote at the end of his first week, "there aren't any words to tell you how much I love you. But you know that our love can stand this being apart." A few weeks later, he wrote from the combat zone, "It gives me a feeling of serenity knowing there will be a place waiting for me, a place where I can settle for good, and try to make up to you in part for all of the things you have had to put up with. There are times when I get to feeling pretty low about the whole business, but then when I realize that it is tough for you too, and how uncomplaining you have been about it all, it makes me feel pretty cheap."

The more Nancy read, the more bewildering the letters seemed. Looking at them, it was impossible to imagine that Jimmie had abandoned Tommy and his mom—but then, why did Jimmie's brothers insist that he had? Why did they swear he'd called them from California, and that they'd driven out to see him, arriving at Jimmie's apartment just as he slipped away—leaving his neighbors to confirm that he was alive?

Nancy tried to ask Tommy what else he knew, but Tommy just winced and shook his head. He knew nothing, he said. He wished he knew less. He wasn't even sure of his dad's rank, let alone what sort of man he was. Every time Tommy saw the letters, his throat closed up.

"I just couldn't look at them," he said. As the months went by, he never did.

Neither did Casey. "I was against my mother bringing all this up," he said later. "You just didn't talk about this. You didn't talk about it because Dad didn't want to. So when Mom started reading all the letters, I was like, 'Mom, please don't bring it up. Dad doesn't like it.'"

But Nancy wouldn't stop. She wasn't even sure she could. There had to be an answer, some way to make it all make sense. She started placing phone calls to learn more about Jimmie. She called the Department of Veterans Affairs to see if they knew his combat history. She called the Army's human resources office to request his service records. She even called a local Army recruiter to find out if there was anything left from his enlistment—some scrap of paper or hidden detail that might point toward an answer. But no matter where Nancy looked, she came up empty. The Army didn't have a personnel file, they said. They had no record of his enlistment, no file on his missions, no information on his squadron or his crash. In fact, they didn't have much more than his name in a database. Everything else about Jimmie Doyle, they said, had disappeared—probably burned up in a fire in Saint Louis.

"I was skeptical," Nancy said. "I kept telling them to look, but they kept telling me everything burned. I thought, *Everything?*"

A year passed, then another, and Nancy's hunt trailed off. She knew only fragments, and they didn't add up. From the letters, she could see that Jimmie's unit moved across several islands in the South Pacific, and she gathered from Tommy that Jimmie had been a tail gunner on a B-24 bomber, manning a machine gun at the back of the plane. But where did he fly? What targets did he hit? How much combat did he see? And why did his return address show a promotion to sergeant in midsummer? Nothing in the letters explained what Jimmie might have done to earn the rank. There were only vague references to the war. "I can't tell you any details," he would write, "but the Japs are sorry I'm here."

Nancy found a few other letters in the trunk, written by Jimmie's friends after he disappeared. But those letters brought up more questions than answers. "I have talked to some of the fellows who flew the same day and saw what happened," one man wrote. "I'm sorry I can't tell you now the whole story. But when I return to the States, I am coming to see you." There was no sign he'd ever come.

As Nancy's search faltered, so did her confidence. Maybe it had been a mistake to read the letters. Maybe Tommy and Casey were right. Maybe it was better to live with the scar than to reopen the wound. She'd wanted to make sense of Tommy's past, but now it made less sense than ever.

By May 2000, six years had passed since Nancy first opened the trunk. She'd stopped making calls and asking questions about Jimmie, but she was always on the watch. As she skimmed through the newspaper over Memorial Day weekend, she spotted an article in *Parade* magazine. Some doctor in California named Pat Scannon was searching for missing airplanes. He was tracking down men like Jimmie who disappeared in Palau. There was a picture of Scannon on the opening page, a leathery figure with a gray beard, who stood before a vintage bomber with a climbing rope tossed over his shoulder. The article described him as "the Indiana Jones of military archaeology," and Nancy practically ran to the computer to find his phone number. She left a message at his office, and a few days later, Scannon called back. His voice sounded weary. He'd been flooded with calls, he said. He wanted to get back to everyone, but it was hard.

Nancy swallowed. "Well," she said, "I just wanted you to know that my husband's name is Tommy Doyle and his father was Jimmie Doyle . . ."

Scannon's voice perked up. "And his plane went down on September 1, 1944," he said, "and the tail number ended in 453, and the pilot was Jack Arnett, and . . ."

Nancy listened in disbelief as Scannon rattled off a dozen details she'd never heard. When he paused, she whispered, "But how did you *know* all that?"

"Because," Pat Scannon said, "I've been searching for that plane for six years."

TWO

WRECKAGE

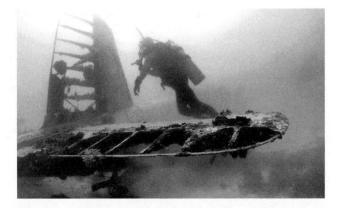

The first time Pat Scannon went to Palau, he wasn't sure what he was searching for. He wasn't even sure why he'd come. Officially, he was part of a scuba expedition looking for a sunken Japanese ship, but Scannon wasn't a very good scuba diver, he didn't know much about the ship, and he hadn't even heard of Palau until a few months earlier.

It was 1993, and Scannon was not the kind of guy who typically disappeared on exotic vacations. He was a medical researcher in his midforties who worked for a small biotech company in a suburban office park in California, and he was sufficiently disinterested in the great outdoors that his wife, Susan, had long since given up asking for his help in the garden—where instead of pruning or planting or weeding he tended to stare into the distance, thinking about work. Though he was licensed as a physician, held a PhD in chemistry, and had actually founded the company where he worked, Scannon also had little interest in corporate affairs. Years earlier, he'd given up control of the company to a team of experienced executives, preferring to focus his own attention on esoteric research into therapeutic monoclonal antibodies. He sometimes confessed to his friends that he'd only built the Xoma Corporation because he wanted a job there, and having built it, he arrived for work each morning with his plastic ID tag dangling from a lanyard around his neck, disappearing inside his office to spend ten or twelve hours under the fluorescent lights. A typical workweek for Scannon consisted of sixty hours at Xoma, plus the hour's drive to and from his stucco home on a dead-end street in town.

Like most things in Scannon's life, the invitation to Palau came while he was at work. One of his colleagues at Xoma was a man named Chip Lambert, who ran the company's infectious disease program. Like Scannon, Lambert had spent his career studying the intersection of chemistry and medicine, but their similarities ended there. Where Scannon was shy and unassuming, with a light, airy voice that tended to wash away in a crowd, Lambert was tall and burly and strode the hallways of Xoma with a gruff exuberance. He had a mop of curly hair and a brushy mustache that danced above a mischievous grin, and he was a world-class scuba diver who'd spent much of the 1970s tooling around the Middle East— working for the king's hospital in Saudi Arabia, then briefly at the World Health Organization, while zipping away each weekend to dive the earth's finest waters, from Scotland to New Zealand and throughout the Red Sea. Now that Lambert was back in California, he and his wife, Pam, ran a small scuba shop on the weekends. When Lambert offered diving classes to his colleagues at Xoma, Scannon was among the first to sign up. Over a few weekends, he earned a basic scuba certification, but mostly enjoyed soaking up Lambert's stories about Cyprus, Vanuatu, and the Poor Knights Islands, a world that Scannon could hardly imagine. Then Lambert started talking about Palau, and Scannon wondered if they were both imagining it.

There was gold on the islands, Lambert said. Hidden gold, mountains of it, stolen by the Japanese during World War II and buried in secret hideaways throughout the Pacific. For half a century, treasure hunters had been tracking down various deposits. They called it "Yamashita's gold," after a notorious Japanese general, and the total value was said to be $100 billion. There were books on the treasure, and lawsuits over it, and more than a few ruined lives. A year earlier, Imelda Marcos of the Philippines confessed that most of her own fortune came from the gold, but a man named Rogelio Roxas claimed that Marcos had stolen it from him, after he uncovered a secret bunker in the Philippine hills full of gems and swords and a golden Buddha whose head was stuffed with diamonds. That case was making its way through the US courts, which would soon award Roxas $22 billion in damages.

Meanwhile, several of Lambert's friends were tracking another deposit of the gold. They had sources in the Japanese government who said that a hospital ship had been sunk in 1945 while ferrying some of the treasure past Palau. By studying old maps and documents, Lambert and his friends hoped to find the ship and bring home the gold. But first they were planning a preliminary trip to generate publicity and funds.

Scannon listened with his jaw hanging open. It sounded like something from a serial film, or a comic he might have read as a child. *Tintin and the Golden Buddha*. But Lambert was just beginning. The preliminary trip, he explained, was a search for the first combat kill of President George H. W. Bush. During the summer of 1944, Bush was a young naval aviator flying photographic reconnaissance missions over the islands. One day in July, he sank his first enemy vessel, a 150-foot trawler. The mission report placed that strike on a northern atoll called Kayangel (*kayh-ang-el'*), but after half a century of diving and fishing in the area, no one had found the trawler. Now Lambert's team had come across photos taken during the mission, which showed the ship going down beside a distinctive patch of coral. They planned to bring the photos to Palau, locate the patch of coral, and drag a magnetometer through the water to pinpoint the ship's metal. Then they would shoot underwater video of the sunken wreck, and produce a documentary on the forty-first American president's virgin kill. They would use all the money and publicity from the documentary to fund the search for Yamashita's gold.

"What we wanted to do," Lambert said later, "was find the wreck, make the movie, and sell the documentary to raise funds for the treasure hunt."

If the whole thing sounded vaguely cartoonish, the divers and historians on Lambert's team put Scannon's doubt to rest. The leader of the group was Dan Bailey, a renowned historian of the islands, whose most recent book, *WWII Wrecks of Palau*, had already become the definitive guide to the island waters. It was Bailey who came up with the mission photos, from a Navy photographer named Bob Stinnett who flew in Bush's squadron. At seventy, Stinnett couldn't join the mission himself, but he was closely involved in the planning. The team also included a scuba pro named Dave Buller, who'd helped discover some of the most famous shipwrecks in Palau, along with several notable sites off the California coast, where he spent his free time scouring the continental shelf for abalone snails as large as a soccer ball, prying them loose while holding his breath and hauling them up for supper. Both of the Lamberts were also coming, and had spent enough time in Palau that the cover of Bailey's book was actually a photo of Pam gliding past the gear shaft of a sunken destroyer. The team had even secured a TV crew to film underwater.

When Lambert suggested that Scannon tag along, Scannon found himself grinning and nodding. He didn't have much to offer the team, but he didn't much care. As a doctor, he could always bandage a scraped knee. But what really mattered to Scannon was that, after a decade of working sixty-hour weeks, which had brought his first marriage to an end and left little time for his second, he finally had a way to break up the routine with a shot of adventure. In fact, his second wife, Susan, was an accomplished diver herself, and he convinced her to join him after the mission for a few days of sightseeing on the islands. So, on a cool summer afternoon, Scannon headed west—through Hawaii, then Guam, before landing on Palau, where he joined the team on the beachfront estate of a resort hotel to watch the red sun cannonball into a sea of surprises.

BUT THE MISSION was already changing. Through a bizarre coincidence, on the same week that Scannon landed in Palau, the September issue of *Harper's Magazine* was landing on newsstands with an article that would throw his vacation into headline news.

The story consisted of just two pages, which were mostly filled with a reproduction of the mission report from Bush's attack on the trawler. But in a series of pullout annotations, a writer for the magazine claimed that the old document offered "strong circumstantial evidence that George Bush committed a war crime as a rookie Navy pilot."

As Scannon gathered with Lambert, Bailey, and the rest of the team for breakfast in the open-air lobby of the hotel, they huddled over the *Harper's* story to figure out what the reporter meant. Though Bailey had a copy of the mission report and had read it dozens of times, he was baffled by the suggestion that it revealed anything nefarious. In most respects, it seemed to him like a thousand other wartime documents. There was a brief description of the 250-mile flight from an aircraft carrier to the islands; a list of the planes in Bush's squadron, known as VT-51; and a terse account of the strike on the trawler, noting that Bush scored the vital hit. The final sentence concluded, "The trawler sank within five minutes, with its crew taking to two life boats, which VT strafed." Except for the brief reference to a future president, nothing about the document struck Lambert, Bailey, or the rest of the team as unusual.

But for the *Harper's* writer, the line about lifeboats was crucial. Depending on how one interpreted it, the attack could have been illegal. If, as the *Harper's* writer suggested, the language implied that Japanese soldiers boarded their lifeboats without weapons, and then Bush swooped down to strafe "defenseless combatants," it would indeed be a war crime. But the document said nothing of the sort. Like so many wartime reports, it had been hurried together by a harried officer who was already focused on the next day's events, and it left out far too many details to draw such precise conclusions. It didn't say, for example, that the Japanese soldiers were defenseless. They might just as easily have climbed into the lifeboats with their sidearms for protection, or even the lightweight Nambu machine guns common to the period. Nor did the mission report say which pilot strafed the lifeboats. Maybe it was the same pilot who sank the trawler, Ensign George Bush. Then again, maybe not.

As it happened, those very questions had been circulating in Washington for several months. During the final weeks of the 1992 presidential campaign, nine months earlier, the mission report materialized in the mailboxes of several prominent reporters. Though the timing reeked of an October surprise, the allegations were serious, and some of the most venerable names in news, including the *Los Angeles Times*, *U.S. News & World Report*, and *Newsweek*, launched investigations. As their reporters scoured the US and Japanese archives in search of clarifying detail, they came up empty. By Election Day, not a single magazine or newspaper had discovered enough evidence to justify a story. Nor had the *Harper's* writer uncovered anything new. The closest he came was a single quote from a gunner on the mission, who said he couldn't remember the incident but allowed that "it might have happened."

Still, with the *Harper's* article on newsstands, the floodgates were open for other news groups to "follow up" on the story. While Scannon was on his way to Palau, a deluge of television reporters had been tracking down veterans of Bush's squadron, including Bob Stinnett, who pointed them toward the team in Palau. As phone calls lit up the switchboard of the waterfront resort, Bailey and Lambert found themselves inundated with media requests. By the time they boarded a flat-bottomed boat for their first day of diving, three days had passed and they'd struck a deal with *Nightline* to provide video for an exclusive segment.

All of which Pat Scannon watched in a state of dazed amusement. According to Bailey and Buller, the most striking thing about Lambert's friend was how utterly disengaged he was—a cheerful spectator who wandered the hotel grounds while the rest of the team scrambled to take phone calls, secure gear, and coordinate logistics. "If Chip wanted him along," Bailey said later, "that was fine. But he wasn't a major part of the team."

"He didn't really contribute," Buller added. "He just came along."

As the boat finally sped north toward Kayangel, Scannon stared west to where the shallow water of the archipelago plunged into the fullness of the sea. The whole peculiar madness of the journey seemed written upon the landscape—these lost islands, a thousand miles from anywhere, filled with buried treasure and sunken warships and rumors of a president's crimes. Who cared how much of it was true? He had come to the islands to recharge himself with change, and whatever else he might see or discover, he had already found that. It was everywhere around him, in the gleaming iridescent ocean, the teeming jungle, the screech of wild birds, and the pile of mesh scuba bags strewn across the floor of the boat beside boxes filled with video equipment and the long, torpedo-shaped magnetometer.

After two hours, the boat slowed down and Kayangel came into view, a tiny cluster of four mint-green islets poking through the water's surface. Bailey dug into his bag for the mission photos. He raised them up against the horizon, squinting as he compared the images with the landscape before him. He turned the photos left, then right, and frowned. The pictures didn't match. Where they showed a long, continuous arc of coral, the reef before him was mostly flat with a bulging promontory in the middle. The reef could change in fifty years, but not by that much.

The sun was creeping past its zenith as the small boat puttered through the water. Bailey laid the photos down and pulled out a map. He studied the surrounding landscape as a realization hit him: The photos didn't match Kayangel because they *weren't* Kayangel. There was another atoll just five miles north and nearly the same size. The islanders called it Ngaruangel (*ner-angle'*), but it was virtually unknown to the outside world. In fact, it probably did not appear on World War II maps. If the trawler had gone down on Ngaruangel, aviators like Bush would have written down the name of the nearest atoll. That would explain why, in fifty years of diving Kayangel, no one had seen the ship. It was never there.

It took only a few minutes to speed north to the Ngaruangel reef. As the boat drew close, Dave Buller dropped his magnetometer into the water, crouching over the handheld monitor to watch for signs of metal. Bailey picked up the photos again, comparing them with a new horizon. They motored slowly along the edge of the shoal, and as they moved, Bailey saw the transformation unfolding. Like the shifting lines of a kaleidoscope, his perspective on the landscape morphed until it matched the pictures.

"Hey!" he cried out to Buller, "we've gotta be almost on top of it!" But even as the words came out, he heard Buller calling back: "I'm getting hits!"

There was a palpable tension as the boat pulled to a stop and the team began to suit up. *It's almost too easy*, Bailey thought. They had been on the water just a few hours, and in Ngaruangel for only a few minutes. But the combination of pings on the magnetometer and a match with the photos made it difficult to tamp down expectations. As the team stretched into neoprene wetsuits, strapped on weight belts, and slipped into tanks, Pam Lambert hit the water first. Scannon dropped in behind her, swimming down hard through the darkening water to maximize his time on the bottom. After forty feet, he saw the seafloor and righted himself in the water. He blinked and stared at the landscape around him.

The wreckage was unmistakable; it was everywhere. A dusty haze drifted across the massive hull of the ship, ripped open by the blast from Bush's bomber, with its gear strewn in all directions and encrusted in half a century of staghorn coral. Scannon saw Bailey and Buller a few yards away, moving across the debris field together. He drifted over to join them, following as they pointed out the telltale signs. Not only was the ship fitted with mounts for a seventy-five-millimeter cannon, but the cannon shells were packed into a ready box nearby, and the seafloor was strewn with thousands of rounds of linked machine-gun ammunition. *So they were armed*, Scannon thought. In hindsight, it seemed obvious. Only a fool would throw down his weapon as he boarded a tiny lifeboat with enemy planes circling overhead and an ocean of sharks below.

For thirty minutes, the team swept through the twisted metal, finally coming to the surface with whoops of joy. None of them doubted what they'd found. Whatever else the Japanese sailors had been—young, naïve, filled up with nationalistic bravado, even honorable in their own way— they had clearly been armed. By finding the wreckage, Bailey and his team had solved a fifty-year mystery and, they were now certain, exonerated a president. In the days ahead, as they returned to the States, they would broadcast their discovery on *Nightline* for the world to see. Only Scannon would stay behind.

He picked up Susan at the airport, and over dinner on their first night, they nursed a pair of beers while Pat leaned across the table, whispering excitedly about the rush of discovery and having felt so close to history. By the time they returned to their hotel that night, they had decided to scrap their plans to visit tourist sites like the Blue Holes and Blue Corner. Instead, they would spend the next four days exploring World War II wreckage on the islands.

They hired a local guide, Hudson Yalap, to drive them into the hills and jungle, stopping to wade through elephant grass, past the ruins of Japanese encampments and the cindered spires of old radio towers that rested like dinosaur bones in the damp earth. And on their final morning, they boarded a small boat with Yalap and a second guide, Lucky Malsol, to visit underwater wrecks. Neither of the Scannons had any idea where the guides planned to take them, and as the boat slipped away from the dock, they stared forward at the open water, never imagining how long the journey ahead would be.

———

EVEN AFTER HALF A CENTURY, the waters of the archipelago were strewn with relics of war. In shoals that were sometimes just a few feet deep, a casual snorkeler could drift away from a hotel beach through the glimmering surf and discover a pile of unspent ammunition, or the barrel of a ship's cannon, or even a whole Japanese seaplane resting on the sandy bottom. With a scuba tank, it was possible to swim inside the plane, climbing into the cockpit to tug at the controls and shoot down passing fish like a pilot in some aquatic fantasy.

With so many wartime wrecks to choose from, Yalap and Malsol might have taken the Scannons to one of the popular sites: maybe the Japanese mine-laying ship filled with stacks of military helmets, or one of the Mitsubishi Zero fighter planes crumpled in the shallows. But instead, the guides steered the boat to a bay just south of Koror Island, weaving a course between small islets before slowing to a crawl. Malsol guided the boat to the edge of a little island, not much bigger than a house. In the waist-deep water, colorful fish darted away from the hull. Scannon frowned. It didn't look like a wreck site; it looked like a typical tropical beach. *This is nice*, he thought, *but why are we here?*

Then he saw the wing. As Malsol pulled around a bend in the coral, the whole thing came into view at once: a massive strip of metal, at least fifty feet long and gleaming in the sun. The aluminum skin was peeled back in places to reveal a lacework of struts inside, and as Malsol lowered the throttle to approach it, Scannon called over the engine, "What kind of plane?" But the guide only shook his head.

There was a long silence as Malsol flipped off the engine and retrieved an anchor from the foredeck. Wavelets lapped against the boat. Scannon stared at the wing. As soon as the anchor hit water, he leaped over the gunwale, striding quickly toward the wing. He heard Susan behind him.

There was a propeller mounted on the leading edge, and as Scannon got closer, he could see that the blades were bent and fractured from impact with the coral. A few feet away, there was a second engine attached to the wing, and Scannon felt his heart pound as the significance sank in. "This was a four-engine plane," he whispered when Susan caught up. She nodded, and walked toward the second engine, crouching for a look.

"Pat," she said. She pointed at the engine mount. He stepped over and peered in. There was a number stamped on a bolt—*a number*, he realized, *not a character*—and beneath it, an ID plate with clear black lettering said "eneral Electric."

Scannon felt a chill wash over his body. He was surprised by how much it really felt like a chill—as if the temperature of the water had plunged to nearly freezing. It began with numbness in his lower legs, then crept into his thighs, through his waist, and up his torso to his neck, until the skin on the crown of his head felt tight and his hair stood at attention, all the feeling in his body draining away. *This was an American plane*, he thought. Then he corrected himself. *This is an American grave.*

As Susan moved toward the wide end of the wing, where the metal was gnarled from breaking free, Scannon circled to the opposite end and searched the shallow water for pieces of debris. Where was the rest, he wondered. There had to be more. He drifted into deeper water, where the reef dropped into a channel, and he followed the edge of the channel west for 150 yards. There was no sign of the plane. He turned and headed east, but still found nothing: not a fragment, not a scrap of metal, just fish and sand and coral. He glanced back at Susan, who was still inspecting the root of the wing, and he dropped into the water to swim a few yards into the channel, scanning the bottom for signs of the wreckage, but there were none. By the time he turned back, Susan was climbing into the boat.

For her, he realized, *it's just another wreck.* Of course it was—she'd grown up in Singapore and Bangkok, where her father worked as an oil executive. For years she had spent summers and holidays swimming through debris fields in the Gulf of Thailand, the South China Sea, and little inlets and waterways so remote they didn't have names. Since then, she'd been on wreck sites from Tahiti to South Africa. She had joined an archaeological expedition to study shipwrecks in England from the fourteenth century. By the time she and Scannon met in the 1980s, she had a collection of cannonballs from her travels. She would later say that she found the wing interesting, and Palau pleasant enough, but she didn't particularly care to see either again.

As Susan settled into the boat, Scannon's gaze drifted back to the wing. Nothing about the experience was familiar to him. He glanced at the small island just behind the metal, its limestone cliffs rising fifteen feet to a tangle of vines and small trees on top. Without knowing where he was going or why, he called for Susan to wait; then he was splashing toward the island and scrambling up, grabbing clumps of dirt and roots until he reached the top and, with a final surge, rolled forward into the jungle.

It was another world. Under a thick canopy of leaves, the air was wet and cool, and it was streaked with narrow blades of light that sliced past fluttering birds and giant spiders looming on five-foot webs. The roots and vines were so thick, he could only crawl through on his belly, and he slithered deeper into the island, studying the ground as he went. Even a strip of aluminum, he thought, even a single bolt would show the wreckage was there. He wriggled across sharp branches, through piles of fallen leaves, his fingers biting into the soil, his knees dragging in the mud, but he found nothing more than an old wooden crate filled with green sake bottles.

After thirty minutes, Scannon turned back. He dragged himself to the edge of the island and splashed down into the water. On the boat, Susan and the guides were watching him and shaking their heads. Mud caked his face and wetsuit, and his hands were scraped raw. He scrambled back through the water and climbed into the boat. Malsol started up the engine and began to pull away.

Scannon flashed an apologetic smile, then stared back at the wing, watching as it disappeared behind the island. Then he slid into his seat, oblivious to the cheerful patter of Susan conferring with the guides.

Something inside him was changed, but he couldn't place what. He had come to the islands to escape the pressure of daily life, yet he found himself overcome by an even greater sense of purpose. Somewhere nearby, young men died. They had come spiraling down in a plane with one wing and probably either died on impact or drowned in the sea. Did anyone know? Was there a record of what happened? Had someone come to find them? Or were their remains still resting in the carcass of the fallen plane? And where was the plane? Did their families know? Did they even care?

Later, when Scannon tried to explain the feeling that came over him that day, the sense of duty and responsibility that would consume the next two decades of his life, that would bring him back, year after year, to swim and dive and hike and climb and fly small aircraft over the islands; when he tried to describe the sensation that gripped him as he gazed upon the wing, words would always fail.

"I just came around that bend in the coral," he would say, "and I was a different person."

BACK IN CALIFORNIA, Scannon found himself drifting to the islands: at work, at home, and in between, the questions always lingered. Where was the rest of the plane, and how many other planes were nearby? The guides had taken him and Susan to another site, four miles north, where a lone American propeller rested in water so shallow that during low tide its blade poked into the air like a thin, gray beacon. Four miles was probably too far for the propeller to have come from the same airplane as the wing, but as Scannon asked around—at the hotel, in dive shops, and among various guides—no one seemed to know where either part came from, or where the rest of either plane was. There didn't seem to be any record of the lost planes on Palau.

Now that Scannon was home, he could see that there wasn't much record of the air campaign at all. The ground and naval battles against

Japan filled hundreds of volumes, from the intimate memoirs of Marines, to tactical studies of carrier battles, to popular histories of the island-hopping campaign by General Douglas MacArthur. For each of those battles, American men on ships and beaches were backed by a raging sky of planes, which pounded the earth and swooped low across enemy bunkers with a fusillade of bullets that blackened the midday sun. But the story of those fliers was always relegated to the margin, eclipsed by the gruesome infantry landings and the grandeur of the Navy fleet.

Then, too, Palau itself was missing from many accounts of the war. The islands were home to some of the most savage fighting in the Pacific, but most Americans had never even heard of them. Other island battles were much more famous but comparatively short. The horror at Tarawa extended for three blistering days; the fight for Iwo Jima, about a month; the battle for Okinawa dragged on for three months; and the eruptions at Guadalcanal, six. But the fight for Palau was spread across eighteen months of combat that dyed the white sand red. When historians did account for Palau, they tended to divide the battle into its constituent operations, like the naval strikes in March 1944, the Army Air Forces' bombardment that summer, and the Marine invasion on the southern island of Peleliu in the fall. Yet on the ground those distinctions were meaningless; on the ground, the islands were simply at war—pummeled by ships and planes and landing vehicles, day after week after month, so that on the final day of the war, the north was still held by Japan and the south in Allied hands. No other Pacific island territory was contested so bitterly for so long. The fight for Peleliu Island alone was among the bloodiest engagements of the war. In his epic work *The Pacific War*, historian John Costello wrote of Peleliu, "The bloody, grinding warfare was to reach a savagery the 1st Marines had not encountered even in their long struggle on Guadalcanal." At the National Museum of the Marine Corps, historians called Peleliu "the bitterest battle of the war." And to veterans of Palau, the archipelago was simply "the Forgotten Corner of Hell."

As Scannon devoured histories of the Pacific, he began to realize that the lost wing could only belong to one kind of plane. Most of the American aircraft over Palau had been small, tactical ships, like the Avengers flown by naval aviators and the Corsairs used by Marines. But those planes had a total wingspan of just forty to fifty-five feet, with a single engine mounted on their nose. The wing in the water had come from a plane twice as broad, with four times as many engines. As far as Scannon could tell, that left only one possibility: the B-24 Liberator. The Army Air Forces had flown Liberators over Palau at several points in the war, but the most notable period was in the late summer of 1944, just before the Peleliu invasion.

Not that Scannon could find a detailed history of those missions. The books in his collection that mentioned the Army Air Forces didn't mention Palau, and most of the books on Palau didn't mention the Army Air Forces. Even Dan Bailey's book, which he now understood was by far the most thorough account of the campaign, with exhaustive detail on hundreds of Navy and Marine aircraft, included only a glancing reference to the B-24 missions that laid waste to the archipelago that summer, dropping more than a million pounds of ordnance and destroying "the majority of above-ground buildings and installations."

Fortunately, Bailey himself was a font of information beyond the book. When Scannon asked what else he might know about the B-24 missions, Bailey passed along the phone numbers for two B-24 veterans' groups that served in the campaign. Then he told Scannon about a photograph in his collection. It was taken by a military photographer on a flight over Palau, and it showed a Liberator plummeting toward the islands in flames. Bailey promised to send Scannon a print by mail.

When the photo arrived, Scannon stared in disbelief. It wasn't just a photo of a B-24 crashing on the islands; it was a B-24 falling into the very same bay where he and Susan had seen the wing. Not only that, but the plane in the photo was in the process of losing a wing. There was only one problem: it was the wrong wing. The one the Scannons had seen on the islands was a starboard, or right-side, wing. The one breaking off in the photo was a left wing. Everything else in the pictures was oriented correctly, so he knew the negative wasn't reversed. But unless the plane had lost both wings within moments of the photo, he was looking at a second plane going down in the same spot. Was that possible?

In the morning, Scannon shut the door to his office at Xoma and began calling the reunion groups to track down B-24 veterans; at night, he disappeared into his home office to pore over old mission reports that oozed from his fax, scouring each document for any reference to a missing plane, while Susan passed down the hallway, rolling her eyes at him.

"All of a sudden, he's calling all these old guys and just charging into it," she said. "He just kept going and *going.*"

"I was possessed," Scannon admitted. "I had no idea where it was heading, but the one thing I promised myself was that I was going to let it take me where it took me."

Everything Scannon could find out about the B-24s suggested that three, not two, had crashed near the southern bay. He could only assume that all three had been trying to bomb the same target, and had been shot down by the same well-concealed anti-aircraft guns in the hills. Of those three, it was easy to guess which one he and Susan had seen. It was the only one that had lost its right wing. The crash had been on August 28, 1944, two weeks before the Peleliu invasion. The pilot was a man named William Dixon. He'd gone down with a crew of ten.

The other two B-24s had each lost their left wing. One went down three days after Dixon. It was flown by a pilot named Jack Arnett. Then eight months later, a third Liberator went down with a pilot named Glen Custer at the helm. One of those two had to be the plane in Bailey's picture, but there was no way to figure out which. The image showed no serial number or identifying marks. Scannon asked surviving airmen, but none of them knew, either. When a plane went down in enemy territory, they said, that was all you knew.

Scannon wasn't satisfied. Three months after his return from the islands, he had dozens of wartime documents, but the collection was spotty at best. There were random pages from mission documents; fragments of missing aircrew reports; and portions of the individual aircraft records that listed a plane's equipment—but nearly all of the documents were missing pages, and there was no way of knowing how many other documents he didn't have. Most of the records from the Army Air Forces in the Pacific seemed to be housed at Maxwell Air Force Base in Alabama. That was two thousand miles away, and there was no guarantee that anything inside would point toward the missing planes.

Still, Scannon went. On December 9, 1993, he boarded a flight to Alabama with two changes of clothing and an artist's sketchbook filled with huge white pages and bound in hard black covers. As he crossed the country at thirty thousand feet, he cracked open the book to the first page, writing in tiny letters at the top:

"This is the opening of my log on World War II. I am interested in the period of February 1944 to March 1945 in the Palau area for several reasons: It is an almost forgotten campaign. This is the 50th year after the air battles. The AAF involvement has been totally neglected. Other areas of the Pacific have been covered extensively: Guadalcanal, Truk, Iwo Jima, Okinawa. But I'm not interested in the scale of the operations. I am interested in how individual crews, albeit in a lesser campaign, came under intense fire, lost their lives, and have, by necessity, been forgotten. Some of the crews remain in water where they impacted 50 years ago. It is time someone acknowledges their efforts and perhaps lays to rest the outcome for their family members."

At Maxwell, Scannon passed through a small entry station and made his way to a brick research building, where he signed his name into the guest book, listing his organization as "self." He posed for a visitor photo in his pressed white shirt and blazer; then he asked a librarian to bring him every document related to B-24 missions over Palau. Waiting at a row of Formica tables, Scannon glanced around him. Air Force officers were paging through arcane battle summaries, and Russian authors and scholars examined stacks of loose paper, and for a moment, he suppressed the instinct to bolt from the room. But as the boxes began to arrive on wheeled carts, he squared his shoulders and popped open the first one.

Hours ticked by in the small archive as Scannon ground through the tedium of research. His eyes glazed over, his ears began to buzz, he shook his head and stretched to stay clear. Each time he found a reference to a Liberator crash, he would race to the copy machine and add another page to the stack piling up beside him. The sun fell. The building closed. He crashed in a motel. Then he was back to pick up where he left off. Consciously, Scannon still had no idea what possessed him. He simply read, and copied, and collected documents on instinct alone. "It took two days," he said later, "and nine million dimes."

With each document, Scannon's understanding of the war became more clear. In a folder on the Custer crash, he found the same picture Dan Bailey had sent him, along with three others, all showing the plane on its descent toward the southern bay. In a folder on the Dixon crash, he found two photos. One showed the plane's right wing plummeting toward a small island, where he and Susan had seen it fifty years later. The other showed Dixon's fuselage coming down in a trail of smoke that raced across Koror Island to the northern shore.

Finally, in a third folder, Scannon found a report on the Arnett crash. Flipping through the pages, he felt his heart rate jump. There weren't any photos, but there was something even more specific: two witness statements that described parachutes floating through the air as the plane corkscrewed down. "Two crew members were seen to bail out and their chutes open before hitting the water," one witness wrote. There was even a map of the archipelago tucked into the report, with the big island of Babeldaob (*bobble-dop*) at the top and Koror near the center, and in the narrow channel between them, two small Xs. Beside one of them, someone had typed, "Plane down here." Beside the other, "Crew member down here."

As Scannon packed up his files for the journey home, he felt sickened by the crash reports and everything they described: more than thirty men trapped on those planes as they swerved through a burning sky toward the enemy below. But Scannon no longer had any doubt what he planned to do. No one seemed to know where the wreckage of those planes lay: not the commanders who sent out search teams for them, or the veterans who spent sixty years wondering what had become of their fallen friends. Now he would find the answers. He would bring the photos and map to the islands and find those missing planes. He would honor those airmen, and leave behind a record of where they lay.

He'd already found the Dixon wing, and he had a photo of its fuselage streaming toward the north shore of Koror. For Custer, he had four photos showing the plane's trajectory toward the bay. And for Arnett, he had a map prepared just a few hours after the crash. It was too small to provide exact coordinates, but the X on the channel was unmistakable. A B-24 was a colossal machine, sixty-seven feet long and twice as wide. It weighed thirty-six thousand pounds empty. It was resting on the bottom of a narrow passage, in water less than one hundred feet deep.

How hard could it be to find?

THREE

AIRMEN

Most men facing a B-24 did not share Scannon's enthusiasm. With its square walls and blocky nose, its skinny wings poking out, the Liberator looked less like an airplane than a freight car pierced by a missile.

Stepping on board the plane did not improve the impression. It was designed to deliver a heavy payload across long distances, but it rattled and shook the whole way, lurching and bobbing in the crosswinds, while its crew shivered in the back under a howling wind that pierced the seams. When a B-24 was hit by enemy artillery, it tended to catch fire, yet the corridor that ran down the center of the plane was so cramped that a pilot wearing a parachute could not squeeze through to escape. Especially for men accustomed to the sturdy B-17, the new bomber seemed like a cross between an insult and a joke. Some men called it "the Pregnant Cow."

Others, "the Flying Coffin." One navigator on Guadalcanal drew a car-
toon of the Liberator with the caption "The Army's New B-24—Will the
B-24 Ever Replace the Airplane?"

By the onset of the war, in 1941, the B-24 had been in production for
two years, but most American commanders didn't want it. Nearly all the
early models had been shipped to the French and British, and by the time
of the attack on Pearl Harbor, there was only one B-24 on the adjoining
airfield, which had reached the base just two days earlier on a secret photographic mission and was promptly blasted to pieces in the Japanese
attack.

Even as the United States advanced into Europe, many American
commanders remained skeptical of the Liberator. None were more vocal
in their objection than General Jimmy Doolittle, who commanded the
Twelfth Air Force in North Africa, then the Fifteenth in the Mediterranean, before taking the helm of the legendary Eighth in England. In a
letter to the Air Forces' chief of staff, Doolittle made his critique of the
new plane clear. "Upon being put into operations in the European Theater," he wrote, "it was found that the armament and armor of the B-24
were inadequate, and in order to operate without prohibitive losses it was
necessary to make emergency modifications immediately." Doolittle
beefed up the Liberator's plating and installed additional guns, but this
"substantially increased the weight, reduced the aerodynamic characteris-
tics and, although increasing the firepower, eventually unacceptably reduced the overall utility of the aircraft." For those units where Doolittle
was required to maintain a few Liberators, like the Third Air Division, he
tended to fly them as a separate wing near the back of the formation,
where their wobbly flight path wouldn't jeopardize his B-17s. Being in the
rear, of course, only added to the plane's disadvantage: by the time the
Liberators reached a target, the enemy was alert—and the planes took an
extra beating, which only confirmed their bad reputation.

On long flights, the B-24 fared better, but it would always fall in the
shadow of the B-17, and a handful of spectacular failures would tarnish

its record forever. The worst of these was the raid on Nazi oil refineries in August 1943. Situated near Ploesti, Romania, the refineries were more than a thousand miles from a major Allied airbase, which was beyond the usual reach of the B-17 and gave the B-24 a chance to prove its utility. On the morning of August 1, a formation of 177 Liberators departed from Libya, sweeping over the Mediterranean and up the western coast of Greece, past Albania and Yugoslavia, to reach the Ploesti refineries. But as the 1,700 fliers approached their target, they ran into a heavier defense than anyone expected. As a hail of anti-aircraft fire lit up the sky, the B-24s shattered and dove through smoke and flak, airmen leaping to their deaths in the burning refineries below. With 660 fliers lost, it was the deadliest mission in Air Force history, known as Black Sunday. Yet the impact on the Nazi machine was negligible. According to an intelligence committee at the newly built Pentagon, the Ploesti raid accomplished "no curtailment of overall product output."

The Pacific, of course, was a different battle, and sometimes seemed a different world. By the middle of 1942, the Japanese empire swept across the ocean in one of the largest imperia of human history. The expansion had begun in the 1860s, when the Meiji Restoration inspired a military surge in Japan, but the impulse to extend the empire seemed to accelerate with each decade. Between 1894 and 1910, Japan fought two wars with Russia, seized the Korean peninsula, and occupied Taiwan. Then, as World War I broke out in Europe, the Japanese captured German territories in the Pacific, and by the end of the war, the empire stretched from the edge of Siberia to the Caroline Islands and around the belly of Indonesia. And it was still growing.

To modern eyes, Japan's push into mainland China in the 1930s may seem savage, and by modern standards it was. The Japanese atrocities in Manchuria and Nanking still resonate among the great horrors of modern history. Yet it was difficult for Allied countries at the time to object on principled grounds. The American conquest of the West, which dominated the preceding century, spilled no shortage of blood in the name of political destiny, while the British Empire sprawled across a quarter of the globe.

What the Japanese saw in China was not just opportunity. They saw a resource they could scarcely live without. Japan's population had been growing since the turn of the century, until the home islands were filled with more than four hundred people per square mile. At the same time, the country's military economy was faltering, and the American stock market collapse had eviscerated the demand for high-dollar exports like silk. The combination of a growing population and a sinking economy was devastating. With labor strikes mounting in Tokyo, and food and land in short supply, Japanese political leaders gazed achingly across the sea toward the lush, fertile, and largely open Chinese mainland. As Iris Chang explained in *The Rape of Nanking*, "China was twentieth-century Japan's manifest destiny."

But with the Japanese assault on China came a defensive mandate: the greatest threat to the imperial project was not Chinese resistance but the massive US naval fleet parked on the Pacific. To American leaders, the Japanese expansion represented both a military and an economic threat, and by the time of the attack on Pearl Harbor in December 1941, the carnage may have been shocking, but the war itself was not. US commanders had been planning for it all year, flying spy missions over the Japanese islands, patrolling the region with submarines, and fortifying US bases in anticipation of trouble. All of which made the strike on Pearl Harbor seem sensible to Japan: if war with the United States was inevitable, then the best option was to strike first, strike hard, and keep striking, so the Americans stayed on their heels.

The Japanese advantage held into 1942, as imperial forces followed Pearl Harbor with a race across the Pacific: northeast to the Aleutian islands of Attu and Kiska near Alaska, southeast to Tarawa and the Solomon Islands, and southwest across a constellation of larger islands—Sumatra, Java, Borneo, Celebes, New Guinea, and the Philippines, which together comprised about twice as much land as Germany, France, and

Italy combined. Some of those captured islands were rich with natural resources, while others, like the diminutive atolls of Truk, Yap, and Palau, served mainly as a strategic buffer. Within six months of Pearl Harbor, the Japanese controlled a radius of three thousand miles in some directions, across a string of disparate islands. Any effort to restrain the empire would require American forces to beat a path through those islands and the garrisons stationed on them.

Suddenly, the clunky, clumsy B-24 was essential. Whatever its flaws, the Liberator was the only heavy bomber capable of crossing the vast distances between many Japanese islands. As US forces prepared to push across the Pacific, production of the B-24 surged like never before. Soon there were assembly plants in San Diego, Dallas, Fort Worth, and Tulsa— but none would symbolize the rise of the Liberator like the facility near Detroit known as Willow Run.

Managed by the Ford Motor Company, Willow Run was in some respects a greater engineering feat than the planes it produced. It was the largest factory in the world, spread across 3.5 million square feet, with 28,855 windows and 152,000 fluorescent lights. The assembly line traveled so far that, when it reached the edge of the county, designers built a fifty-foot-diameter lazy Susan to rotate the line and avoid paying extra taxes. As American forces drove into the Pacific in 1943, the pace of production at Willow Run doubled, then doubled again. In January 1943, the plant produced 31 B-24s. In February, it was 75. In March, 104 and rising.

To keep the plant humming, Ford hired workers in unprecedented number. When there weren't enough local men, they recruited throughout the region, and when the region came up short, they offered moving incentives to men as far away as California and the Deep South, building dormitories to house them and a shopping mall to serve them. When there still weren't enough men, the plant began hiring women, and at the same wage. Soon, there were twelve thousand salaried women on the line, and the plant's output continued surging: to 400 planes a month, then 500, then 650.

Pilots and crews would arrive at the factory, wait for a plane to come off the line, and then climb aboard and fly the eighteen-ton behemoth off to war. The most famous pilot in the world stopped by from time to time. Charles Lindbergh had, like Henry Ford, opposed American involvement in the European war, and he was regarded in many circles as a Nazi sympathizer. He had resigned his own rank in the Air Corps to protest US intervention, but in the aftermath of Pearl Harbor, he had been calling for an assault on the "Asiatic intruder."

Unmatched as a pilot, Lindbergh toured American airfields and manufacturing plants to offer advice on everything from airplane design to combat tactics. "The Willow Run factory is a stupendous thing," he wrote in his journal after a visit to the plant. "It is a sort of Grand Canyon of a mechanized world." As for the lumbering B-24, Lindbergh was less enamored. "I am not overly impressed with the qualities of this bomber," he wrote. "When I flew it for a few minutes in the air, I found the controls to be the stiffest and heaviest I have ever handled. Also, I think the gun installations are inadequate and the armor plate poorly installed. I would certainly hate to be in a bomber of this type if a few pursuit planes caught up with it."

Yet as the war with Japan raged on, production of the B-24 would outpace not only the B-17, but all other planes. No other multi-engine aircraft had ever been manufactured in such numbers, nor has any since. Though assembly of the Liberator ended with the war, in just five years of high-intensity production, more than 18,000 models were built. By comparison, fewer than 13,000 B-17s were manufactured, and fewer than 4,000 B-29s. In forty years of production, only about 1,500 Boeing 747s have been assembled.

A 1945 advertisement for Ford boasted of Willow Run: "Raw material went in one end, planes came out the other." A newsreel crowed,

"Relentless. Unceasing. On time. As methodical as a great river fed by its tributaries."

By the dawn of 1944, it was a river rushing toward the Pacific, and tiny islands like Palau.

WITH SO MANY BOMBERS coming off the production line, the Army needed more men to fly them, and engineers in Nevada set about revamping a sleepy airfield in Tonopah into a massive B-24 training school. With $3 million in new runways, roads, barracks, and hangars, it would be the job of Tonopah to manufacture airmen as quickly as Willow Run produced planes.

They arrived in Tonopah from all across the country, having finished specialty programs like the navigation school at Selman Field, Louisiana, or the gunnery school in Laredo, Texas. But it was in Tonopah that a cluster of ten random men became a crew, bringing their skills together for the first time. Day after day, they roared across the Nevada desert in training. They learned to fly close, in a box formation called "javelin-down," while spitting bullets from the guns in their nose, tail, waist, ball, and top turrets. After a day of flight, they would find their way back to base by triangulating from the nearby mountains, or by following a lone radio signal, or by charting the night stars.

For many of the men, those stars were the only familiar sight. Born in the 1920s, they had come of age in an endless depression, and many had never left home before or had any idea where they were going. Their uniforms would be their first suits; their barracks, their first homes with lights and plumbing.

At twenty-five, Jimmie Doyle was one of the oldest men in his crew. He came from the flatlands of West Texas, raised by a single dad who'd left his mom and four siblings in Arkansas years earlier, heading across the High Plains with only Jimmie at his side. Growing up in the heart of the Dust Bowl, Jimmie had gone to work with his father—helping to lay stone walls and build fences on the Llano Estacado caprock. They spent one summer pouring a road base for Route 180 between the towns of Lamesa and Snyder, staking the shoulder with wooden rails and pouring in stone and crushed lime, then hitching up horses to drag a chain across the top. At night, they bedded down with the animals, cooking over a campfire with the other men.

Jimmie's hands were calloused and strong but he still had the lanky physique of a teen. His blond hair was perpetually tossed over a boyish face of freckles. One day at gunnery school in Laredo, he was struggling with a heavy pack, the blisters bleeding on his feet, when his wiry frame gave out. He felt a surge under his arms as another private hoisted him up, carrying him down the field until his strength returned. After that, Jimmie and Johnny Moore were rarely apart. They bunked together, ate together, and stayed up late talking. Jimmie told Johnny about life on the plains, the shade of the elm trees he longed for, and the little boy, Tommy, he'd left behind with Myrle, the only woman he'd ever loved. Johnny told Jimmie about the sultry woods of Arkansas, a place that Jimmie no longer remembered, but where his mom and siblings still lived.

Johnny was five years younger than Jimmie, but he was a head taller and laced with muscle. His dark brown hair scooped into a swirl, and he beamed the easy sideways smile of a lifelong country boy. Growing up on the Des Arc Bayou, he was the youngest of nine kids and the second son, but he was named for his father. Most folks in Des Arc called him John Junior. His dad and sister called him Bud. In the service, he was Johnny.

Life in Des Arc hadn't changed much in a century or two. Johnny's dad woke early each morning for a bowl of corn mush and a mug of hot water, then headed out to fish the hidden corners of the White River, bagging catfish and buffalo fish as big as fifty pounds. In the evening, he dragged them home to put on ice and ship to Saint Louis. When Johnny was little, he stayed home with his mom, Addie, a husky, whistling figure who tended the chickens and milked the cow and raised fields of cotton and corn beside the jumble of beans and peas and potatoes in the household garden. The older kids sometimes helped Addie do laundry in the outdoor washtub, or hang the clothes to dry on a line between trees. When things got busy, Johnny hung by his sister Melba, who was six years older. "He was my pet," Melba said. "He was my baby. He was my doll."

In place of toys, Johnny had cousins and nephews to race and chase through woodland acres. Two of his sisters were so much older that one had a son, Doyle, who was just ten months younger than Johnny, and another had a boy named Charles born just two years after that—the year the White River climbed so high in Des Arc that it breached the pages of the *New York Times*. By the time the three boys were old enough to walk, they were running. They'd skinny-dip in the river behind the cemetery and climb up high in the persimmon trees to ride the branches to the ground. When school began, they made the two-mile walk along railroad tracks by the river, tossing rocks into the water to see who could make the biggest splash. The year Johnny turned thirteen, the river surged over the banks again, sweeping through the first floor of the house. Johnny was surging that year, too: In high school, he was six feet tall, with size $11\frac{1}{2}$ shoes. His hands were strong enough to crack a walnut.

On weekends, Johnny and his dad would slip away together, crawling up the malarial gulches of the river to hook fish. Johnny would clean them with a cleaver he'd cut from a railroad plate. Back home, he rounded up his cousins and nephews to smack a baseball or hurl a football until they were all falling down. Then they'd clamber into someone's kitchen to belt down beans and broth. Once a year, on the Fourth of July, the town filled with farmers, everyone converging to park their wagons by the river and bustle into Caskey's Hardware, or chop a hunk of cheese from the block on the counter at Robinson's Mercantile. At dusk, they drifted back to the waterfront, eating together at long picnic tables and sleeping below their wagons under lilting cricketsong.

When Johnny got a football scholarship to junior college, he trundled off to spend four days each week on campus. Then he'd hurry home for long weekends, demanding a pile of fresh biscuits from whichever sister he found first—Melba, Mary, Flossie, it didn't matter; they all had Addie's recipe.

One day at Melba's, Johnny spotted a new girl across the road. She had downturned eyes and a broad, open face, and she'd just moved with her family from the little town of Hazen. Her dad had a job in the rice fields. Dirty work, but it paid. By summer, Johnny and Katherine Price were dating. By fall, they were hinting at marriage.

Whatever passion some men had for war, Johnny had none. The thought of combat was alien to him, and the thought of leaving Katherine worse. When the draft notice came, he handed it to his mother and she ran away. His dad's face turned red and he swore he'd never vote for a Democrat again. Johnny's sisters reassured him. "It's only a while," Melba said. "You'll be back before you miss us." But Melba knew it wasn't true, and Johnny knew it, too. On the last day before he shipped out, he stood with Melba on the front porch. They looked across the road to Katherine's house and the woods beyond.

"Melba," Johnny said quietly in a voice she'd never forget, "I don't think I'm ever going to see you again."

"Oh," she snapped, "don't say that, Johnny."

"Well, I just don't think I will," he said.

Johnny met Jimmie at gunnery school, and then they were off to Fresno. He married Katherine on a visit home, then he was in Tonopah.

Most of the men on Johnny's crew were about his age, but they came from places he couldn't imagine. Earl Yoh was a gunner from the snowy plains of northwest Ohio, one of thirteen kids crammed into a house with no electricity or plumbing. At night, Earl and his family would gather by the downstairs fireplace to play records on a windup Victrola, or else they'd tune in to the battery-powered radio for episodes of *The Shadow*. Then the kids would trudge upstairs to the cavernous second floor, with no insulation or dividing walls. The girls took one end of the room, the boys the other—except in the deepest part of winter, when they might burrow together under a mountain of blankets to stay warm.

Earl played baseball and basketball well enough to be named the "Best Boy Athlete" in his yearbook, but with soft brown hair and wide blue eyes, high cheekbones and a chiseled chin, he spent nearly as much time under the stage lights of the auditorium—starring in theater, the chorus, and the glee club, and singing his way into the hearts of local girls. In the annual "Will" section of the yearbook, his classmates wrote, "Earl Yoh leaves his way with women to Wayne Zielke"—a junior who, judging by photos, must have been grateful for the help.

Leland Price happened to grow up just a few miles from Earl on the banks of the Auglaize River, where his grandparents, aunts, and uncles shared a large house on a forty-acre farm, while Leland and his parents lived in a smaller home nearby. At five feet six and 130 pounds, he was small but not slight; his powerful shoulders and arms made him a natural fit for the cramped turrets of a B-24.

In Tonopah, they all bunked together, ate together, and raced together into the sky. Each time they lifted off, Johnny felt the pressure building in his nose, throbbing as they gained altitude until the blood came trickling down from an old football injury. He'd try to pin his nostrils shut, but never had much luck, laughing to the other boys that, damnit, he'd been hit. Then he'd belly up to the waist gun, raining hell on the desert floor.

"I've been on two gunnery missions this week and fired 500 rounds," he wrote to his sister Mary in March. "I almost shot a hole in the tail of the plane. Scared the heck out of me!"

After dark, the boys would retreat to their barracks—enlisted guys playing cards and drinking beer together, while the officers disappeared into separate quarters. Only one of the officers routinely visited the enlisted men. He was the navigator, Frank Arhar, a massive kid from a coalmining family near Johnstown, Pennsylvania, who loomed even over Johnny at six feet five, with a jutting jaw and short hair parted down the middle. At navigation school on Selman Field, he'd been issued a small booklet that he carried with him. It gave instructions to officers on how to relate to enlisted men. "If you do not have a sense of humor, cultivate one," it said. "Lack of it is worse than a disease. A disease affects only the person who has it, whereas a lack of a sense of humor is a wet blanket over all with whom you come in contact. Do not be afraid to laugh with your men. It will only go to show that you are human, and will add a little cement to the bonds that hold them to you."

More than any other officer the men had known, Frank Arhar lived those instructions. He would join them for a hand of cards and a drink and a laugh, and in time they gave him the nickname "Big Stoop," after the good-natured giant in a popular 1940 serial film. When they reached the war zone and got their own plane, they said, they would name it *Big Stoop*, and they would be the Big Stoop crew.

That day was coming. Each morning it seemed another crew departed Tonopah, and soon it would be their turn. They would fly to Hamilton Field, California, pick up a gleaming silver B-24J, and head west, to war.

THE WAR WAS PICKING UP. As the Big Stoop boys finished their training in Tonopah, Mussolini was hiding in the strongholds of northern Italy, Allied raids were leveling German positions in Belgium and France, and final preparations were under way for the landing at Normandy. But if the war in Europe was reaching an apex, the Pacific was at a crossroads of its own.

Since the beginning of the drive in 1942, US forces in the Pacific had formed along two primary lines of attack. The northern line, led by Admiral Chester Nimitz of the Navy, was pushing through the Central Pacific toward Taiwan. The southern line, led by the Army's General Douglas MacArthur, looped through Fiji and the Solomon Islands, and across New Guinea toward the Philippines.

If the two-column advance had some tactical benefits, they weren't entirely deliberate. Mostly, the twin approach reflected two different strategies for the war. The northern column embodied the Navy's conviction that the best way to reach Japan was in a relatively straight shot. But in the Army, MacArthur was just as adamant that only the southern track would work. Driving through the Philippines, he insisted, was a strategic and a moral necessity. Strategic because the islands offered a choke point to stop the flow of oil from Japanese refineries, including those of Balikpapan, Borneo, known as "the Ploesti of the East." But the southern route was also a moral necessity, MacArthur believed, because two years earlier he'd been driven from the islands himself and promised, "I shall return." Any strategy that failed to keep that promise was a betrayal of America's good name—not to mention his own.

Faced with two competing strategies, President Franklin Roosevelt chose both. His friend and military chief of staff, Admiral Bill Leahy, advised him to let each column proceed and see which fared better. Along the way, the two could protect each other at the flank, and they would give Roosevelt the greatest number of options as he drew closer to Japan. It was the sort of kitchen-sink strategy that could only make sense to an emerging superpower. As the military historian Max Hastings put it, "The twin-track strategy, sustaining both MacArthur's invasion of the Philippines and the navy's drive across the Central Pacific . . . represented a broadcasting of resources acceptable only to a nation of America's fantastic wealth."

The biggest downside of the two-column approach, other than expense, was that it split the Pacific command in half. Nowhere was the potential for bureaucratic confusion more obvious than in the Thirteenth Air Force. Much smaller than the Eighth and Ninth Air Forces pounding Europe, the Thirteenth had been cobbled together as an afterthought in 1942, when commanders realized that the ragtag ensemble of fighters and bombers they had sent to the South Pacific would need an organizational home. Yet as the Thirteenth Air Force stood up in January 1943, its position remained unclear; unlike other Air Forces in the Pacific, such as the Seventh in Hawaii and the Fifth in Australia, it had no standing base. Instead, its "headquarters" jumped from island to island, following MacArthur's front line, while for administrative reasons, it fell under the command of Nimitz. On any given morning, the airmen of the Thirteenth might fly in support of either column: north to cover Nimitz in the Central Pacific, or west to back MacArthur's advancing line. In time, the small, mobile Thirteenth became known as "the Jungle Air Force."

The first unit of the Jungle Air Force to embrace the B-24 was the 307th Bombardment Group. In fact, the 307th converted to Liberators even before the Thirteenth officially stood up. During the first major Allied offensive of the war, as the legendary First Marines pushed back Japanese defenses on Guadalcanal, the airmen of the 307th had flown the longest mass bombing mission in American history, pouring munitions on the Japanese airfield at Wake Island from their Liberators. It was a flight so risky, bloody, and effective that, two weeks later, Nimitz himself awarded the commanding officer of the mission the Distinguished Flying Cross. By the time the Thirteenth Air Force came into being a few days later, the 307th was its most decorated unit, with the nickname "the Long Rangers."

Over the next two years, while the Jungle Air Force hopped across the South Pacific, the Long Rangers remained invisible to the public. Just as the Marines who rushed onto Pacific beaches would always fall in the shadow of their counterparts at Normandy, the airmen of the South Pacific would never know the fame that fliers in Europe enjoyed.

But the Long Rangers knew. One of their earliest members was the Olympic runner Louis Zamperini, immortalized in the biography *Unbroken*; one of their last was the film director Robert Altman, who completed his fiftieth mission in the summer of 1945 and returned to California without a single bag of luggage. In between, the Long Rangers would cover a region of four million square miles, rarely stopping anywhere for more than a few weeks.

By the spring of 1944, they had made their way to a small island in the Admiralty chain, known as Los Negros. Two hundred miles south, the sprawling battlefield of New Guinea swarmed with Japanese troops; a thousand miles north, the Navy was preparing a strike on the

Mariana Islands. And to the west, Japanese troops were fortifying their defenses.

Faced with a string of losses on their outer islands, Japanese commanders were pulling back to a new defensive perimeter. They called it the Absolute National Defense Zone, and it hooked up from their claim on Timor, through central New Guinea, around the Caroline and Mariana Islands, and back to the Japanese home islands. Just getting the Japanese Army and Navy to agree on the new boundary involved a fierce debate; now that the line was in place, both had orders to defend it to their last man.

At the heart of the new perimeter lay tiny Palau. Since the first American strike on the islands by carrier planes in March, many Japanese commanders were convinced that Palau would be the next major US target. To defend the archipelago, the prime minister of Japan, General Hideki Tojo, dispatched one of the most vaunted divisions of the Japanese military. The Fourteenth "Shining" Division had, since its founding in 1905, won a string of battles in Siberia and Manchuria, and was one of the most honorable assignments in the Imperial Army. At the head of the Shining sat Lieutenant General Sadae Inoue (*in'-no-way*), a square-jawed man with large round spectacles, stiletto cheekbones, and a black triangular mustache, whose wife described him as "strict, but actually quite warmhearted."

Inoue had been leading the Shining for about a year in China, but when Tojo summoned him to a private meeting in Tokyo, his new instructions were clear: Palau was vulnerable, exposed, and possibly indefensible. But it was Inoue's job, and the job of the Shining, to hold it. If Palau was to be the next American target, Inoue was to make it the bloodiest target they'd ever taken.

Inoue landed on Palau just as the Big Stoop crew left Tonopah. As they made their way toward Los Negros, he was settling into the islands: digging intricate caves and bunkers through the hills, and girding the new defensive perimeter for the coming assault.

FOUR

DISCOVERY

Thirty thousand feet in the air, Pat Scannon cracked open his massive black sketchbook and rested it on the tray table in front of him. It had been two months since his visit to Maxwell Air Force Base, and his fixation on the missing B-24s spilled across the pages of his logbook in pencil and red ink. Each night he devoured history books and archival records, taking notes on the arc of Japanese colonial power, the aerodynamic details of the B-24, and the controversial role of Palau in the Pacific campaign—a debate still lingered among historians over whether it had been worth so much blood for such a small group of islands.

Scannon had also been planning his return to the islands in meticulous detail. He memorized topographic maps of Koror, cross-referenced them with vintage photos, and studied the witness statements in the mission reports. He contacted the Eastman Kodak Company to learn about the chemical properties of infrared film, hoping that with the right equipment he might be able to peer through the water of the channel and spot Arnett's plane. That channel, he now knew, was called Toachel Mid (*tow-ah'-kul mid*), and in a few days he expected to be there. Five months had passed since his first trip to the islands, but this time felt different.

He felt different. In all his years of medical school, the doctoral program in chemistry, and professional projects, he had always been able to maintain exacting focus, but the focus he now gave to Palau eclipsed anything he'd ever known. The six days he spent working at Xoma paled beside the seven nights he studied the islands, reviewing his plans and preparations into the hazy hours. Now that he was on his way, it was time to step back—to review everything he'd learned and what he hoped to accomplish.

Scannon flipped through the sketchbook until he found a blank page, and he popped the cap of a black felt-tip pen, writing in the upper left corner: "4:30 pm, over Pacific. I'm going back alone to Palau to find out more on B-24s. Because this is an expedition, a series of goals is proper. But first, after more than five months of research, what do I know?" He quickly summarized the leads he'd found. The wing that he and Susan had seen "is most likely the wing of Dixon." The rest of the Dixon plane appeared in photos to be heading for the north shore of Koror. The Custer plane seemed to have crashed somewhere near the Dixon wing—"south and east of Koror, into mangroves." And finally, the B-24 flown by Arnett "fell north of Koror and south of Babeldaob, but exactly where is unknown."

Next, Scannon listed his priorities:

- Locate Dixon wing, and see if other debris can be seen.
- Attempt location of Custer plane—also wing just west of plane, about 100 yards in water near outlet. Also, see if anything can be seen on adjacent island.
- Fly between Babeldaob and Koror to see if Arnett can be located.

But even before he delved into the jungle and water, Scannon wanted to speak with Palauan islanders. He would only have one week on the archipelago, and it would be easy to waste it trudging through all the wrong places. Places that appeared small on a map could be dangerous or inaccessible, and he also didn't want to spend his time searching for something that someone else may have found. He knew that the veterans of the 307th Bombardment Group had no record of where the B-24s crashed, but that didn't mean a Palauan islander hadn't found the debris. The islanders were expert fishermen and hunters who dove and trekked every day. They might easily have found a plane without bothering to notify the US Army. The smart approach was not to begin searching on his own, but to spend a few days meeting guides and elders who could tell him what the islanders already knew.

When Scannon's plane touched down at the airfield on southern Babeldaob, he descended a staircase to the runway in darkness. It would be his first time alone on the islands, and it filled him with a combination of excitement and fear. This time, he wouldn't have experienced travelers like Lambert and Bailey to help him arrange logistics and navigate the serpentine roads that led through the islands and their customs. As he walked across the airfield under a moonlit sky, he realized he was just a few hundred yards from the Toachel Mid channel. Everything about the islands was as unfamiliar and alien as that watery grave. The hot, moldering air clung to his skin and the sounds of the jungle echoed through the sky, yet somehow it all felt strangely reassuring, as if his body knew he belonged. He picked up a rental car in the terminal and drove slowly across the bridge to Koror, passing through the low concrete buildings of downtown, by gas stations and shuttered groceries and children bicycling through the night. When he found his hotel, he stumbled into his room with the realization that he'd been traveling more than twenty-four hours. In bed, he cracked open his journal and scribbled, "Travel—Overnight—Ugh—Jet lag." Then he passed out.

In the morning, Scannon headed to the Belau National Museum, a white stucco building with a red tin roof in a clearing above the southern bay. Like the traditional spelling of its name, the Belau museum focused on the islands' early history. It was nearly empty when Scannon arrived and an employee named Kemphis Mad walked him through the exhibits, pointing out ancient tools and weapons, dioramas of traditional villages, and a special collection of photos from the war, showing bombed-out Japanese fortifications and starving Palauan islanders huddled in the jungle.

As they walked, Scannon explained to Mad the purpose of his trip, how he'd come to the islands a few months earlier for a temporary diversion, but felt something deeper stirring when he saw the Dixon wing. He described the research he had been doing, how he riffled through archives and dug up photos of the lost bombers, and how all three of them seemed to have fallen just a few hundred yards from where they stood. As Scannon spoke, Mad listened and nodded. To the islanders it was hardly news that the archipelago was filled with missing planes and men. The mystery was why it had taken so long for someone like Scannon to come find them. "I can help you," Mad said, writing a series of names on a scrap of paper. If anyone had seen the planes come down, or if someone had found them since, the guides and elders on his list would know it.

For two days Scannon worked his way through neighborhoods and small towns, following a trail of introductions that began with Mad's contacts, then caromed between their relatives and friends, rumors and fading memories. It seemed that every few hours he would pull up to some new home in a remote community, to find a small group of islanders sitting in the bright sun, usually chewing a mixture of betel nut and crushed coral wrapped in a local leaf, which swished together in their saliva to make a chemical reaction that turned their lips orange. As Scannon took a seat, he would explain where he had been, who he'd met, and who had sent him, then he would ease into the conversation until finally he found an opportunity to pull out his photos and maps, asking, "Have any of you seen this plane? Do you know anyone who has?" Each time, the islanders would shake their heads, and give him another list of friends to ask, and he would follow another byzantine set of directions to another group of elders in the sun.

With every dead end, Scannon pushed down the urge to race to the dock and rent a boat and begin searching on his own. He reminded himself that working blindly was a fool's method. One man could never hope to discover in a week what the islanders had seen all their lives. Someone, somewhere, must have seen the bombers go down. It was just a matter of finding that person.

And then he met Xavier March.

IT HAPPENED SO FAST it was dizzying. One minute, he was pulling up to the young guide's home in central Koror, shaking hands, sitting down, and pulling out the photos; the next, they were driving to meet one of March's uncles, Demei Temol, at the home of another elder, named Belsam Lekesel. Then they were all sitting together on the stoop in front of Lekesel's tin-roofed house, chewing betel nut and sweating pools in the sun, while Temol and Lekesel flipped through Scannon's photos, saying, "No, no. There's no B-24 on Koror."

But the photos clearly showed the Dixon fuselage streaking down near Lekesel's house, and Scannon insisted that it had to be nearby. "I kept asking," he said later, "'Could it have gone over here? There?' and they said, 'No, no. Absolutely not. No bombers crashed on the island.' And I just couldn't think of another question, so I finally said, 'Okay, I appreciate your talking to me,' and I got up. And they said, 'You know, you never did ask about the wreckage in the *water*. . . .'"

Minutes later, Scannon and March were hurrying down a jungle trail, which burst into the open coastline of the north shore, where ankle-deep water lapped at the beach and, twenty feet out, a dense knot of metal the size of a car sat plunked in the surf.

Like it fell from the sky, Scannon thought with a smile. He rushed into the water, not even bothering to take off his shoes, and as he approached the wreckage, he could feel fragments of debris in the mud beneath his feet. When he reached the metal, he knew immediately that it was a plane—the sheets of aluminum joined by rivets, the bombardier's window cut into the side. It was the nose. The cockpit. He crept around it, peering into its core. There were pulleys inside, and a lever with a small button on the tip, which he recognized instantly as the bomb-release handle of a Liberator. *Dixon's plane*, he thought. It was just as it appeared in the photos—struck by the anti-aircraft guns over the southern bay and streaming over the island in flames to land here.

Scannon examined the cockpit for several minutes; then he sloshed toward the shore. He was exhilarated by the discovery and yet unnerved by the presence of death. William Dixon had probably died in this spot. In fact, he was probably still there, along with his navigator, Duncan, their bombardier, Tenton, and who knows how many of the crew. There had been a young lieutenant flying with them as an observer. He was probably in the cockpit, too.

When Scannon reached the shore, he glanced down at the sand. There was a glint of half-buried metal, and he reached to pick it up. It was a seventy-five-millimeter shell. He turned it over in his hands, confused. It was the same kind of shell used by the anti-aircraft guns on Koror, the kind that would have shot Dixon down. But those shells would still be in the hills with the guns, not here with the wreck. Scannon glanced back toward the water and did a double take. Directly over the crumpled nose, there was a rainbow forming. He laughed to himself and shook his head. He was a chemist, a physician—a lifelong empiricist. He stared at the rainbow a long time. Later, he wrote in his journal, "It was almost too much."

In the morning, he and March met up to follow another lead. The same two elders who knew about the Dixon cockpit also knew a man named Ichikawa Tadashi, who had seen another B-24 go down. It was, they said, somewhere in the southern bay. From his research, Scannon knew it had to be Custer.

They stopped by Tadashi's home on Koror. He was a frail man with tentative legs and a long scar down his forehead, but he agreed to take a boat to the site where he'd seen the plane go down. As they barreled toward the dock in Scannon's rental car, Tadashi recalled the crash.

Like many Palauans, he'd fled the city during the war. The only shelter he could find was a cave. It was carved into the limestone wall of a small island in the southern bay, where he could see the daily formation of Liberators as they came on the horizon. Most of the time, he would wait out the bomb strikes inside his cave, but one day in May 1945, the bombers arrived while he was foraging on Koror. From the shoreline, he could see his cave across the water, but there wasn't enough time to swim back. All he could do was duck into the mangroves and watch the US bombers sweep overhead, laying a string of bombs across Koror while the Japanese gunners lit up the sky.

As he crouched in the mangroves, Tadashi recalled, he saw one of the American planes take a hit on its left wing, and he watched as the wing floated down to land on an island near his cave. The rest of the fuselage was coming straight toward him, a stream of smoke and fire that hit the earth with a concussive blast as shards of metal rained down, slicing into Tadashi's arm and thigh and carving the long, deep scar that Scannon had noticed on his forehead.

Scannon searched for words to respond, but found none. Tadashi had nearly been killed by Custer and his men, the very airmen he was now taking Scannon to find. As they pulled into the marina, Scannon glanced outside, suddenly overcome by another memory. It was the same dock where he and Susan had met their guides on the day they found the Dixon wing. Now, as he watched Tadashi hobble from the car toward the pier, he couldn't shake the feeling that everything he had seen since then, from the discovery of the wing, to the photographs at Maxwell, to the crumpled cockpit in the water, even the scar on Tadashi's face, was all part of some invisible path that he was merely following.

When March had secured a boat, he and Scannon helped Tadashi aboard and pulled into a channel. They steered past the southern promontory of Koror and around to the southern bay, passing a series of small islands, including the one that held the Dixon wing, which Scannon now knew as Ngetkuml. Just to the north, there was an even smaller island, Iberor. It was where Tadashi had seen the Custer wing land.

As they crept toward Iberor, rain began to fall, pattering at first, then rising to a deluge. Scannon held a hand above his eyes and stared at the shimmering limestone walls. When the boat stopped a few feet from shore, he jumped out and splashed toward the cliffs. They were slick and slippery in the rain, but Scannon scrambled up. Directly above him, he could see a piece of the wing extruding through the foliage. There was a white star painted on the bottom, against a blue background. When he reached it, he grabbed the metal and hoisted himself up. He pushed into the subcanopy and found a second piece of the wing wedged between two trees. He could hear Tadashi and March shouting for him to come back, but he pulled off his backpack and found his underwater camera, snapping a few photos of the wing. He paused to offer a moment of silence, then he was rustling back to the cliffs and down to the boat.

Heading east, they passed another small island and Tadashi pointed to an opening on the cliffs. It was his hideaway during the war, just barely large enough to hold a man. It seemed impossible that Tadashi had lived there for months on end, but Scannon was learning that everything about the war was impossible to comprehend. The verdant hills had been carved with tunnels and strewn with cannons and military bunkers, and if it was difficult to grasp the full scale of the terror and violence, he knew he should be grateful that it was so hard.

The northern rim of the bay lapped against the shoreline of Koror, and Scannon stared up at the hills rising from the water. There was a Shinto shrine somewhere near the top, and beyond it, a massive gun emplacement known as Battery Hill. The area had been remade into a luxury hotel and putting green, but during the war, the guns of Battery Hill had probably shot down all three B-24s.

Tadashi gestured to a mangrove swamp to the east, and as March steered the boat closer, Scannon could see debris trailing into the jungle darkness. He stepped gingerly into the mud and waded toward the shore, past rods of metal jutting up from the ground and electrical equipment scattered in branches. He found a single piece of landing gear resting upside down. There was a large tropical plant growing in the wheel well, and without quite knowing why, he tried to pull it out, but the roots were bound deep in the metal and he couldn't break them free. Scannon removed his camera and took a few pictures of the wreckage, then he stopped to take it all in.

He wondered what sort of man Glen Custer had been. It was easy to imagine the airmen as gallant young heroes, but of course they weren't. They were all sorts of men, as prickly and troubled, crude and foolish as anyone else. He wondered if Custer had been alive long enough to see the jungle rushing toward him, and Tadashi crouching in the mangroves, his eyes wide with terror. He wondered how many of Custer's crew had survived the crash. He knew that the navigator, Wallace Kaufman, parachuted into Japanese hands. Some of the postwar reports described what happened to Kaufman. He tried everything to stay alive; at one point, he even attempted to convince his guards that he was Franklin Roosevelt's cousin. But the Japanese soldiers killed him. Took off his head with a sword. Scannon wondered if anyone had made it off Dixon's plane. He wondered what had happened to the airmen who parachuted from Arnett's.

In two days of searching, he had found two of the three B-24s. He'd done it with patience, and by asking the islanders for help. They were eager to share what they knew, and they knew more than he ever would.

Scannon could only begin to imagine what else Tadashi could tell him—about the years of Japanese occupation, the treatment of the islanders, and the fate of men like Wallace Kaufman. On the islands, none of those things seemed so far away. The Palauans also reminded Scannon that the search was much larger than himself. It wasn't about the thrill of adventure, or finding a pot of gold. It wasn't even about the lost planes. It was about memory. It was about preserving the past. It was about the feeling that came over him when he saw the Dixon and Custer wreckage, though it would be a long time before he understood where that feeling rose from in his past.

"On both the Custer and Dixon sites, I was emotionally overcome," he wrote in his journal. "Seeing the wings in the photos and in their final resting places, realizing the bits and pieces that I see once carried crews of Americans every bit as hopeful for a future as I was at that age, I have gotten to know these crews a little. To them, it made no difference that they died in a backwater campaign. They died young and violently. They are to be remembered."

ON HIS LAST AFTERNOON in Palau, Scannon drove up a long, winding road to the luxury hotel and putting green overlooking the bay. As he walked among the tropical shade trees, he felt the soft Palauan soil give beneath his feet, and he was struck again by the distinctive smell of the islands, a fusty aroma of jungle flowers, salt water, and decay, of wood fire mingling with diesel smoke, as if a thousand years of history wafted through the air at once.

In his research on the islands, he had been surprised by how long they were isolated. For centuries, European explorers simply called them "the Black Islands." Even modern archaeologists saw the archipelago as a puzzle. They could confirm just enough about the ancient people who inhabited them to be mystified by who they were. There were signs of civilization everywhere, from the old stone ruins covered in vines, to the tops of huge mountains that appeared to be sheared off. The hillsides were dribbled with evidence of settlement that traced back three thousand years. But the genetic composition of the islanders seemed to have shifted drastically in that time. It was difficult to say exactly who had lived there, or when, or for how long. The only thing certain was that people had been on the islands continually for thousands of years, their tribes merging together and warring, and building cultures that transformed from one to the next.

The nearest neighbor was Yap, a cluster of four small islands three hundred miles away, yet for centuries, the two were locked in a blood feud, passed down by legend and by oral tradition, and manifest in the odd Yapese habit of sneaking onto Palau to carve giant stone discs from the limestone hills and ferry them home. Some of those discs were twelve feet in diameter and weighed several thousand pounds, and their value on Yap was measured precisely in the danger of obtaining them. On Yap, a disc could be traded like currency to buy land or pay dowries, while on the shores of Palau, tribal sentries stood watch for raiding Yapese moneymakers.

The first European to sight the islands was Ferdinand Magellan in 1522, but another half century passed before Sir Francis Drake came ashore, then another century before the Spanish claimed the islands, and yet another before the English stayed long enough to meet the natives. That was in 1783, when the British ship *Antelope* crashed into the archipelago on a journey that the historian Daniel Peacock has called "a secret voyage to China." The British were reeling from the American Revolution, at odds with France and Holland, and found their merchant ships in Asia besieged by marauders. They had sent the *Antelope* to chart a course to China along a less traveled route. If the journey was successful, it would reopen the doors for English commerce in Asia.

The journey was not. The *Antelope* had been designed by the master shipwrights of Newburyport, Massachusetts, to be light and fast, but not especially sturdy. When it slammed into the western island of Ulong, the men on board were shipwrecked for months. By the time they had pieced together a new ship from the fragments of the old, they'd become so friendly with the tribe on Koror that they offered to bring the chief's son, Prince Lee Boo, back to England. He packed a woven mat to sleep on, and a rope made from coconut fiber, which he tied in knots to count the days at sea.

London changed all that. Lee Boo moved into the home of the *Antelope*'s captain and began squiring his way through British salons in a pink overcoat with a green collar. He sang at parties, flirted with older ladies, and learned the proper way to pass a bowl of cherries at dinner, before dying of smallpox five months later. In 1788, the story of Lee Boo and the *Antelope* became a best-selling book in London, putting the islands of Palau briefly on the mind of England.

In Palau, the impression of England was even more brief. Long after the departure of the *Antelope* crew, the islands remained a tribal land of family, village, honor, tradition, and internecine war—especially between the people of Koror and those of the Melekeok (*meh-lek'-ee-ok*) region on Babeldaob. It would be another century before Spanish diplomats brokered a peace between the two, then promptly sold the island chain to Germany in a package deal that included the Marshall Islands and most of the Marianas for about $4 million.

Under German control in the early 1900s, technology poured into the archipelago, as phosphate miners tunneled into the hills of Angaur Island to the south. But the German influence would disappear as quickly as it began: with the start of World War I, Japan seized control of the islands, and by 1920, all that remained of German Palau was the shrieking colony of pet monkeys that had escaped into the jungle of Angaur, soon to be known as Monkey Island.

Japan launched an immediate program of development on Koror, turning the sleepy village into the regional headquarters of its Micronesian empire, with responsibility for two thousand islands and three million square miles. Into the 1930s, the archipelago teemed with Japanese officials, merchants, and commercial fishermen, so that by the end of the decade there were three times as many Japanese residents as Palauans. They mined Babeldaob for bauxite to make aluminum, established a major army garrison on Koror, and oversaw the commercial behemoth of the South Seas Trading Company.

By the time Scannon reached Palau, most of the Japanese influence was fading, but the islands remained in political limbo. Since the end of World War II, they had been listed as a "trust territory" of the United Nations. But now, as Scannon walked the putting green above the southern bay, the country was on the verge of independence. That fall, it would become a sovereign republic for the first time. With a growing number of dive shops and hotels, restaurants and tourists, the islands maintained a fragile balance—at once a burgeoning vacation mecca and a nation anchored to the past, with no large-scale industry to mar a landscape of ancient ruins, pristine water, and sunken warships that shimmered beneath the screams echoing off Monkey Island.

While Scannon crossed the grassy expanse of the resort, the only other visitor in sight was a Japanese man in shorts and a Hawaiian shirt who was practicing his short game on the putting green. Scannon wandered to the edge of the lawn, where a pair of rusty iron tubes protruded from the ground. With a shudder, he realized they were anti-aircraft guns, probably from the Battery Hill emplacement. In fact, there was a good chance these guns had shot down Custer, Dixon, or Arnett. They seemed so small and harmless now, just spears of rust pointing at clouds. He glanced down the hillside to the glimmering water of the southern bay. Custer's plane was down there, and behind it, Tadashi's cave, and beyond that, Dixon's wing, all of it nearly forgotten.

The sun was burning down the horizon and he suddenly felt aware of the absurdity around him, that he could stand on this deadly hilltop in the padded embrace of luxury, where the only other man was a tourist like himself. Fifty years earlier, they would have seen each other only as Japanese and American, and they would have rushed headlong into a clash from which only one could survive. He listened to the quiet click of the man's putter striking the plastic ball. He turned back to the setting sun and squinted. Custer's plane had approached in a twenty-two-plane formation. They were flying at nine thousand feet, on a heading of fifty degrees. He tried to picture the planes approaching on the horizon. "I tried to hear the anti-aircraft rapid fire," he wrote later in his journal, "while the blast and vibrations of salvoes, as well as well-aimed bombs, went off to my right. I tried to imagine seeing a single B-24 hit, and come down in flames to crash just below my feet, while, first, a wing flutters down on a small island nearby. . . . I tried, but I could not imagine what it really was like. I felt empty, as if I wanted to feel more but couldn't."

As Scannon boarded a flight home the next morning, he watched the islands drop away. Then he ordered a tomato juice and leaned back in his chair. He thought of the week behind him. He had come to the islands with a list of three planes, and he had found two. But finding them only made the Arnett plane loom in his imagination. It was in the channel. It had to be. He hadn't had time to look, but he would come back. He would scour the bottom for as long as it took to find the last plane.

Scannon reached into his bag and pulled out the black sketchbook. He flipped to a blank page and wrote:

Dixon—found.
Custer—found.
Arnett—needs to be found.

FIVE

LANDFALL

For Jimmie and Johnny and the Big Stoop boys, the South Pacific was a pleasant surprise. The base on Los Negros had an unexpected lightness and an almost fantastical air. Just a few weeks earlier, when the unit first landed, it hadn't been so welcoming, with nests of coral snakes and adders that slithered through an impenetrable thicket. But a flurry of clearing and construction had transformed the camp into one of the most comfortable the unit had ever known.

It didn't hurt that the island was scheduled to become a new headquarters for the Thirteenth Air Force. With that distinction came a heightened building effort that included not only the usual Navy Seabees and Air Force Camp-Building Echelon, but also a crew of more than one hundred native men, who, for $2 a month plus a ration of canned food and tobacco, bustled about the camp carrying panels of thatched roofing made by the women of their villages, which they lashed together to form an instant village of administration buildings. By the end of May, there was a central office on the island with cubicles for pilots and squadron leaders to type their reports; an elaborate hospital, flush with supplies; a church; a chapel; a library stocked with a wide selection of titles, including *Swann's Way*, by Marcel Proust; and an officers' club perched on stilts above the beach, where men could try their luck at cards, ping-pong, or the Red Cross nurses passing through. Music was piped into the mess hall for dinner, and when the men returned from a mission, they were often met on the airfield by nurses carrying trays of cold juice and cookies.

There were two airfields on the island and two others nearby, but the Long Rangers had by far the best. Mokerang Field perched at the tip of a long peninsula that stretched into the South Pacific, with immaculate beaches and pristine water all around. The airstrip offered a dual runway, with one lane used to taxi and the other to lift off, and there were new service and supply buildings to one side. Just south of the airfield, Tent City was tucked into a shaded grove of coconut trees, which had once been part of a plantation and provided the men with as much fruit as they could stomach.

Arriving at the camp in early May, one man from the 371st Squadron wrote in his journal, "I already feel it may be the South Pacific island I dreamed of one day finding: a long, narrow palm tree–covered finger of land which gently curves to the northwest. . . . The surf, sometimes thunderous and threatening, is quiet and gentle at night. The steady on-shore breeze will keep us mosquito-free and cool. Rustling palm fronds, the soft hissing of shifting sands beneath the unfurling sheets of foam-speckled water, will lull us to sleep."

By the time the Big Stoop crew reached Mokerang and began to unpack their gear, the island was beginning to look like a Hollywood set. In photos taken by the unit that month, the roadways sway with straight lines of palms, while airmen relax on sandy beaches and sail the shallows in makeshift boats. The men erected volleyball courts, baseball diamonds, and horseshoe pits throughout the camp, where officers would play against the enlisted men in round-robin tournaments.

Some of the men also took time to expand their tents, building elaborate tiki-hut additions and tables for playing cards. During the move to Los Negros, the unit store had been folded into a larger PX, but the larger facility would not accept the unit's alcohol or tobacco. Since beer and cigarettes made up roughly 70 percent of the Long Rangers' inventory, commanders had little choice but to give away the goods. Beer flowed freely throughout the camp.

One of the Long Ranger squadrons had a Scottish terrier as a pet, and the men posed for crew photos with the dog, even painting its likeness on the flat panels of their planes. Other men collected local wildlife, like lizards, birds, and snakes. "The natives used to get inner tubes from the planes to make slingshots," a gunner named Al Jose recalled. "They'd shoot a rock at a parrot to bring it down, and they'd sell wounded parrots to the crews as pets. Of course, you'd go on a mission and come back, your goddamn tent was in a shambles." In film shot by the unit on Los Negros, one man can be seen patrolling the airfield with a pet monkey on his shoulder, which would periodically leap into the window of a B-24 and swing from the waist gun.

In his letters home, Jimmie Doyle tried to capture the sensation of discovering an island paradise at war. "Wish you could have been with me today," he wrote to Myrle. "I spent all afternoon on the beach, swimming and trying to take the hull off of coconuts. Johnny and I found one of those big lizards, about like the one you and I saw at Tonopah, only this one was about twice as big. We would chase him awhile, and then he would chase us, but finally he found a tree, and got away from us. There are a lot of pigeons here, all colors and kinds, but they all make a noise about like rubbing two pieces of rusty iron together. . . . About the biggest problem is getting anything to read. We don't have papers or magazines, and I guess I've read about all there are here."

In the large green tent that the enlisted men shared, they arranged their cots against the walls, hung their belongings from the poles that supported the pyramidal top, and traded wisecracks in the darkness.

Only one member of the crew had not trained with them in Tonopah. His name was Ted Goulding, and he was a quiet kid from Yonkers, New York, with padded cheeks and sad eyes and the faint beginnings of a mustache. He'd been through Tonopah at about the same time, but would now transfer into their crew as radio operator. Ted had a soft, clear voice and a studious air that belied a limited education. He'd dropped out of school in his midteens and run away from home to escape the domineering presence of a hard-drinking father. By the time he was sixteen, he'd settled into a job at a dog kennel in Westbury, Long Island, where he tended and groomed show dogs for a woman he addressed only as Mrs. Tucker.

Long Island in those days, and especially Westbury, was home to some of the most famous airfields in the country, known collectively as "the Cradle of Aviation." Just two miles from Mrs. Tucker's kennel sat the nation's busiest airport, Roosevelt Field, where Charles Lindbergh departed in 1927 on the first solo nonstop flight across the Atlantic. Next door to Roosevelt was Mitchel Field, another legendary airstrip, where a young Jimmy Doolittle had completed the first "blind" flight in 1929—lifting off, navigating, and landing with only instruments to guide him.

Living among the airfields of Westbury offered Ted a kind of daily proof that even the loftiest dreams may rise. He was infatuated with aircraft, and studied the various models of the era with an intensity he'd never found at school—memorizing their dimensions and mechanical features in the way other boys knew baseball or movie stars. Inside his tiny bedroom at Mrs. Tucker's, he collected flight magazines and sent away for model kits, which he built up carefully and brought into her backyard to fly. He had been mesmerized when Jimmy Doolittle led the first American raid over Tokyo in April 1942, and whenever he was outside with his models, he would keep one eye on the horizon for air-planes landing in the fields nearby. Who knew, one day it could be General Doolittle himself.

One afternoon while Ted was in the yard, he struck up a conversation with two young boys kicking about the neighbor's property. George and Phil Graziosi were two of the youngest in a family of twelve kids, and soon they were bumbling through the small gate to help Ted in the kennel in exchange for a few pennies and a turn at his model planes. Then Ted was passing through the gate to join the Graziosis for dinner—hoisting little George and Phil into the air and posing for photos with one boy on each shoulder and a billiard pipe clamped in his teeth.

It wasn't long before Ted noticed the Graziosis' daughter, Diane, and then his dreams weren't just about airplanes anymore. In the summer of 1942, he spent his savings to buy a sporty green 1936 Oldsmobile coupe from Mrs. Tucker's boyfriend, a proud figure named Grayson Neff who always wore a three-piece suit. Neff had mounted two small bronze statues of Airedale terriers on the front fender and Ted adored them, but he folded away the backseats to give the interior a sportier feel. Then he ushered Diane into the passenger seat and whooshed her off to the movies. Afterward, he would drop her back at home, park the car, and climb up to the second-floor balcony by her bedroom for a kiss good night. In his own room at Mrs. Tucker's, he would stare at the ceiling for hours, buoyed by the memory of Diane and flipping absently through airplane magazines, dreaming of life in the sky. Within a year, Ted and Diane were married: Ted moved into the Graziosi house, Diane got pregnant, and Ted got drafted.

As Ted wound his way through training in Miami Beach and Chicago, Diane's family moved to a small farm in the gentle folds of Marlboro, New York. They rested Ted's car on blocks in a barn, and in the evenings, little George and Phil would traipse down to see it, standing in the shafts of light and wondering when Ted would come home. In July 1943, while he was still in training, Diane gave birth to a son. She named him Ted

Junior. Another three months passed before the youngest of the Graziosi boys, Paul, was playing outside and spotted Ted at the foot of the driveway, walking toward the house with a duffel bag over his shoulder. Paul Graziosi stared, frozen, then raced inside to tell.

They got seven days together, taking picnics by the river and staying up late to walk the moon across the stars. Ted checked on the Oldsmobile and played with the Graziosi boys, but mostly he stayed near his son, cradling the boy to sleep and posing for a photo in his bomber jacket, with his goggles on his forehead, and Ted Junior nestled into a mountain of white swaddles in his arms. Then Ted Senior was back in training, and then he was off to war.

As he settled into the green Big Stoop tent and got to know the rest of the crew, he could only wonder when they would see combat. Each morning, the veteran fliers of the unit would hurry to the airfield, climbing aboard their Liberators and speeding down the runway, while the new arrivals shuffled into a thatched building for advanced training. Jammed in their seats, they listened to a droning spiel about island topography, enemy tactics, target identification, and sea survival, and when the classes ended at lunch, the afternoon yawned before them. They would wander off to play cards, or amble down the beach, throwing shells back into the water and swimming along the coral coast. In the evening, they watched as the Liberators returned, clattering onto the airfield with wings holed by Japanese artillery, medics racing the injured men to the island hospital, while the rest of the fliers tossed back a glass of juice, grabbed a cookie, and stumbled back to their tents to descend into a haze of beer. At dinner, they would leave empty seats for the men who hadn't made it back, turning their cups and plates upside down. Then they would walk through the darkness to a huge white sheet stretched between palms, where the unit broadcast nightly movies sent by the War Department. The films were often several years old, but familiarity was its own reward.

On the last night of May, at a screening of the 1938 film *Alexander's Ragtime Band*, Jimmie Doyle found himself drifting back to the day that he and Myrle first saw the movie at the squat brick Palace Theater on First Street in Lamesa, Texas. When the reel fluttered out and the screen went dark, Jimmie shuffled up the coral road. He lit a candle inside the tent, stooping over a small lined notepad to write a letter home. "Do you remember when you and I saw it," he began, "back in those golden days when there wasn't a war? Sweetheart, I sure wish you could be with me, to help me gather coconuts. There are a thousand new things to see, and you should see some of the blossoms that grow here. There is one red one that grows at the top of a tree, and it is the prettiest flower you ever saw."

As the days of training dragged by, the boys grew restless. They began to grouse in letters home about the tedium of training, and the long, aimless days. Some began to call the island Camp De Luxe. Lying on his bunk the night of June 15, Jimmie wrote to Myrle, "I go to the show about three times a week, and drink my two bottles of beer. . . . The rest of my time is spent dreaming about coming home." Across the tent, Johnny was finishing a letter to Katherine when a loud thump broke the silence and a coconut rolled through the door to Jimmie's bunk.

Jimmie looked up. He grinned. "Now that," he said, "is real service."

But the slow pace of life on Los Negros was about to end. What Jimmie and Johnny couldn't know as they finished their letters that night, was that two dramatic changes were already unfolding that would alter history and their lives. A thousand miles north, in the Mariana Islands, American forces were landing on the island of Saipan, sending shock waves through the Japanese military that would eventually shatter the imperial command. And closer to home, that same day, the Long Rangers had a new commander of their own: after eighteen months in the northern column led by Nimitz, they had been transferred into MacArthur's line—putting the Army's Thirteenth Air Force under the Army's command for the first time. In the days to come, the Big Stoop boys would not just fly their first mission. They would enter the war at a pivotal moment, with Japanese forces reeling on Saipan and the Thirteenth Air Force coming into its own.

THE AMERICAN LANDING on Saipan was more than just a beachhead. Though the Mariana Islands were barely a speck on the regional maps issued to Long Ranger navigators, their importance went far beyond size. Like Palau, the Marianas lay near the center of the new Japanese perimeter, and a victory there would be the first breach of Japan's inner line. It would also provide the Air Force with a base just 1,500 miles from Japan, putting the US heavy bombers within reach of Tokyo. In time, the Marianas would launch the *Enola Gay* toward Hiroshima.

For the Japanese, the Saipan landing was also a political disaster. All year, Prime Minister Hideki Tojo had been girding for an assault on Palau, and he had personally dispatched Sadae Inoue to defend the islands with twenty-five thousand men. Now that US troops were swarming across a different archipelago, Tojo's judgment and his position were cast in doubt. As the military historian Mark Peattie wrote in *Nan'yō*, "The attack on the Palaus [three months earlier] had convinced Imperial General Headquarters that the next American amphibious blow would fall on those islands, a conviction in which both Tokyo and the Thirty-First Army [in the Marianas] persisted up to the very last days before the American invasion of Saipan."

If the balance of power in the Central Pacific was shifting, so was the power of the Long Rangers. Unit commanders had never been happy about their position in the northern line. It wasn't just that they answered to the Navy there; the bigger problem was that under Nimitz they had to give up operational control of their fleet. With the transfer to MacArthur, they would not only come under Army command, but would gain control of their planes, equipment, and staff for the first time. As the historian of the Thirteenth Air Force, Benjamin E. Lippincott, wrote in the 1948 book *From Fiji through the Philippines with the Thirteenth Air Force*, "With operational control, it may be said that the Thirteenth came into its own.

There was a distinct improvement in morale at headquarters; men could now see and feel that the Air Force was performing the function for which it had been designed." A keepsake volume assembled by the Long Rangers in 1945 described the transfer like this: "This move seemed to symbolize in our minds the opening of a new era. Like a boxer who has been seasoned by a number of successful preliminary bouts, the Allied forces were now ready to step into the big ring, confident of the devastating punch they could deliver."

In a fitting gesture, the first mission the Long Rangers would fly under MacArthur was to support Nimitz on the northern line. As the Central Pacific ground forces pushed onto Saipan, the Japanese Navy responded with a massive assault on American support ships offshore. By June 19, the fight for the Marianas was raging on land and water, when a US reconnaissance plane spotted a bevy of Japanese reinforcement ships heading to join the fight. Nimitz dispatched a special task force to cut them off at Yap, but if the task force failed, the whole campaign could tip.

With so much on the line in the Central Pacific, MacArthur sent the Long Rangers to cover their former commander. Their instructions were to find the Japanese ships, sink them, and destroy the imperial infrastructure on Yap while they were there.

Just getting from Los Negros to Yap was a navigational feat. The flight crossed more than one thousand miles of uninterrupted water, with no major landmarks or points on the horizon to help chart the way. In a rare feature on the Long Rangers, the *New York Times* declared Yap "the most important single target in the Southwest Pacific area," and praised the unit for having already completed three hundred successful combat missions in less than two years.

While the Long Rangers prepared for the mission, another plane was lifting off in California on a very different journey. It was a medical airlift heading to rescue the wounded on Saipan, and a small troupe of entertainers had hitched a ride on board. The leader of the group was Bob

Hope, who was still in his early forties but already a legendary figure around the world. Hope had spent the previous year touring military bases in England, Sicily, North Africa, and throughout the United States, but he was heading to the Pacific for the first time.

To join him, Hope brought some of his favorite performers, including the singer Frances Langford, the comedian Jerry Colonna, the musician Tony Romano, the dancer Patty Thomas, and a joke writer named Barney Dean, who had been working with Hope since his early days in 1920s Chicago vaudeville. When the airlift touched down to refuel in Hawaii, the entertainers transferred to one of Douglas MacArthur's personal planes, the *Seventh Heaven*, to complete their journey south. Over the next two and a half months, they would travel thirty thousand miles across the South Pacific, performing 150 shows that would change Hope forever. According to biographer William Robert Faith, the comic remarked at the end of the trip, "Everyone claims I'm a little more serious than I was. . . . Those men, those soldiers, they're not just a bunch of crap-shooting, wolfing guys we like to joke about. These men are men, with the deepest emotions and the keenest feelings that men can have about everything life holds dear."

While Hope circulated through the islands, the Long Rangers were gearing up for Yap. In their first strike, they took the Japanese garrison by surprise, plastering the harbor and airfield with enough bombs to destroy nineteen planes and damage fifteen more, all without losing a man. But they hadn't found the Japanese ships, and were surprised to discover how extensive the fortifications were on Yap. They were planning a series of follow-up missions, but they knew the surprise was lost.

The return to Yap would also mark the first combat mission for a member of the Big Stoop. As part of each crew's preparation, the pilot and co-pilot were required to fly one mission as observers with another crew. On the morning of June 23, under a blanket of cumulus clouds, the pilot of the Big Stoop crew—Norman Coorssen—climbed aboard a silver B-24J to see his first day of battle. The plane was so new that it had only completed eight missions, and it had no name or artwork painted on its nose; it was known only by the last three digits of its serial number, 453.

But that was a number Coorssen would never forget.

COORSSEN WAS A STRAPPING KID with blond hair and blue eyes and the faintest hint of a sarcastic smile. He came from the town of Amesbury, Massachusetts, just above the harbor of Newburyport, where shipwrights had built the *Antelope* in the nineteenth century for its journey past Palau. In the years since, Newburyport had diminished as a shipping center—its waterfront yards giving way to railroad tracks, then parking lots, while its remaining docks echoed not with maritime traffic, but with the vestigial ruckus of longshoremen carousing.

The town of Amesbury, meanwhile, was nestled up the Merrimack River and its tributary, the Powwow, far enough from downtown Newburyport to sustain its own social strata. Tucked below the New Hampshire border, it was about as far north as one could go in Massachusetts, and the Coorssen family was as far north as one could go in Amesbury. They owned the last big nautical company in town, the Henschel Corporation, which made telegraphs and consoles for ships in a massive brick warehouse that employed 10 percent of the town.

For the Coorssens, the Great Depression had been something in the newspaper. Norman and his older brother, George, enjoyed the sort of crisp New England privilege that seems rinsed in sepia even to those who were there. "It was almost a caste system," George's wife, Helen Coorssen, said. "It's embarrassing to say it now, but the Irish were still not accepted. There was a large French population, who were the workers. Then there were the Protestants, who lived at a higher level. And then there were five or six families like the Coorssens—for them, it was a wonderful place to live. They had no competition. They all sort of played bridge and golf, and liked their drinking. The whistle blew at noon, and everybody went home for lunch."

Like the other leading families in Amesbury, the Coorssens kept a summer cottage at nearby Plaice Cove, where Norman and George spent teenage afternoons swimming and sailing and chasing all the right kinds of girls. For high school, they attended Phillips Exeter Academy. For college Norman chose Williams, and George, MIT.

But while George adapted well to collegiate life, Norman had trouble. "Norman liked to play a lot," Helen said. "He was handsome, blond, crispy-creme, and all that—just *loved* the parties." After the Pearl Harbor attack, George volunteered for officer training in the Navy. Norman continued to enjoy himself at Williams, until the draft notice came.

For the first time in his life, Norman Coorssen was on the wrong side of fortune. "It was like a rug pulled out," his nephew, Gary Coorssen, said. Under the draft, Norman would not only enter the service as a lowly private, but he was slated to serve in one of the most dangerous jobs of the war, as an infantryman in a reconnaissance battalion. "That's when he started to think, 'Gee, that's the front line—maybe I should become a pilot!'" Gary said.

"He must have been a wretched private," Helen added. "He used every wile he had to get out of it."

Somehow, by the spring of 1943, Norman had managed a leap that few men could make, from the enlisted ranks to the officers' club, from grunt to pilot. How he did so, even his family wasn't sure. But he arrived in Tonopah at the head of a crew filled with men who weren't so lucky: Jimmie and Johnny and Ted and Earl and Leland—the Big Stoop crew. Now, as Norman climbed aboard the 453 bomber for his observation flight to Yap, even those men were gone. He was heading into enemy territory with a crew he didn't know.

Norman listened to the familiar rumble of engines as the 453 rolled down the coral taxiway, turning at the end to face the open runway, then surging forward to sweep into the sky in a formation of six. Through the window, he could see the other five planes in the squadron fanned out against the horizon, and beyond them, two other squadrons, for a total of eighteen planes from the Long Rangers, plus another formation of the same size from the Fifth Bombardment Group, which was stationed a few miles south on Momote Airfield.

Together, the Liberators climbed through the clouds until they reached the open sky, looking down on pillowy cumuli that seemed to rest upon deep black water. The hours crept by, the horizon unchanging. Norman Coorssen waited. When the formation finally drew close to Yap, the planes circled above a nearby island, Sorol, pulling into a tight box formation for the bombing run.

Leaving Sorol, the 453 was near the back of the formation. Norman watched as the Fifth Bombardment Group led the way toward Yap. As the first squadron approached, a swarm of Japanese Zeros leaped from the airfields toward them, zipping around the Fifth bombers and dancing in the air above them, swooping down like knives to slice through them, rattling them with machine-gun fire, and then looping overhead again to drop phosphorus bombs that exploded into tentacles of white-hot liquid dripping down the clouds.

It was like watching sailboats in a storm. The artillery pumping up from the ground filled the sky with a haze of shells, and there seemed no way for the Fifth planes to avoid being hit. Within seconds, one was streaming down, a thick plume of yellow smoke trailing from its right wing as it swerved across the enemy islands with two Japanese fighters chasing it. Norman watched as they sprayed the Liberator with an endless torrent of fire.

On the radio, he heard the pilot of the wounded Liberator call out. The damage was too great. He would have to ditch the plane. The bomber sank toward the water. It skirted the whitecaps at 150 miles per hour, and for a moment it seemed to stabilize, but then a slight wobble tipped the right wing too low, snagging on the water's surface and bowling the whole airframe forward on its nose. A geyser shot up as the wing broke off. Then the fuselage folded and snapped in half. There were five more Zeros bearing down. They tore through the air above the wreckage, spattering it with machine-gun fire.

Norman felt a drop in his belly as his own plane lifted. They were over the enemy position and their bombardier was beginning to drop the payload. The 250-pound bombs plummeted toward the ground. From the cockpit, Norman could see explosions on the runway below. The first bomb struck the shoulder of an operations area, and the rest walked north toward the taxi loop, where a collection of parked planes dissolved in black smoke.

Norman felt another surge and now the plane was dropping. The pilot had the controls forward, diving to 5,000 feet, then 3,000, then 1,200, then they were just 250 feet above the water, scooting over the surface in search of the downed plane—but there was no plane, just fragments of wing and landing gear sinking into a yellow stain of foam, while a lone survivor floundered madly in the oily surf. There was a commotion in the back of the 453 as crewmen tossed a life raft through the rear door, but there was nothing else they could do, no way to land or help. They turned the Liberator back toward Los Negros for the journey home.

Night was falling as Norman climbed down to the white coral runway. He made his way back to camp, disappearing inside his tent. In the morning, he would have to return to the airfield. He would have to return to those islands. He would lead his crew on a mission that he knew they could not yet imagine. They had missed his first day of war, just as he would miss their last.

SIX

ARNETT

A*rnett.* Scannon stared at the name. It was the last B-24 on his list, but like the missing piece of a jigsaw puzzle, it made the whole project feel incomplete. The more Scannon studied the islands, the more mysterious the Arnett plane seemed.

For one thing, it was the only one for which he had no pictures. According to the mission report, there had been six aerial photographers flying on other planes that day. Their job was to document bomb strikes, but during the Dixon and Custer crashes they turned their cameras to record the planes going down. In fact, some of the same photographers who shot the Dixon crash had been on the Arnett mission three days later. So why did they photograph the first crash and not the second?

It was also curious that the mission documents placed the Arnett wreckage between Koror and Babeldaob. Now that Scannon was more familiar with the islands, he knew how improbable that was. The narrow channel, Toachel Mid, was not just any passage. It cut between the two primary islands in the chain and served as one of the busiest throughways of the archipelago. Hundreds of boats passed through Toachel Mid on any given day, and it was striking that, over half a century of regular traffic, no one had ever caught a glimpse of the Arnett wreckage, and no stray line had ever snagged it, and no fisherman's sonar pinged it.

Other aspects of the report were equally bewildering. The witness statements were only a few words long, and they made no effort to describe the crash in detail. Staring at the fifty-word summaries, it was tempting to read between the lines for clues, but Scannon had seen first-hand on the Bush trawler how dangerous that could be—how easy it was to imagine hidden meanings that weren't there. The men who wrote those wartime reports had done the best they could, but with the benefit of time and distance it was clear how much they'd left out. Scannon would never forget that the Bush report listed the wrong atoll, and he knew that if he wanted to find Arnett it wouldn't be enough to keep searching the same old documents for details. He needed new documents, new information, and new witnesses—but where?

At night, he punched in phone numbers, following a trail of connections that began with veterans in the Long Ranger reunion group and bounced through their friends and crewmates, until sometimes he wound up calling a flier he knew only by a nickname. Occasionally he would get through and discover that the man had recently died. Other times, the man would pick up but have no memory of the war. With each conversation, Scannon heard the tick of time on the line, as if the last memory of the Arnett crash might vanish at any moment. He kept calling.

In the summer, he flew to a reunion of the Long Rangers, milling through a crowd of old men with slicked white hair and name tags clipped to their Hawaiian shirts. He choked down plates of warmed-over chicken and gobs of mashed potatoes, asking everyone he met whether they had been in the unit during the summer of 1944. When someone said yes, he would sit rapt for hours, absorbing every story the old airman could recall—how members of the group snuck off one night, on a base with dirty water, to dig up the plumbing supply of a nearby Australian unit and tap a branch line for themselves; or how, on the endless flights over enemy territory, they often had no better place to empty their bowels than the boxes their lunch came in, which they would drop whenever they crossed a Japanese island, laughing at bombs away.

Even in the bright, bland light of the hotel conference center, Scannon felt a strange intimacy with the Long Rangers. All his life, his friends and family had known him as intensely private, given to long interior spells lost in thought. He had always been more interested in contemplating biochemical bonds at work than in forging them over drinks, and he knew that his first marriage had suffered in part from that unreachable aspect of himself. When the marriage ended, he'd made the long drive north to visit his daughter each weekend, privately suspecting that the distance made him a better father, that it forced him to set aside time for Nell that he might not have found otherwise. Now she was a teenager who seemed to share his singular drive; he felt they understood each other in unspoken ways. But with the fliers, Scannon felt a different kind of kinship. He felt as if somehow he had always been among them, as if laughing with them and slugging a beer and leaning back in his chair, he belonged, and he was entranced by even the most trivial minutiae of their wartime memories, the intricacies of the islands and the bombers and the bases.

He began to visit the airmen at home, recording interviews that could stretch for hours or days or only a few minutes. One weekend, he drove 150 miles to spend two hours in the living room of a gunner who had seen both Dixon and Arnett crash. Scannon spread his records on the table, tracing the path of the Dixon plane in the mission photos; then he pulled out the pictures he'd taken of the wreckage fifty years later— the pristine wing, the mangled nose plunked in shallow water. He listened in awe as the gunner recalled the sight of Dixon falling, and the strange sensation that came over him, a combination of unbridled hatred for the Japanese and unalloyed joy at having been spared.

But when Scannon pulled out a map of the channel and asked where Arnett went down, the gunner just shook his head. It might as well have been a map of the moon, she said. After half a century, he could still see the plane's left wing bursting into flames. He could see it folding off, and the plane swerving right, then left, before it hit the water, while two parachutes popped into the air and floated through the clouds. But the precise location of the wreckage had vanished from his memory.

Back home, Scannon continued reading, calling, and studying the mission reports, when yet another anomaly caught his eye. The men who crashed with Arnett had never flown with him before. On every other mission that summer, they flew with another pilot, Norman Coorssen. So why did they join Arnett on their final mission?

Scannon called the historian of the 307th, Jim Kendall. Over the prior year, they had spoken many times. Kendall had given Scannon some of his first mission documents, pointed him toward the archive at Maxwell Air Force Base, and introduced him to surviving airmen from the Palau campaign. In fact, Kendall himself had flown with the unit that summer, and he regaled Scannon with colorful stories about life on base. But when Scannon asked Kendall why Arnett had flown with a different crew on his final mission, he could hear the dread and weariness seep into Kendall's voice.

Arnett, Kendall explained, had problems with his crew. A few hours before the mission, they refused to fly with him. There was no way to resolve the conflict in time for the mission, so commanders brought in another crew to fly with Arnett. They'd never flown with him before, and the whole thing was a breach of protocol. It would have led to a disciplinary investigation, except the plane crashed.

Scannon's eyes grew wide as he scribbled into his journal in black ink: "Crew voted him out! Navigator, co-pilot, and bombardier refused to fly with him. A serious complaint was filed, and another crew flew on that day." Yet as he hung up with Kendall, he realized that he still had no idea what it meant. Why would Arnett's crew refuse to fly with him? Was it personal, or did they question his ability? And was it a coincidence that his plane went down the same day? The timing seemed too neat to dismiss, but there was no other evidence to go on. There was no record of the crew change in the mission documents. There had been no investigation, as far as he could tell. And Kendall said he didn't know any other details.

It would be a long time before Scannon did.

THE DEEPER SCANNON'S FIXATION with Palau became, the more baffling it was to Susan. She had never shared his overpowering awe at the Dixon wing, and after a childhood in the Pacific she saw little magic in the war-torn islands. "The Pacific isn't exotic to me," she would say with a shrug. "To me, Switzerland is exotic."

Yet privately, Susan was delighted by Scannon's budding obsession. She enjoyed a raft of her own pursuits that rarely involved Pat—writing plays and sewing her own clothes and gardening and attending symphonies, while Pat's hobbies had always been: work, work, and more work. If he suddenly felt a hankering to hump through a distant jungle and unravel the mysteries of war, well, the only thing that worried Susan was the possibility that he might resist that urge out of some misplaced deference to her. One night as he was rustling through yet another stack of papers, she poked her head into the room and watched for a moment.

"Patrick," she said.

He looked up.

"You need to go back."

A flash of confusion crossed his face, and she said, "You need to do this. Go. Stay as long as you want." Then she smiled. "It's nice to cook for one."

Scannon went back.

He spent a week on the islands in 1995, but lost the first four days staring through the windows of his hotel room as a deafening gale rattled the streets and pelted the sea. When the storm finally broke, he raced to the airport to hire a charter flight over the islands with a pilot named Spike Nasmyth, who was an old Air Force flier himself and knew what it meant to be shot down. In 1966, on a mission over Vietnam, Nasmyth had been hit by a surface-to-air missile and fallen into enemy hands, spending the next six and a half years—2,355 days, he liked to say—in the same Hanoi prison as John McCain, beaten senseless by guards and tied in knots until his limbs were a tangle of cartilage and scars. Now he listened as Scannon explained about Arnett and pointed to Nasmyth's Cessna, saying, "I want you to take the door off and bank over the channel, so I can hang through the opening and get a bird's-eye view."

"Sure," Nasmyth said with a shrug, "but if you fall out, it's your problem."

Then they were coursing over the channel with Scannon lashed in the doorframe by a ganglion of ropes, reeling off hundreds of photographs with infrared film, but as he returned home and developed the pictures, he saw nothing in the water, just a vast expanse of churning sediment that washed through the channel.

Scannon felt deflated. He had spent another week on the islands and come home with nothing. Looking at the photos, what he saw most clearly was his own naïveté. The same channel that had seemed so small on the little map at Maxwell Air Force Base now stretched out before him like an angry void. It might take years to search the silty water, one dive at a time. Working alone, in fact, it could take the rest of his life.

Scannon assembled a small team for his next trip. At the top of the roster were Chip and Pam Lambert, and then two diving friends, and for fun he invited his daughter, Nell, to come along with her boyfriend, Jed. As the two-week expedition wore on, the search devolved. Each morning, they boarded a flat-bottomed boat and motored out to the channel, trailing an echo finder behind them in a series of long passes. Whenever they heard a promising ping, they would drop in for a look, but the current was strong and the visibility poor and the weather grueling. As the days passed in blasts of frigid rain and broiling sun, they broke off a little earlier each day, pointing the boat toward a glimpse of something more hopeful—the explosion of life on a barrier reef perhaps, or the giant mollusks at Clam City, or the transfixing verdancy of small islands rising up from the water.

One afternoon, Scannon and Chip Lambert scaled the walls of an especially steep island, and when they reached the top, they peered over the side to discover that it was hollow—the center bored out like a volcano, with two marine lakes at the bottom. They climbed down carefully into the lush vegetation, with sounds reverberating around them. "It was like we had gone into prehistoric times," Scannon said. "There were these white birds flying, and eerie echoes. Honest to God, if we had seen a pterodactyl, I would not have been surprised." But when they paused for a moment at the bottom and gazed across the landscape, Lambert cried out, "My God, Pat! Do you know what you're leaning against?"

Scannon spun around. It was a boulder, six feet across and nearly flat on top, and he realized that he was looking at a Yapese stone disc. There was a long crack down its face and the edges were unfinished, but the rest was too carefully chiseled to be anything else. Looking around, Scannon and Lambert spotted dozens of others lying incomplete or broken in the island soil. "The whole *area* was a quarry," Lambert recalled. "They had been carving stone money right out of the walls!"

"It had clearly been abandoned," Scannon added. "You could just imagine what happened. The Palauans had a deep hatred of the Yapese, so if they ever got caught, they would have been killed."

Scannon and Lambert walked deeper into the island. They crossed the lake and scaled a wall overlooking the basin, ducking into a small cave. When their eyes adjusted to the darkness, they could see that the earthen floor sloped deep into the rock. They descended past mounds of bat guano until they reached the end, where a tiny set of human bones lay carefully arranged against the wall. There were pieces of jewelry still wrapped around the skeleton, and nearby, the head of an ax.

Scannon felt the chill of death wash through him again, the same sensation he had first experienced at the Dixon wing. He and Lambert whispered quickly in the darkness, deciding not to touch another thing. They hurried outside and back to the boat, speeding off toward Koror, where they passed along the coordinates of the quarry to local preservationists.

As Scannon returned to California, he was filled again with a feeling of defeat. However intriguing the Yapese money had been, however beautiful the islands, he had gone for the Arnett plane and he now felt farther away than ever. In his first solo trip, he had found two B-24s; now, he'd made two more trips and found none. Now, he knew how impossible the task would be: it was impossible to search the channel alone, and just as impossible with the wrong team. Of the six team members he'd brought along, only the Lamberts had the right skills for the task, and even they found the channel dreary and dull. Of course they did. The channel was dull, but to Scannon it was all that mattered. How could he ever hope to find a team who felt the same way, who were willing to fly halfway around the world to one of the most beautiful underwater meccas on the planet, and then spend the whole time mucking around in the murky waters of a shipping channel?

All he knew for sure was that he hadn't found that team yet. "We clearly weren't productive in ninety-six," he said. "It was a feeble attempt to put together a team. I learned from ninety-six what not to do."

SCANNON TOOK A YEAR OFF. Then he took another. Without a team, he had no plan, and without a plan, no reason to go back. Yet the rest of his life seemed to be drained of purpose without the islands. He felt restless, adrift; he tried to re-immerse himself at work, but work was no longer enough. The intricate puzzles of biotechnology still captivated part of his imagination, but now there was another part, one that longed for the physical mystery of the islands and the plunge into the unknown.

One day, without telling Susan or anyone, he drove up to the Yolo County Airport in Davis, California, and signed up for a tandem skydive at a company called SkyDance. As the plane climbed to ten thousand feet and the door cracked open, Scannon flashed back to his flight with Spike Nasmyth over Toachel Mid, and he took a deep breath and dove into the battering void, the instructor at his back as he streaked down, his mind as clear as the cloudless sky. A few days later, he jumped again. Then he was jumping all the time. In the space of only a few months, he racked up more than one hundred skydives, and began training for a high-altitude jump from thirty thousand feet: he spent three days in a hypobaric system at Beale Air Force Base until his blood was accustomed to the same hypoxic levels as a climber halfway up Mount Everest; then he climbed aboard the tiny plane, rising through the jet stream and leaping into air so thin that it didn't even ripple his clothing. But with each jump, Scannon felt his interest waning. It wasn't that skydiving was no longer fun—every time he stepped through the door of a plane, he felt the same terrifying rush of adrenaline—but he no longer doubted that he could do it, and without the doubt, it was no longer an interior journey. "Then it just wasn't satisfying," he said. "It was skydiving for the sake of skydiving."

Finally, in the summer of 1998, after two years off the islands, Scannon pulled his old sketchbook down from the shelf. He flipped through the pages, remembering all the hopes and discoveries and the days of thwarted plans, the business cards taped into the margins, the ideas jotted on yellow stickies. It had been five years since his first trip, and the book was nearly full. He could close it, and leave the last five pages blank, or he could return to the islands and fill some unknown number of books in an endless search of the Arnett channel.

Scannon bought another book. It was identical to the first. He cracked open the front and wrote "Vol. 2" on the inside cover. Then he called the Lamberts and Dan Bailey, and they agreed to go back with him.

For six days in 1999, they trolled Toachel Mid, dragging a side-scan sonar device and staring blankly at the monitor. Each time they got a ping, they splashed in for a closer look, but as the week groaned by in driving wind and rain, they came up empty. In their downtime, at restaurants and bars, they chatted with other divers. Nearly everyone who dove the islands knew of some unidentified wreck, and they began to jot down directions and coordinates. After a few hours on the channel each morning, they would follow those directions, wading through mangroves or drifting through shallow water until they came upon fragments of metal. On the western edge of the barrier reef, they found pieces of a small airplane that looked like it could be a Marine Corsair; in a bay on the western coast of Babeldaob, they came across the remnants of another; and on the southern tip of the islands, they found a Navy Avenger. By the time they went home, they were no closer to Arnett, but they faced a world of new possibility: there were dozens of small American planes yet to discover. Scannon knew less about them, but he resolved to learn everything he could. He had started with a search for three airplanes; now he would search for hundreds.

By the time he got the call from *Parade* magazine in the spring of 2000, he was planning his sixth trip to the islands, and he'd put together a long list of Avengers and Corsairs he hoped to find. He regaled the *Parade* reporter with the story of his first mission with Lambert and Bailey, described their discovery of the Bush trawler, and explained how he'd gone to find Dixon and Custer. He told her about his return with Lambert and Bailey a few months earlier, finding Avengers and Corsairs, and his plan to find more on the expedition to come.

He left out the Arnett plane. It was his great white whale.

When the article appeared on Memorial Day weekend, Scannon bought a copy of the magazine and studied the opening photo. The man in the picture beside the vintage bomber with the rope spooled over his shoulder was almost unrecognizable as the same man pictured on his ID tag from Maxwell Air Force Base just a few years earlier. His hair and beard were graying, but something else had changed as well. His eyes were more alive and focused, his posture more assured. He looked as different as he felt. It was as if he had found another body on the islands.

In the days to come, as calls began flooding the Xoma switchboard, Scannon sorted through a stack of blue "Phone Memo" messages. He saw the names of veterans, families, and historians, all calling with questions and clues. One of the memos said, "Corsair is his baby." Another said, "Bloody Nose Ridge." A third said, "Survivor of Bataan."

And one said simply, "Doyle."

FOR SCANNON, THE *PARADE* ARTICLE marked a turning point in several ways. It was a reminder, first, that his fascination with the air campaign was not a lone obsession. After years of scouring histories for any glancing reference to the Long Rangers, he was suddenly inundated with calls from other history buffs who shared his frustration with the comparatively thin record.

But he also discovered that for families of the missing the oversight was far more personal. To the sons and daughters of the disappeared, the wounds of loss remained fresh, and the lack of answers about what happened to a father, brother, or son was only deepened by a dearth of information about the war he fought. "That was the biggest surprise," Scannon said. "I wasn't sure how many families even *cared* anymore, but when you talk with them, the first thing you find out is that the later generations care even more—it's like there's an empty chair at the dinner table all their lives."

To someone outside the MIA community, this can be difficult to grasp. The special grief of the MIA family is little understood, and only a handful of researchers have ever focused on the issue. One of the first to do so, in the early 1970s, was a student at the University of Wisconsin named Pauline Boss. A doctoral candidate in family studies, Boss was interested in the way that grief can be heightened by uncertainty, and she was beginning to develop a concept that she would eventually label "ambiguous loss." Whether it's the sudden disappearance of a child or the slow erasure of a parent by dementia, the grief process is disrupted because so much of grieving depends on the knowledge and acceptance of what has happened.

When Boss presented her early ideas on ambiguous loss to a conference on family relations in 1973, she was approached by two social scientists who worked with military families. Edna Hunter-King and Ham McCubbin had been counseling the families of missing men and prisoners from the Vietnam War, and they recognized the signs of ambiguous loss in the MIA community. If Boss wanted to focus her dissertation on the military experience, they told her, they could put her in touch with MIA families. "They said, 'We have data on this, but no theory,'" Boss recalled, "'and you have a theory with no data.'"

In the decades to follow, Boss, Hunter-King, and McCubbin would develop a small literature on MIA grief. What distinguished the missing soldier from other combat losses, they found, was that the family was deprived not only of a son, but of a clear explanation for his loss. Without knowing where the man died, or how, they faced a story with no ending, and their inconsolable grief had as much to do with narrative as with death. "When you have someone missing, it does something to the human psyche," Boss said. "It's not logical. It's not natural. There are no rituals for it. The rest of the community doesn't know what to do. And grief therapy doesn't work. They don't have closure, and they never will."

Boss was also intrigued by the way MIA grief passed through families. Like Scannon, she noticed that in many cases, a daughter, son, or grandchild would become fixated on the loss of a man they had never known. By 1998, Boss and Hunter-King had documented so many MIA families in which the grief carried into a second or third generation, that they were invited to draft a new chapter for the clinical handbook of multigenerational trauma, alongside entries on the effects of slavery, nuclear annihilation, and the Holocaust.

"Unlike the Holocaust," Hunter-King wrote in the manual, "mothers of MIA children were not suddenly uprooted from their homes and deprived of their possessions, countries, and cultures. They did not lose parents, siblings, and husbands to programmed incineration. They were not subjected to incarceration, underfed, and abused, as were Holocaust victims. . . . On the other hand, most children of Holocaust survivors have not waited for over a quarter of a century in a state of ambiguous grieving, wondering whether their parent is dead or alive, as children of MIAs have done. Both groups, however, have perceived the conspiracy of silence between survivors and society, and between survivors and their children. . . . For most of these MIA adult children, unless they are convinced that the fullest possible accounting has been made, and/or unless the father's remains are located, adequately identified, and returned to the family, their prolonged, ambiguous grieving will continue indefinitely."

Even as Boss, Hunter-King, and McCubbin began to document MIA grief, their emphasis on Vietnam left out the majority of MIA families. Over the past century, some eighty-three thousand service members have been listed as missing, of whom seventy-three thousand disappeared in World War II, and forty-seven thousand in the Pacific theater alone. To put it another way, the number of men who disappeared in the war against Japan makes up more than half of all missing service members, and is nearly the same as the total number of combat deaths in Vietnam. Of course, this is partly a reflection of the difference in scale between those wars, but it also calls forward the special challenge of the Pacific theater. The same watery expanses that made the B-24 essential would later make the task of finding a lost crew nearly impossible.

It may be tempting to imagine that for the MIA families of World War II, the grief and confusion were somehow less acute than for Vietnam families, and that the men and women of the "greatest generation" were imbued with a special storehouse of stoicism that softened the agony of loss. But this is a modern myth. At the military's MIA recovery office in Hawaii, specialists who work with families of the missing say that the lingering pain from World War II is as potent as any other war. This is a point made clear in the unit's main research room, where the words of a letter sent to the Army flash against a blood-red screen: "If those bodies or bones aren't recovered or returned home, I hope all 19 boys haunt you nite and day—until you die." The letter was written in 1947.

By the time the article on Pat Scannon appeared in *Parade* magazine, the Pacific war was half a century past, yet Scannon continued to receive a deluge of calls through summer and into the fall—nieces, grandsons, great-nephews, cousins, and daughters all searching for the final chapter of a family story.

When Scannon spoke with Nancy and Tommy Doyle, he could hear the same longing in their voices. Though the Doyles did not mention the rumors in Tommy's family, they offered to meet with Scannon for a longer conversation at the next reunion of the Long Rangers, which was scheduled for San Antonio that fall. It would be Scannon's last stop in the United States before leaving on yet another journey to Palau.

At the reunion, Scannon and the Doyles found each other and slipped into a side room. They sat down at a small table beside a model of a B-24. On the wall, a reunion organizer had propped up a poster-sized map of the South Pacific, marked with long red lines to show the movement of the Long Rangers. Scannon opened his briefcase and laid a stack of folders on the table.

"This is everything I have on your father's plane," he said, passing the folder to Tommy. For the next two hours, they pored over mission reports and photos. Scannon walked over to the model plane and explained the crew positions; he stood before the map and described the two-column strategy of the war, and the distinctive position of the Long Rangers, flying in support of both MacArthur and Nimitz. Periodically, Tommy or Nancy would interject with questions, but mostly they listened in wonder.

"I learned more about my dad in the first five minutes than the government had ever told us," Tommy said.

While they spoke, the commander of the unit's 424th Squadron, Jack Vanderpoel, wandered into the room. Vanderpoel had reached the South Pacific just a few weeks before the Big Stoop crew, and became famous for leading his men on their most daring flights. On one mission, he'd engaged in a dogfight with a nimble Japanese fighter plane and somehow chased it away. Even in training, Vanderpoel had been a daredevil pilot. Once, during a night flight, he'd swooped down over a train track, turning off his lights and rocketing toward an oncoming engine, then throwing his lights back on at the last second to blind the terrified engineer, who jammed on his brakes and squealed down the track while Vanderpoel raced into the night sky laughing. That stunt cost him laps on the quad, but his talent was impossible to deny. He was chosen by his classmates as cadet captain, and after graduation, became a flight instructor for the next class. In the half century since, he continued to straddle the line between mischief and command. At reunions, he was notorious for flirting with the wives and daughters of other veterans "on the outer boundary of what was appropriate," Scannon said.

Vanderpoel had been the direct superior of both Arnett and Coorssen, and was one of the only men who could explain the last-minute change of crew. The trouble was, he refused to tell. At an earlier reunion, Scannon had approached him to raise the subject. "I was trying to work around to it carefully," Scannon recalled. "I mentioned the Dixon crash first, and he said, 'Yeah, a tragedy.' Then I mentioned Arnett, and he said very quickly, 'Another tragedy.' But I could see the tone in his voice was different. Like, 'Where is this going?' So I said, 'You know, there are these rumblings about Arnett . . . ,' and that's when the interview ended. He got angry. He said, 'Let the dead rest in peace!' and he took off. I was really shaken. It was the first time I had ever run into a wall. I had to figure, if he didn't know anything about it, he would have said so. But it came across that he did know, and he wanted it laid to rest."

Vanderpoel kept a watchful distance as Scannon conferred with the Doyles. After a while, he ambled off and Scannon leaned forward.

"There's something else," he whispered, explaining that Tommy's dad had been flying with a new pilot when his plane went down. On every other mission that summer, Jimmie and his crew had flown with a guy named Coorssen. There was no official record to explain why they flew with Arnett on their final mission, and none of the veterans had been able to explain the whole story. Vanderpoel knew the truth, but he refused to say.

Listening, Tommy felt his pulse hammer in his temples. He found his own story spilling out for Scannon—how his Uncle Dan had driven from Arkansas to Texas when Tommy was just a boy, to break the news to his mom that his dad was alive; how relatives insisted that Jimmie called them to check in; and how two of his uncles had driven all the way to California to find him, tracking Jimmie to an apartment complex where neighbors confirmed that he was alive.

Now it was Scannon's turn to stare in disbelief. Huddling together, he and Tommy tried to align the two stories, to see how they might fit together, how it all might make sense—but it didn't make sense, none of it, and by the time they parted company, each was more confused than ever.

As Scannon left the reunion and made his way to the islands, he realized that, once again, something in his journey had shifted. He had always known that his search wasn't really about airplanes, but he'd convinced himself that it was about the men on board—about finding those men, and honoring them, and leaving a record of their sacrifice. Now he knew that the search went beyond even that. It reached into a vast network of families, spread across the American landscape and bound together in grief. Theirs was a loss compounded by uncertainty and unresolved by time. When he scoured the archipelago with sonar, when he hung in the open doorway of a Cessna, when he slogged through the jungle and traversed the channel on yet another rainy day, he wasn't searching for the dead. He was searching for the living.

SEVEN

PLEDGE

The human impulse to bury the dead is as old as civilization itself. In Greek mythology, King Priam crosses the front lines of battle to recover his son's body from Achilles. In ancient Egypt, the remains of the pharaoh were entombed to last forever. From the earliest records of Jewish tradition, the principle of *k'vod hamet* called for a body to be cleansed and buried; Christianity and Islam inherit aspects of the same tradition. Among Native American tribes, the burial mound dates back at least three thousand years to the Adena people of the Ohio Valley, and African slaves, after being robbed of their homes, communities, and cultures in the Americas, nevertheless managed to preserve many of their funerary rites through a syncretic merger with Christian tradition.

Yet for most of American history, the fallen soldier was denied the same honor. From the Revolutionary War to the Civil War, soldiers who made the ultimate sacrifice were often denied the most basic thanks, their bodies pillaged by other soldiers and left on the battlefield to rot. As Drew Gilpin Faust described in the Civil War history *This Republic of Suffering*, men on both sides who fell were "thrown by the hundreds into burial trenches; soldiers stripped of every identifying object before being abandoned on the field; bloated corpses hurried into hastily dug graves." To modern ears this may seem barbaric, but in the nineteenth century it was the norm. There were no identification tags for soldiers, no notifications for the next of kin; there was no national cemetery to honor the men, nor Memorial Day to remember them. Today, Faust wrote, "the obligation of the state to account for and return—either dead or alive—every soldier in its service is unquestioned. But these assumptions are of quite recent origin."

After the Civil War, the US government did launch an effort to account for the wartime dead, yet within a decade the program was faltering with tens of thousands still missing. The first dog tags appeared with World War I, but the limitations were obvious. As E. B. Sledge recounted in his lyrical memoir of the Pacific, *With the Old Breed*, even military recruiters in the 1940s would point out the shortcomings of the ID. "When he asked, 'Any scars, birthmarks, or other unusual features?' I described an inch-long scar on my right knee," Sledge wrote. "I asked, why such a question. He replied, 'So they can identify you on some Pacific beach after the Japs blast off your dog tags.'"

Faced with the massive losses of World War II, the military funded an unprecedented recovery effort, pouring staff and funds into a unit known as the Graves Registration Service. But the obstacles were legion. For one thing, there was disagreement among the services about the mission itself. While the Army, Air Forces, and Marines all hoped to recover their dead, the Navy had a split view. Sailors adhered to an old seafaring custom that regarded a sunken vessel as a tomb, while naval aviators believed, like other fliers, that their friends should be recovered even if they went down in water.

Then there was the challenge of logistics in a place like the Pacific. Recovering a body from deep water was impossible with postwar diving technology, but even in shallow water and on land, finding a man in the islands posed a special problem. Unlike the cultivated fields and villages of western Europe, many Pacific islands had never been densely populated, and with the end of the war, they disappeared under a blanket of jungle. While European farmers and construction workers would continue to discover the remains of US troops with regularity, the lost men of the Pacific could linger on small islands for decades to come.

Finally, there was the problem of records. After the Japanese surrender, imperial commanders launched a systematic program to destroy their wartime documents—burning so much paper in some places that the sky turned black. Records that did survive were often trapped in a translation queue, and if they contained information about a lost crew, they could wind up as evidence files in the war crimes tribunals, which continued through 1951. It was not uncommon for information about a downed airplane to reach the Graves Registration Service only after their investigation of that case was closed. By the start of the Korean War in the early 1950s, nearly sixty thousand men were still listed as missing in the Pacific, but only one GRS recovery platoon was still active in the region.

It wasn't until the Vietnam era that the United States launched another large-scale recovery effort, and even then, progress was halting. At the Paris Peace Conference in January 1973, the North Vietnamese government agreed to allow American recovery units to search for missing men in the hills outside Hanoi, but by the time the United States officially withdrew from the war two months later, the question of how to conduct those searches remained wide open. To tackle the problem, the Army created a unit called the Central Identification Laboratory. With offices in a metal warehouse on the Gulf of Thailand, the unit became known as CIL-Thai. While Pauline Boss was delivering her first lecture on ambiguous loss in 1973, the staff at CIL-Thai were ordering their first batch of microscopes and forensic tools—but when one of their first missions to

North Vietnam was ambushed that December, killing the team leader and several members, the program ground to a halt.

Another sixteen months passed before a crisis remobilized the unit. In April 1975, an airlift of orphans being taken to the United States for adoption crashed in South Vietnam. The Army had nowhere else to send the children's bodies, so they shipped them to CIL-Thai. When the remains overwhelmed the lab, the Army sent more refrigerators and staff.

One of the first officers to arrive that summer was a tall, dour figure named Johnie Webb, who had spent most of his Army career in the logistics office of Petroleum, Oil, and Lubricants, which helps supply fuel for trucks and airplanes. When Webb received orders to fly to Thailand and manage something called the Central Identification Lab, he couldn't imagine what it was. "I said, 'What is that?'" he recalled, "and they told me, and I said, 'Well, I'm not interested.' And they said, 'You don't understand. It's an emergency requisition. They need an officer. You're going.'"

Webb arrived at the CIL in June 1975, and spent the rest of the summer waiting for instructions. It was still unclear whether the American families who wanted to adopt the orphans should be legally responsible for their burial, or if it was the Army's responsibility to dispose of the bodies. As the weeks passed, Webb recalled, "it turned out that nobody was really willing to take that responsibility." Finally, at the end of August, a judge ordered the Army to handle the remains. "So then it became an issue of, what now?" Webb said. "What happens to the remains of all these orphans? And I'll tell you what happened: Those of us that worked there took up a collection. We bought a burial plot in Thailand. We had a headstone made. And many of us took the weekend and went down to a local monastery and cremated the remains of those orphans. We had them buried in plots that we bought with our own money."

For members of the CIL staff, the experience proved to be as galvanizing as it was tragic. The unit began to cohere with a new sense of camaraderie and purpose, and when the Thai government requested a drawdown of US troops in 1976, the lab staff relocated to Hickam Air

Force Base in Hawaii with a dramatic new mission. No longer confined to the Vietnam theater, Webb and the other officers expanded their purview to include earlier wars. In 1978, Webb led the first mission to a World War II crash in the jungle of New Guinea, and soon the lab was adding historians, anthropologists, and forensic scientists to its staff. Dozens of times each year, they would descend on some remote location to examine the wreckage of a ship, truck, or plane, and if it turned out to be a US military vehicle, they would sift through the soil in search of bones. Then they would bring home the remains, use forensic tools to identify them, and return them to a family for burial.

By the early 1990s, while Tommy Doyle pushed his mother's trunk into a back room and Pat Scannon discovered Palau, Johnie Webb was wrapping up twenty years in the CIL. He had transformed the unit from an isolated morgue in Thailand to one of the most ambitious recovery operations in the world, and had come to think of it not so much as a military operation but a humanitarian mission, less concerned with the waging of war than its psychic toll. When Webb finally retired from the military in 1995, he took a civilian position at the recovery lab, serving as the primary liaison for grieving families. He also began to make new inroads with foreign governments: In 1996, he opened a dialogue with North Korea, and sent a recovery team across the Demilitarized Zone— the first American troops permitted to cross in four decades. Over the next ten years, he sent another twenty missions over the DMZ, bringing home the remains of more than two hundred missing service members. In 2002, he helped coordinate the first US recovery mission to Burma, one of the most isolated countries on earth, and in 2003, the CIL ascended from its position within the Army to become a joint operation of all military branches, with a new name: the Joint POW/MIA Accounting Command, or JPAC.

For the four hundred men and women who worked in JPAC's campus of trailers and warehouses on Hickam air base, there would always be a fragile balance to the unit's work. On the one hand, members of a JPAC recovery team had to excel in the logistics of military deployment—preparing for and enduring long encampments in remote places, sorting and transporting mountains of technical equipment across inhospitable terrain, and coordinating tens of thousands of man-hours toward a single purpose. Yet there was also a profound intimacy to the job—the delicate task of handling a man's remains, the haunting awareness of his family's grief, and the daily struggle to maintain emotional distance on a recovery site. At a fundamental level, it was the unit's job not just to bring home remains, but to provide each family with answers, in the hope that truth would allow life, finally, to go on.

It was with this delicate goal in mind that JPAC field teams could be found, on almost any day of any month, in the most rugged environments on earth. No other unit of the US military deployed so often in both peacetime and war. A typical member of a JPAC team could expect to spend between five and ten months in the field, every single year. At each location, she would combine her own area of expertise with those of other scientists and historians, and with site-specific experts drawn from throughout the military. At one site, there might be a specialist in land-mine disposal; at another, an authority on altitude sickness. There could be forensic dentists on the mission, or Navy deep-sea divers, or moun-taineers trained to navigate glacial ice—each member arriving in civilian clothing to spend the coming weeks and months serving an archaeologi-cal team.

Meanwhile, Johnie Webb spoke for them all. Most of the family mem-bers who contacted JPAC wound up on Johnie's line, and he would take the call in an office stuffed with memorabilia from around the world, leaning back in his chair to offer information, or just to listen. He kept a small, plain box on the corner of his desk to remind him of why he was there. Once in a while, he would lift the lid and remove a silver bracelet, twirling it gently between his fingers.

"This was for a young NCO in the Special Forces during Vietnam who was lost in a helicopter crash," he explained one afternoon. "Over the years, I got to know his family very well. We became, I would say, friends. A very patriotic family. But I watched over the years as we searched for their son, and they began to lose some of their patriotism. I can remember the father telling me many, many times, 'Johnie, I don't want you to send me a bunch of bones. I gave the government my son. I expect you to give my son back to me.'"

Webb stopped and swallowed. He stared at the bracelet in his hand and shook his head, and it seemed obvious that, however much Johnie Webb believed in his work, he did not, strictly speaking, love it.

"Shortly after we excavated the site for his son," he continued. "I met the dad at a National League of Families meeting. I told him, 'You know, you need to prepare yourself. We're going to have some information for you in a short period of time.' And again, he reminded me that he didn't want any bones. He wanted his son back."

Webb cleared his throat. "Well," he said, "eventually we made the identification. There was a huge military funeral. A lot of politicians turned out. And after maybe three weeks, I received a packet in the mail. It had a very simple card with the POW/MIA logo on it and a note that said he wanted to thank me for all that we had done. He wrote, 'To show my appreciation, I am sending the POW/MIA bracelet of my son that I have worn for the last twenty years. . . .'"

Webb's voice cracked, and he ended the story.

IN THE SUMMER OF 2001, a new anthropologist arrived at Webb's lab. Eric Emery was still in his early thirties, but he had the worn eyes and compact physique of a lifelong outdoorsman. Just two weeks before he reached Hawaii, he'd been on a tall ship at the end of a fifty-thousand-mile journey around the world by sail, rounding Cape Horn at the tip of South America, and the Cape of Good Hope in Africa, sleeping under the giant moai heads on Easter Island, and swimming with the manatees of the Galápagos Islands. With a master's degree in history, a PhD in archaeology, a lifelong mistrust of authority, and a general aversion to rules, Emery came to the crisp confines of the lab for one overriding reason: to develop a new program for underwater operations.

It was not so much a job for Emery as the fulfillment of a personal mission.

Growing up in northern Vermont, Emery had always been a creature of the water. His family spent summers on Lake Champlain, where he swam and fished and joined his dad on a small Bristol sailboat for week-long jaunts. On a typical trip, they would bring fishing gear and little else, enjoying the rough simplicity and the raw wear of nature, but the summer Emery was twelve, his dad tossed a scuba rig in the cabin. It was a primitive system, just an old steel tank with a heavy chrome regulator that he'd picked up years earlier on a trip to Key West. "This was back in the day, when you didn't need to be certified," Emery said. "You could just go in and buy the equipment and use it." The gear had been languishing in the family garage, but once his father dusted it off and brought it to the lake, Emery was determined to try it. They hauled the tank to a gas station one afternoon, filled it using an air compressor behind the store, and dunked it into a garbage can filled with water to make sure it wasn't leaking. Then they headed offshore to give the thing a try. The last thing Emery's father told him as he stood on the deck with the tank in a backpack and the regulator strapped to his face was "Never stop breathing."

"And what I think he meant," Emery said, "was that the number-one rule in diving is not to hold your breath—because if you change your position in the water column, you could embolize yourself." Years later, when Emery thought back on his father's advice, it would mean much more.

As the summers passed and Emery moved through high school and college, he continued to use the tank and regulator until they were as familiar as well-worn shoes. But it wasn't until he began a master's program in American history at the University of Vermont in 1992 that he discovered a link between his studies and his hobby. He was walking down a hallway in late spring when he spotted a flyer on the wall: it was an invitation for students to participate in an archaeological project nearby. As Emery read through the details, it was like seeing a Venn diagram of his life.

The project would take place on Lake Champlain. Documents from the American Revolution described a floating bridge on the water, which linked the star-shaped Fort Ticonderoga on one side with a peninsula called Mount Independence on the other. But there was no longer any sign of the bridge, and no one knew why. Some people thought it had floated away; others wondered if it had ever really been there. Now a research team from Texas A&M University, led by an underwater archaeologist named Kevin Crisman, was coming up to find it. For Emery, it would bring together his graduate studies in history, his love of diving, and his connection to Lake Champlain. He signed up.

Scuba diving was by then a popular sport, first made famous by Jacques Cousteau in the 1950s, and brought to the mainstream in the 1960s by the organizations NAUI and PADI, which certify divers. But underwater archaeology was something else. It was a young field, still looked upon with skepticism in many corners of the archaeological world, where the prospect of conducting a professional dig in a cloud of muddy water seemed dubious at best.

Though the earliest cases of underwater archaeology could be traced to the fifteenth century, with the discovery of ships built by the emperor Caligula under a lake near Rome, the effort to salvage treasure from shipwrecks had not become common until the mid-1800s, and the first academic exploration of underwater sites did not begin in earnest until the 1930s, when helmet divers examined a four-hundred-year-old Swedish warship in the Baltic Sea.

By the time Emery arrived at the excavation site on Lake Champlain that summer, only a handful of universities offered a degree in underwater archaeology. Among them, Texas A&M was widely considered the best.

Emery tried to maintain a low profile as he watched Crisman and the

Texas team work. He was there to check equipment and help carry gear, but he wanted to learn as much as he could. "I didn't know anything," he said, "but I think that helped me, because it allowed me to go in there and be a sponge." As the days turned into weeks, he watched in amazement as Crisman moved through the water with minute precision, documenting each detail of the subaquatic landscape. When the team began to uncover evidence of two-hundred-year-old pylons to support the bridge, Emery felt his own future shifting in the water around him.

Suddenly, he was acutely aware of his frustration with written history. It told a story of the past, but like any story, it was vulnerable to the whims of memory and perception. Archaeology seemed to offer a more tangible approach. All the theories and doubts about the bridge on Lake Champlain dissolved in the presence of Crisman's research, and to Emery, the endless conjecture of historians seemed like a flimsy substitute for science. "I'm not sure who it was that said history is just the best string of lies," Emery said, "but what appealed to me about archaeology was that you could confirm or refute those stories." By the time he received his master's degree in history, he had already enrolled in Crisman's underwater program at Texas A&M.

To cover his tuition and expenses, Emery worked summers and took the occasional semester off. He became a kind of journeyman archaeologist, flying to remote locations to help with underwater recoveries. By the spring of 1999, he was in his fourth year of the program when he accepted a position with a French team in the Ecuadorean mountains. There were ruins from a Cañari Indian civilization buried in the sediment of a high-altitude lake, and he would spend two months living in a pup tent while he retrieved them.

Or anyway, that was the plan. Within days of Emery's arrival, the seasonal rains picked up, and as the weeks rolled by, he spent most of his time trapped inside the tent with another archaeologist, Jon Faucher. Day after day, they stared out the screen window of the tent as canyons of mud opened on the hillsides. Their supplies grew thin. The team helicopter sat grounded in the rain. "It was ugly," Emery recalled. "Just solid rain for weeks, and we were fully exposed."

Finally, during a break in the weather, Emery and Faucher decided to get out. They scrambled their things together and climbed aboard the chopper with one other member of the team, rising over the lake and looking down at the bamboo huts trailing into the valley, when suddenly there was a deafening grind and the chopper hung right, lurching and twisting as it plunged toward the water, its tail whipping into the surface.

Emery yanked at his seat belt as the water rushed in. He still wasn't sure what had happened. He glanced around and saw Faucher kicking open the door, but Emery's seat belt was jammed. He felt the water creeping higher as the chopper slid down. He pounded the buckle and pulled frantically at the strap, trying to wriggle free, but the water was rushing into his mouth. He held his breath. Then he gasped. Then the world went dark.

Outside, Faucher paddled furiously to stay on the surface in heavy clothes. He glanced around in search of Emery and saw the other team member and the pilot. Faucher shouted to see if either of them had a knife, and when the pilot called that he did, Faucher swam over to grab it. He tried to ignore the pain in his back. It was broken in two places, and his trachea was crushed, but he turned back toward the chopper with the knife, heaved a breath, and dove.

Faucher swam down to the door of the sunken bird. He saw Emery's lifeless body inside, tangled in canvas, wire, and metal. He grabbed Emery's seat belt and began to saw through it with the knife, but the material was thick and he was running out of air. His lungs surged. His back spasmed. When he couldn't take any more, he shot up for another breath, then plunged back down, back to Emery, hacking and sawing at the seat belt until at last it tore apart. He grabbed Emery and pulled him free, kicking his way to the surface.

Time seemed to have stopped. It might have been five minutes or twenty; Faucher would always wonder. Looking at Emery's body, one thing was clear. Emery was gone. "He was gray," Faucher said, "and his eyes were open and fixed. That was the worst part."

Treading water, Faucher began to blow air into Emery's mouth, a scuba-rescue technique he'd learned in training. Between breaths he studied Emery's dead eyes for any sign of life. Finally, a trickle of water bubbled through Emery's lips, and his eyes began to blink frantically with confusion. Faucher dragged Emery to shore. Other members of the team rushed over to wrap them in blankets. Faucher could not stop staring at his friend. He had not only saved a life; he had brought Emery back from the dead.

They spent a final night on the mountain, and in the morning a new chopper came to get them. After two weeks fighting off infection at an Ecuadorean hospital, Emery went home.

That's when Eric Emery decided to give up. To give up archaeology—to give up his studies, his plans, and the sense of purpose he'd felt in his life since the day he saw that flyer. He felt lost. He felt mistaken. He had always believed that life was a journey of calculated risk, but to risk his life on a jumble of ruins and broken pottery at the bottom of a lake? "You know how they say your whole life flashes before you?" Emery said. "Well, the thing that flashed in front of me was 'What the hell am I doing here?' After that, I pretty much decided that I was getting out of archaeology."

BACK IN TEXAS, Emery retreated from the world. Kevin Crisman had left town for the summer, and offered Emery the keys to his house. Emery stayed inside for weeks, quietly nursing his wounds.

Physically, he felt fine. A few cracked ribs, and his left hand was numb from nerve damage, but nothing like the back brace strapped to Faucher. "The long-term effect for me was psychological," he said. "I just withdrew that summer. I needed time to regroup and think." Periodically, he would leave the house to collect groceries, or to wade tentatively through

Crisman's pool, but it wasn't until the end of the summer, when his classmates returned to town, that Emery began to tell them about the crash.
At a party one evening, he found himself sitting with another student,
Rich Wills, who was a few semesters ahead in the program. To the outside
eye, Emery and Wills seemed to have little in common. Where Emery
had a weather-beaten air and the sturdy build of a 1940s boxer, Wills was
slim and lanky, with a goofy smile and a vaguely adolescent mien. But
when Emery confided that the disaster in the Andes had shaken his passion for archaeology, Wills nodded. "You should look into this place in
Hawaii," he said. For two years, he'd been helping the CIL on jungle recoveries, and it had given him a radically different view of what archaeology could be. "It just feels like it has a purpose," he said.

Emery was skeptical but intrigued. He had no experience in the military and, if he was honest with himself, no talent for following orders.
The thought of answering to a formal chain of command rubbed every
fiber in his body the wrong way. But Wills told him the unit was hoping
to develop a program for underwater operations, and there was something about the idea that Emery couldn't shake. Just a few years earlier,
everything in his life had seemed to align toward a future in underwater
archaeology. The most painful result of the helicopter crash was the loss
of that purpose, the nagging sense that the pieces of his life no longer
added up. But the prospect of helping to liberate men trapped in a watery
grave, and to bring their remains back to the surface as Faucher had done
for him, well, that was a purpose Eric Emery still understood.

He sent an application to the lab, only half expecting a call, and while
he waited to hear back, he took a job as a history teacher on a tall ship that
doubled as a school. Over the next year, he sailed from Amsterdam
through the Strait of Gibraltar, around the Mediterranean, across the
Atlantic to Panama, past the Galápagos and Easter Island, and around
Cape Horn, then back across the South Atlantic to the Cape of Good
Hope. When he finally received an email from the CIL at an Internet café
in South Africa, offering to hire him as a staff archaeologist and let him

build the water program, Emery was only half sure he still wanted the job. He wrote back that he would need a few months to finish sailing around the world. Then he continued up the coast of Africa and back across the North Atlantic, pulling down the Saint Lawrence River from Nova Scotia to Montreal, where he docked less than one hundred miles from his childhood home. He hopped ashore with four bags of luggage and caught the next flight to Hawaii. Two weeks later, he was leading a recovery operation in the jungle of New Guinea.

Over the next three years, Emery would remain in motion—scuttling, like so many CIL employees, from one mission to the next. On his shortest year, he spent five months traveling; on his longest, he was gone for ten. But as the months crept by, he stayed entirely on land. "I was brought in for underwater work," he said, "but there weren't any underwater sites." Whenever he had a few months in Hawaii, he would make plans for the underwater program—drawing up a list of the gear he'd use, and how he would adapt the unit's methods to the water, and waiting, year after year, for an underwater grave to recover.

EIGHT

COMBAT

M ost crews landing in the South Pacific during the summer of
1944 did not receive a bomber of their own. After two years of
combat operations, with planes constantly in for repair, the commanders
of the Long Rangers had discovered that it was easier to rotate the working ships than to assign a dedicated plane to each crew. On any given
morning, the airmen arriving at Mokerang airfield might be given a
shiny, silver Liberator that was fresh off the line at Willow Run, or an old,
green, tattered warhorse like the *Babes in Arms*.

Even among veteran planes, the *Babes* stood apart. Early in her career,
she had been the regular ship of two different crews, who adorned her
fuselage with symbolic art. There were three dozen bomb icons painted
below the cockpit, marking successful combat missions, a collection of

painted Japanese flags to indicate enemy planes shot down, and near the tip of her nose, her name was scripted lovingly in white.

Early on the morning of June 24, Norman Coorssen climbed aboard the *Babes* to lead his first mission. Less than twenty-four hours had passed since his observation flight to Yap, and the sight of the Fifth Bombardment Group plane disintegrating on the ocean was still with him. He was the only man on his crew who had seen the war, and the memory would not fade quickly.

The sky was overcast and a light rain fell as the Big Stoop crew settled on the *Babes*—the new radioman, Ted, at his console; the gunners, Jimmie and Johnny and Earl and Leland, all checking their positions; and Frank Arhar, the Big Stoop himself, crouched by the navigation table before a mountain of maps.

In the cockpit Norman watched other planes fill with men, then he fired up the engines and steered the *Babes* down the coral taxiway, turning at the roundabout and streaking up the runway to the sky.

In theory, each plane in the squadron was designed to carry eight thousand pounds of bombs, but in practice, it was all a question of where the bombs were going. For a short flight, it was possible to carry a good deal more; on a longer flight, the plane needed extra fuel, which had to be stored inside the bomb compartment, cutting into the space for munitions. For a record-setting distance like the flight to Yap, there was so much extra fuel on the plane that the bomb load was drastically reduced. That morning, each plane in the squadron carried only three midweight bombs. Accuracy was everything.

The five-hour flight was mostly over water, and the Big Stoop boys waited in the cabin. Any journey into hostile territory was attenuated by the unknown, but for a crew on their first combat mission, crossing an unprecedented distance, the anticipation was as thick as the clouds outside. Did the Japanese garrison know they were coming? Would they have their fighter planes ready to scramble? Of course they would, and it didn't help to think about it, but you did, and there you were.

An hour slipped by, then another, in the roar of the four-engine plane. Outside, the storm clouds darkened and the rain picked up. It pelted the airframe in a loose, tinny drumbeat, and the *Babes* shuddered, then slumped in the air. Something was wrong. The plane was slowing down. It was falling out of formation.

Norman worked the throttle to pick up speed but it was useless. One of the left engines was running weak. It was probably the supercharger— an easy fix, but not at seventeen thousand feet. The only thing he could do was reduce power on the right for balance, but that would slow the plane even more. There was no chance of catching the formation, which left only one good option. On the radio, Ted hailed the squadron leader and made a plan: while the rest of the formation disappeared over the horizon, the Big Stoop boys hurtled forward on a mission of their own.

The day before, bomb crews on their way to Yap had seen a small radio tower on the rendezvous point at Sorol Island. There couldn't be more than a few Japanese troops guarding it, but if they used the tower to call Yap, it would give the Japanese garrison an hour to prepare for the raid. If the Big Stoop crew couldn't join the attack, at least they could protect it. They would fly to Sorol and drop their payload on the tower. With three bombs in the belly of the plane, they would have three chances to nail it.

Streaking forward to Sorol, the *Babes* was alone in the sky. Suddenly, Frank Arhar's role as navigator took a deadly turn. Sorol was nearly as far away as Yap, across hundreds of miles of undifferentiated water. It was a daunting challenge for a navigator on his first mission. As Frank huddled over his maps, checking and rechecking the course, Art Schumacher tried to decide what to do about the bombs. For the flight to Yap, he had set the fuses with a slight delay. That would allow the bombs to penetrate a building or bunker before they detonated. But for a tower, it made more sense to rig the bombs with instantaneous fusing. Then he could aim for the top of the tower, and if the strike was perfect, the bombs would explode at the very tip, with a downward blast that would shatter the tower and wipe the island flat.

Trying to re-fuse a bomb could be risky under any circumstances. Doing so in the middle of a flight was borderline lunacy. To reach the bombs in the belly of the plane, Art would have to squeeze down the catwalk, stretching and contorting himself around fuel tanks to reach them.

Within minutes, he was there.

By the time Sorol appeared on the horizon, the fusing was complete. Art scrambled back to the bombardier's compartment, while Jimmie and Johnny clipped into their guns and Norman pushed forward on the throttle, nosing closer to the water as the tower came into view. It began as a black speck on the horizon, then grew into a spike, and kept growing, metastasizing, as Art clutched the bomb lever in one hand. His thumb hovered over the release button as he counted silently, and when the tower was about to pass below, he punched the button to release the first bomb—watching in horror as all three trailed down. They exploded 150 feet from the tower.

Art stared in shock. It was almost too much to believe. After months of training on US bases and weeks of waiting for a mission, after an engine failure in midflight and a sudden change of target, after being forced to leave the formation and navigate alone, after climbing through the pitch-black bomb bay to re-fuse the payload, they had finally crept over the tower and missed by a hair—but instead of having two more chances to hit it, they would have none. The release mechanism had failed and dropped all three bombs at once. The mission was already over. The tiny island disappeared behind them as Norman looped south for the long flight home.

On their second mission, they returned to Sorol and laid waste to the island, and on the third, they flew west across the rim of New Guinea to cover MacArthur's men at Numfoor. Then they turned north again to join the assault on Yap, returning for three consecutive missions through an endless string of fighter planes that churned the sky around them. One day, the Japanese planes came so close that two of the Liberators collided, torching the clouds as they plummeted down, while Johnny Moore stood at the left waist window, scanning the sky for something to shoot. When he saw a dark black fighter plane racing toward him, Johnny held his fire. He waited, watching, tracking the plane until it was almost on him, then he unleashed a barrage that burst the fighter into a thousand pieces, the Japanese pilot waffling down like a rag doll tossed from a skyscraper.

The more action the Big Stoop saw, the more alien their return to base each night. In the sky, in the glow of phosphorus bombs and the streams of anti-aircraft artillery, there was no time to question where they were, or why. But the return to Los Negros after a mission, slinking back to camp in the horizontal evening light, to spend another night in the sluggish mist of drink, could be even more disorienting than the missions themselves.

Even the movies became a reminder of their dislocation. Stretched out together before the big white sheet, they were neither at war nor at home, but in some vapid purgatory between. One night, they might see a mind-numbing musical like *Footlight Serenade*. The next, it would be a gritty war drama like *Journey for Margaret*. Then it would be a farce like *Blonde Trouble*, and they would find themselves laughing drunkenly, a bottle of warm beer propped beside them in the sand, half-ashamed at the spectacle of themselves loafing on the beach at war.

The Fourth of July came and passed and Johnny dreamed of home, of the wagons and horses down by the river in Des Arc, the crowds milling through town. "First time I was ever away from home on the fourth," he wrote to his sister Mary. "Next year—I hope." He and Jimmie spent the afternoon wandering through the surf at low tide, collecting shells in shallow water. They split the largest one in half, promising that someday the shells would be matching ashtrays in their homes, a reminder of the islands and each other.

Then they were back in flight, surging through hostile airspace; then on the beach again, or picking coconuts, or chasing another lizard. In the middle of July, when their top-turret gunner fell ill, they took on a replacement, Robert Stinson, and they all lined up for a new crew photo in their combat uniforms, with the old *Babes in Arms* behind them, Johnny's hair swept up in a pompadour, Ted's mustache finally coming in, and Norman Coorssen kneeling in the front with a surly stare, while Frank Arhar's face lit up with a huge, buoyant grin. In the back row, Jimmie Doyle squinted at the camera, eyebrows arched, a tiny smirk playing at the corner of his mouth. He was the only man who'd forgotten to wear a belt.

On a good day, mail lit up the camp with encouraging news from home. "The only thing that saves boys out here from flipping the lid is the mail from home," Bob Hope commented from a nearby island. "When they get a letter, they get a new personality." But when the mail brought bad news, the transformation was not so welcome. Some men discovered that their children were sick, or their parents dying. Others learned that their wives were pregnant, or leaving them, or both.

Jimmie and Myrle were not immune to the strains of distance. During his training in Fresno, Jimmie had become friendly with a gunner named William Crum, but when Jimmie transferred to the school in Tonopah, Crum's girlfriend began writing him letters. She was intrigued by Jimmie, she wrote, and wanted to get to know him. Jimmie immediately wrote to Crum, letting him know about the letters, and when Myrle came to Tonopah for a visit, he let her read them. At the time, Myrle had been unconcerned, but now the distance crept in; now she was writing Jimmie to ask if there was anything he hadn't told her.

Jimmie could feel the suspicion emanating from Myrle's letter and it left him ill. Sitting in his bunk, he lit a candle and spread out four sheets of airmail paper to respond. "Darling," he began, "you know how very glad I was to hear from you, but you also can't know how surprised I was for you to write about that 'correspondence,' as you put it. Dearest, I can understand how you feel about it, but I thought that you knew what I told you was all there was to it. I never dreamed you had thought any more about it, and I'm sure I never have. As you know, I have never met the girl, who is probably Mrs. Crum by now, and all I ever heard about her was just from the talk Crum put out, and he was pretty crazy about her. I am very sorry you ever thought there was anything important about the matter at all, and I'm sure I never thought for a minute that you would think I was keeping any thing from you."

"I have no secrets from you," he added, "and I hope you know by now that I never will have."

WHILE THE BIG STOOP CREW struggled with the balance between combat and life on base, the bloody battle for the Mariana Islands slogged on: by mid-July, Allied forces had finally routed the Japanese on Saipan, and were continuing their drive down the island chain toward Guam.

Nowhere was the Marianas battle more deeply felt than Tokyo. Though the capital was 1,500 miles away, it was now within range of US heavy bombers, and the loss put Prime Minister Tojo in a precarious political position. It had been Tojo, after all, who dispatched the Fourteenth Shining to the wrong islands, and now he would pay the price. In the third week of July, he was relieved as prime minister, and then stripped of his military rank. He retreated to his home in the suburbs of Tokyo and slid into an agitated ennui, pacing the garden in worn clothes and a straw hat, and stopping occasionally to pick vegetables or scrawl notes in a journal.

"He had too much time and he didn't know what to do with it," the general's wife, Katsuko, told his biographer, Courtney Browne. Tojo himself confessed, "If only I could write a poem or something. I ought to have taken more of an interest in those things."

The same day Tojo lost his military rank, President Franklin Roosevelt was nominated for a fourth term. It was an unprecedented tenure and, depending on whom you asked, either a landmark moment in Democratic history, or the least democratic moment in American history. Either way,

Roosevelt wasn't there to enjoy it; while the convention revelers carried on in Chicago, the president was on his way from Washington to San Diego, where he boarded the warship USS *Baltimore* for a tour of the Pacific. His wife, Eleanor, stayed behind. His Scottish terrier, Fala, came.

The *Baltimore* was a heavy cruiser, barely a year old, but already hardened from battle. Since her arrival in the Central Pacific, she had been part of the Battle of Makin, and then the Battle of Kwajalein, and most recently, the vast carrier battle in the Marianas. Now, with the Japanese fleet in tatters, she had returned to California for a few days at the port of San Diego, before turning back toward the war with the commander in chief on board. Roosevelt's health was dwindling, and he had no plans to enter the combat zone. But he was well aware that during an election year a visit to the troops was politically savvy, especially if he arrived on the deck of a triumphant warship.

While the *Baltimore* steamed west from San Diego, other ships from the Marianas battle were moving on to new targets. No archipelago in a thousand-mile radius was more heavily defended than Palau, with twenty-five thousand Japanese troops digging furiously into the hills. On July 25, as Roosevelt closed in on Hawaii, the carrier USS *San Jacinto* sent a small squadron of planes over Palau on a photographic mission. By the end of the day, Ensign George Bush would sink his first enemy ship, setting the stage for Pat Scannon's journey fifty years later.

But the farther American troops advanced, the more urgent the strategic question became. Only one of the two columns could make the final push into Japan. The trouble was, even most American commanders were unsure which track to recommend. Many had changed their preference multiple times throughout the war. As the leader of the northern column, Nimitz embodied the Navy's strategy to seize Taiwan, but on a personal level, Nimitz was not convinced that the plan was better than MacArthur's. One of his leading commanders, Admiral Bull Halsey, supported a combination of the two strategies, while the Army's chief of staff, General George Marshall, vacillated between support for MacArthur's plan, and distaste for MacArthur himself. Trying to keep track of each commander's latest assessment could be a dizzying task. As the historian William Manchester described the strategic landscape in his biography of MacArthur, *American Caesar*, "Individuals changed their minds from week to week. Marshall was beginning to side with MacArthur. Hap Arnold, eager for B-29 bases on [Taiwan], continued to support King. Nimitz, wavering, instructed his staff to draw up plans for assaults on all possible objectives, including the Japanese homeland; he had begun to listen to Halsey, who wanted to seize Luzon, ignore Formosa, and pounce on Okinawa. The Joint Chiefs reflected the general confusion."

By the time Roosevelt landed at Pearl Harbor on July 26, he had made up his mind to end the debate for good. He called for both Nimitz and MacArthur to spend a few days with him in Hawaii, where they would visit military bases, shake hands with the troops, pose for a few politically useful photos, and then retreat to a private mansion overlooking Waikiki to study maps and discuss the options.

It was time for the men leading the war to choose its final path.

CHESTER NIMITZ and Douglas MacArthur were as different as the columns they led. At sixty-four, MacArthur was the most famous general in the Army, and had been for most of his adult life. He'd graduated from West Point in 1903 with the highest academic score ever recorded, been nominated for two Medals of Honor in World War I, and became the youngest major general in the Army at age forty-five. By the time he was named Army chief of staff a few years later, he was known as much for his eccentricity as his precocious command. At his office in Washington, DC, it was not uncommon to find the general sitting behind his desk in a Japanese kimono, waving himself with an Asian fan, and chain-smoking cigarettes through a bejeweled holder. He "increasingly spoke of himself in the third person," William Manchester wrote, "and had erected a fifteen-foot-high mirror behind his office chair to heighten his image."

In 1935, MacArthur left his position in Washington and moved to the Philippines, where he promptly took a position as the leader of the Philippine army, parading about in an embroidered uniform with a golden baton. But as the shadow of Japan loomed over the Pacific, Roosevelt called him back to service as the head of American forces in the region. With the attack on Pearl Harbor in December 1941, MacArthur found himself under siege, and he spent three months hiding in an underground bunker on a small island just south of the Bataan Peninsula, before escaping in March 1942 with his family, their nanny, and a small fortune acquired illegally from the Philippine government. By the time he regrouped to lead the southern column toward Japan, he was as polarizing as any other figure in American life: Some dismissed him as "Dugout Doug" for his months in hiding, while others praised him for having lasted there so long. Parents named their children for him. The Blackfeet Indians called him Chief Wise Eagle.

Roosevelt's view of MacArthur was mixed. They had been friends early in their careers, but by the summer of 1944, the relationship was thorny at best. Just three months before their meeting in Hawaii, MacArthur had finally put to rest a long-standing rumor, circulated by his friend William Randolph Hearst, that the general planned to challenge the president in the fall election. To Roosevelt, it seemed as if MacArthur's denial was a long time coming. For MacArthur's part, the summons to meet Roosevelt in Hawaii came as a personal affront. To be called away from his base, just days after the Democratic nomination, was a distraction he did not take well. On the twenty-six-hour flight to Hawaii, he paced the aisle of the plane, muttering about "the humiliation of forcing me to leave my command and fly to Honolulu for a political picture-taking junket!"

Nimitz, meanwhile, was everything Douglas MacArthur was not. Born to a family of hoteliers in the hills of central Texas, he maintained a crisp and private demeanor, and was allergic to every form of spectacle, including war. As the author Robert Sherrod put it in the Pacific history *On to Westward,* "Nimitz conceived of war as something to be accomplished as efficiently and as smoothly as possible, without too much fanfare."

Unlike MacArthur, Nimitz had risen to power steadily, almost accidentally. His first interest had been the Army, but when he was turned down by West Point, he entered the Naval Academy instead. During World War I, he'd seen no action, spending the first few months on a refueling ship, and the rest in a submarine division, at a time when, as he put it, "undersea craft were regarded as a cross between a Jules Verne fantasy and a whale." While MacArthur's military profile was so prodigious that he'd been recalled to leadership even before the war, Nimitz had only taken charge of the Pacific Fleet after the embarrassment at Pearl Harbor left a vacuum in naval leadership. All of which only underscored the fact that Nimitz was the real thing: a commander who had risen to the occasion, and not been groomed for it. At his headquarters in Pearl Harbor, he insisted on hiring a staff that represented all military services, and he demanded that they wear a special uniform to eliminate branch distinctions. He was meticulous, punctual, and borderline obsessive, with a seven-day workweek, and he expected the same from his men, although he encouraged them to break for thirty minutes a day to exercise. In his own free time, he would repair to the firing range with his pistol. Like Roosevelt, he often traveled with his dog, a schnauzer named Mak that was, in the words of historian Max Hastings, "a mean little dog which growled."

By the time Nimitz left his office to welcome Roosevelt on the docks of Pearl Harbor, he was, at fifty-nine years old, the youngest of the three men called to the meeting and also the oldest-looking, with a strained, pale face, thinning white hair, and ramrod posture. He stood frozen in his dress whites as the president's ship tied off, then he climbed aboard regally amid cheers from a small crowd.

MacArthur, meanwhile, was nowhere to be found. He had arrived an hour earlier, but rather than greet the president, decided to drop his bags at a friend's house and enjoy a steamy bath. Roosevelt and Nimitz waited for MacArthur on the deck of the *Baltimore* for about an hour before giving up. "Just as we were getting ready to go below," one of the president's aides recalled, "a terrific automobile siren was heard, and there raced to the dock and screeched to a stop a motorcycle escort and the longest open car I have ever seen. In the front was a chauffeur in khaki, and in the back, one lone figure—MacArthur."

After a few photos on the deck, the men dispersed for the evening, but they gathered in the morning to make a tour of Hawaiian bases. They stopped at Hickam to visit men wounded on Saipan and watched a mock invasion of a Japanese village at the Schofield Barracks. Finally, they made their way to the hills above Waikiki for dinner.

The vast stucco mansion where they would spend the evening had once belonged to a wealthy businessman named Christian Holmes II, who was heir to the Fleischmann's Yeast fortune and had served under Teddy Roosevelt in the Army. In the years since then, Holmes had been married and divorced three times, much to the chagrin of his mother, who purchased a small tuna-canning company and installed Holmes as president, in order, as she put it, "to keep him occupied." When Holmes was not feeling especially occupied by the canning business, he filled his time with lavish parties, hosting stars and starlets like Amelia Earhart and Shirley Temple in another of his opulent homes, a three-level manse built on a private island, with fish tanks lining the walls of the foyer, and a personal bowling alley and movie theater inside. Outside, he collected exotic animals like giraffes and elephants. For Holmes, the mansion overlooking Waikiki was something of a spare, and he allowed the Navy to use it as a rest home for aviators just back from the war. Five months before Roosevelt's arrival on the island, Holmes had taken his own life with pills, but his estate left the mansion available to Roosevelt as a kind of Waikiki White House.

Though MacArthur had been leading the Army's southern column for years, he and Roosevelt had not seen each other since before the war. The sight of Roosevelt was distressing to MacArthur. Ravaged by illness as a young man, the president managed to hide the paralysis of his legs from the public, but now he was also suffering from massive arteriosclerosis and congestive heart failure, which left him so gaunt, gray, and depleted that MacArthur doubted he would survive much longer. Roosevelt's doctors wondered, too. Just four days before the president left for Hawaii, one of them, Frank Lahey, had written a confidential memo concluding that he "did not believe that if Mr. Roosevelt were elected President again, he had the physical capacity to complete a term." MacArthur described Roosevelt's appearance as "shocking." Later he wrote, "Physically he was just a shell of the man I had known. It was clearly evident that his days were numbered."

After dinner at the Holmes mansion, Roosevelt, MacArthur, and Nimitz moved into an adjoining room to discuss the war. It was a cavernous space filled with antique lamps and luxurious sofas, but the three men perched on a row of bamboo chairs facing an enormous map of the Pacific. Roosevelt turned to MacArthur. "Well, Douglas," he said. "Where do we go from here?"

For the next two hours, MacArthur and Nimitz took turns at the map—pacing before it, pointing at key positions with a long rod, and arguing the merits of each approach. As Nimitz pushed for the northern track across the Central Pacific, MacArthur sat with his head cocked to one side, feigning interest. Privately, he guessed that Nimitz was conflicted. He was a loyal admiral and would promote the Navy plan, but it had been drawn up by his boss, Admiral Ernest King in Washington, and MacArthur had come to the conclusion that Nimitz would be happy with either option. "Nimitz put forth the Navy plan," MacArthur wrote later, "but I was sure it was King's and not his own."

MacArthur was as resolute as Nimitz was uncertain. He not only preferred the southern strategy, he despised the northern one. In addition to the moral and strategic problem of bypassing the Philippines, he realized that the northern strategy would require him to give up command. "All of my American forces, except a token group of two divisions and a few air squadrons, were to be transferred to the command of Admiral

Nimitz," he wrote. This was unthinkable. When it was MacArthur's turn to speak, he grabbed the pointer and swept it over the map in dramatic strokes to highlight the crucial lines. There was the new Japanese perimeter, laying claim to a long trail of islands from Thailand to New Guinea. There was the flow of oil rising up from those islands, past the Philippines, toward Tokyo. And there was MacArthur's column, poised to capture the Philippines, stop the oil, and strike Japan from a position of strength. Any other approach, he insisted, would be ineffective, inexcusable, and ruinous to America's reputation. "I felt that to sacrifice the Philippines a second time could not be condoned or forgiven," he wrote. "I argued that it was not only a moral obligation to release this friendly possession from the enemy, now that it had become possible, but that to fail to do so would not be understandable to the Oriental mind."

The debate continued into the night, but by the time the men parted company, Roosevelt was still undecided. He asked the commanders to meet him again in the morning and trundled off to bed with the direction of the war hanging in the balance.

With it hung Palau. Either strategy would include an assault on the islands, but they were far more important to MacArthur. In the Navy's plan to take Taiwan, Palau was just an outpost on the flank. One of the top Navy commanders, Bull Halsey, was concerned that the islands were not worth taking at all. He'd been arguing since early summer that Palau should be blockaded and bypassed. Yet for MacArthur, the drive from New Guinea to the Philippines went directly through Palau. His planners described the islands as the "key point" in Japan's defenses. If Roosevelt chose the southern option, there was little chance that MacArthur would bypass the islands, especially on the advice of a Navy admiral.

By the time Roosevelt announced in the morning that he'd chosen MacArthur's plan, the fate of Palau was sealed. Although Halsey would continue to argue against the invasion, MacArthur had the islands firmly in his sights. Within days, he would begin to move his heavy bombers into striking range.

NINE

CONTACT

Pat Scannon had the attention of the military, if not the support. The recovery lab in Hawaii was always skeptical of civilians and for good reason. Most of the "amateur archaeologists" who contacted the unit to report crash locations in the Pacific turned out to be little more than treasure hunters who had pillaged the sites for guns and trophies and wanted to sell the coordinates of what remained. On balance, Johnie Webb and the lab staff believed, it was best to approach new faces with caution.

But Scannon was becoming hard to dismiss. His name kept popping up in conversations with veterans and their families, and it sometimes seemed that half the MIA community had either met him at a reunion, spoken with him by phone, or read about his work in a magazine. Then, too, the depth of Scannon's commitment went far beyond the norm. He

wasn't just swimming around blindly, hoping to spot a wreck. He returned to the archipelago methodically, plotting underwater grids and
building a formidable network of historians and scholars to augment the
hunt. Though he still hadn't found the Arnett plane, he was documenting
dozens of smaller wrecks, like the Marine Corsairs he found in 1999 while
taking a break from the channel and the Navy Avenger he spotted near
Peleliu that same year. As Scannon shot close-up photos of those planes
and tracked down their serial numbers, his list of potential recovery sites
in Palau was growing fast.

Then there was the mass grave. One of Scannon's best contacts in the
Pacific was a professor of politics and government at the University of
Guam named Don Shuster. Through his own research, Shuster had come
upon a cache of records from the 1949 war crimes trial of Sadae Inoue,
which included hundreds of pages of transcripts and depositions from
Inoue's men. In them, the Japanese soldiers confessed to a string of executions in Palau, including the murder of local families, indigenous mi-
norities, Jesuit missionaries, and even a few American prisoners who had
been captured as far away as Yap. Many of the victims had been buried
together in a mass grave, and a few of Inoue's men had drawn maps of the
site. When Shuster sent copies of the maps to Scannon, it didn't take long
to recognize the area: it was the long, low ridgeline in southern Babeldaob
where the military police, known as kempei-tai (kem'-pey-tie), kept their
wartime headquarters. The kempei referred to the area as "Gasupan," but
Scannon and Shuster called it "Police Hill." They organized all their files
on the site into a single presentation, and sent it to the military lab.

By the time Scannon sat down with Tommy and Nancy Doyle at the
Long Ranger reunion, the lab was gearing up for its first mission to Police
Hill, and by the time Scannon left the Doyles to make his way to the is-
lands, the lab was already there, searching for the grave.

Still, Scannon had little contact with the recovery unit. Though they'd
come to Palau as a result of his work, he was determined not to interfere.
He stayed in a different hotel, kept his distance from Police Hill, and

spent most of his time on the Arnett channel, continuing the underwater grid in a series of infinite passes—up and down and back again with the magnetometer. Near the end of the trip, they bumped into the recovery team at an Internet café on Koror, and to Scannon's surprise, a member of the lab team presented him with a ceremonial medallion. It was inscribed with the words "Central Identification Lab—Hawaii." The team hadn't found anything yet, but they had seen enough evidence on Police Hill to suggest that it was the right place to look. They were planning to come back for a more thorough search, and if they ran into Scannon, they expected him to have the medallion in his pocket.

For Scannon, the medallion was puzzling. He knew it was a gesture of friendship, but he'd never heard of a challenge coin before. The tradition dated back to the European theater of World War II, when US intelligence services in occupied France used a special coin as proof of identity. In the decades since, it had become common practice for military units to design their own coins, stamped with their name, logo, and motto. Men from the Army, Navy, Air Force, and Marines all traded coins, and if any two guys who had traded coins were to cross paths again, each was expected to have the other's coin in hand. In his journal, Scannon marveled at the strange "gold medallion" from the lab. "They said if they ever met up with me anywhere in the world and I didn't have it, I owe a round of beers," he wrote, adding, "Fair enough."

Scannon was just settling back to work in California when Don Shuster called with another breakthrough on the mass grave. He had found a tribal elder on Palau who remembered where it was. Katalina Katosang had been a teenager during the war, and was close with the Jesuit missionaries living on the islands. A few days after they were executed by the Japanese in 1944, she walked up and down Police Hill looking for their grave. When she found a pair of white, wooden crosses planted in fresh earth, she knelt beside them, crying and praying, and went home with the small comfort that she knew where they lay. Now she was willing to return to the spot and take the recovery unit with her. It was just a few hundred yards north of where the lab had been looking the year before.

Scannon and Shuster called the lab. There was a field team gearing up for a recovery in the Marshall Islands, and they agreed to stop in Palau for one day. The lab invited Scannon to join them and he jumped at the chance. He flew to Koror in November 2001 with two of his skydiving friends.

The lead archaeologist for the lab this time was a stocky civilian named Bill Belcher who, like the lab's newest hire, Eric Emery, was a curious fit on a military team. With a sardonic sense of humor and a prickly temperament, Belcher was accustomed to doing things his way. In his free time, he enjoyed deep-sea diving at depths that went far beyond the usual limits of scuba. Many of the most famous deep-sea wrecks lay at about 250 feet, like the *Andrea Doria* near Nantucket, at 260, or the mystery U-boat off New Jersey, at 230, but Belcher had crept below 400 feet, into the cold, black, oppressive zone where gas roiled in the blood and chemical narcosis took over, drowning men in a crazed euphoria. He knew that his diving experience did not qualify him in the peculiar tools and methods of underwater archaeology, which was why he'd encouraged the lab to hire Emery that summer. But on land, Belcher yielded to no one, especially a hobby sleuth like Scannon. As his plane touched down in Palau, he braced himself for a testy interaction.

"I always have a very, very deep, deep level of skepticism about people involved in this," Belcher recalled. "Particularly with World War II, because a lot of people want it for notoriety, they want to feel important, and it's also the issue that the artifacts are actually worth quite a bit of money to collectors. A lot of times, I'll get in almost a fistfight with divers—like these guys you see holding the skulls of the Germans from the U-boat. I have a real issue with that. They're destroying the sites."

But Belcher also knew enough about Scannon to hold out a glimmer of hope. For one thing, he knew that other archaeologists at the lab had been impressed on the previous mission. Scannon hadn't badgered

them or tried to inject himself in their work, and they found him sufficiently serious to bestow a challenge coin. That wasn't enough to convince
Belcher, but it counted. What counted even more was Scannon's background in science. A licensed MD with a PhD in chemistry was not your
typical scavenger. With most of those guys, Belcher believed, it was pointless to explain how delicate a crash site was, or how, even after half a
century of rain and mud and wind and rummaging animals, the wreckage
had to be treated with microscopic precision. A single touch or movement could obscure a clue, possibly the last one, and if a field site was like
an enormous test tube, it was reassuring to know that Scannon was a
scientist.

Belcher was operating on just a few hours' sleep when he awoke on his
first morning in Palau. He trudged into the lobby of the Waterfront Villa
hotel to meet Scannon for the first time. As they shook hands, Belcher
took a look at Scannon. He was slim but muscular, with a gray beard and
thinning hair, and he wore a faded red bandana rolled around his neck
above a long-sleeved gray T-shirt and loose cargo pants. Belcher wore
an olive bushmaster hat over a khaki shirt, and together the two men
looked as if they knew their way around a jungle.

After a few curt words, they stepped outside to a pair of four-wheel-
drive trucks that Belcher had rented at the airport. They climbed in, and
rolled through the back roads of Koror to pick up Katosang, then crossed
the bridge to Babeldaob over the Toachel Mid channel. As the small convoy barreled north, Scannon gazed out the window. Fields of chest-high
grass waved slowly in the tropical breeze, separated by stands of jungle.
He had been up the road dozens of times to interview tribal elders about
the plane crashes they had seen and the stories they remembered, but he
always found the big island striking. Unlike the rest of the archipelago,
which was mostly limestone rock, Babeldaob consisted of bright orange
clay that had a way of sticking to the fibers of clothing. Many of Scannon's shirts and backpacks were stained with the mark of Babeldaob, and
sometimes as he unpacked his gear at the end of a mission, he would hold

the stain to his nose for a whiff of the warm, tropical smell that always brought him back.

After forty minutes on the serpentine road, stopping occasionally to clear fallen trees, the outline of Police Hill crested on the horizon and the trucks turned right, climbing up a small road over the rutted earth, past outcroppings of carnivorous plants that lay in wait for crickets. At the top of the hill, they pulled to one side and parked. Katosang sprang to the ground, hurrying into the elephant grass alone. She dodged from side to side, as if following a scent. Scannon, Belcher, and the rest of the team scrambled to collect gear, then took off after Katosang.

To the untrained eye, the hillside appeared no different from any other wilderness on the big island. It was a broad expanse of grass interrupted here and there by bare patches of clay. But Katosang saw the past. There had been a hospital a few yards uphill, she said, and a scattering of build-ings down below. She stooped to sift through the dirt and came up with shards of glass and metal. This was from a small wooden building, she said, with a view to the road below.

Katosang continued down the hillside and stopped at a low depression in the earth. Something changed viscerally in her posture. She turned, paused, and nodded. This, she said finally, was it. This was where she'd seen the crosses. This was the mass grave.

Belcher and the lab team fanned out, searching the ground for clues. Scannon stayed close to the depression, studying its shape. He walked a circle around it, then another, widening the spiral as he searched the ground for debris. An hour passed as the team scoured the area. There were no shouts of discovery, no clear signs of the grave or the wooden crosses—but then, Scannon realized, how could there be? Whole build-ings had disappeared into the earth, their lumber swallowed in the clay and grass. A grave would be nearly impossible to find.

For Belcher, the lack of material evidence was troubling but the shape of the depression was unforgettable. It was about ten feet wide and twenty feet long, with corners much too neat to be natural. It could have been a building foundation, but there were no other signs of a building. In the places where Katosang did recall buildings, the remnants were still apparent.

Belcher approached Scannon. They stood together under the gaping tropical sky, the faint sound of breeze and rustling grass in the air. The site, Belcher said finally, was too much to ignore. When he returned to Hawaii, he would recommend a dig.

Scannon hesitated. Then he nodded. He removed his backpack and pulled out a folded American flag. "Would you mind if we had a small ceremony?" he asked. "In case there were Americans?"

Belcher took a corner of the flag and together they unfolded it. They stretched the fabric over the depression as the group converged for a photo. After a moment of silence, Scannon refolded the flag. He tucked it neatly into his backpack and began walking toward the trucks.

Belcher watched. He realized that his doubt about Scannon was gone. The strange, silent doctor was difficult to read, but Belcher had seen enough to know that he wasn't a treasure hunter. He approached the site with an air of sadness, humility, and reverence. He responded to the prospect that they'd found a mass grave not with bravado but resignation. He seemed to want nothing more from the search than answers.

"The thing I liked about him," Belcher said later, "was that he was sincere. He wasn't in it for fame or glory. He just wanted to find these guys."

FOR SCANNON, the connection with Belcher meant the mission had changed. With help from the lab, he would not just be looking for lost men; he would be working to bring them home.

Three years had passed since his skydiving days, but he remained close with his friends from jump school. The founder of the SkyDance program was not just any skydiver. Dan O'Brien was a former world champion who had been featured in the opening ceremony of the Seoul Olympics, where he descended into a stadium of screaming fans to stick a landing at the center, while a swirling mass of performers waved white banners around him. At the jump school, he offered classes for beginners like Scannon, but he also used the building as a locus for elite skydivers to gather. On any given afternoon, depending on who was in town, there might be half a dozen world-record holders in the building. The friends Scannon had brought with him to meet Belcher on Police Hill, Jennifer Powers and Clem Major, were both elite divers. Powers was a world-record holder with more than five thousand jumps, and Major specialized in base diving, with seven thousand jumps. From time to time, Powers, O'Brien, and other members of the SkyDance community would gather in some remote corner of the world to embark on an outlandish odyssey, like trying to organize the largest airborne formation in history. In between, they would regale one another over beers with stories of their exploits, while Scannon traded his own tales from the archipelago.

Something about the skydivers resonated with Scannon in a familiar way. Like the veterans of the Long Rangers, they were disciplined in the sky, with a clear chain of command, while on the ground they eased into an egalitarian ethos born of shared experience. "I don't care if you skydive a thousand jumps or twenty," Scannon said. "Everybody that I ever saw go into the plane had an abiding respect for everybody else. There are rich people who do it, there are people who save every penny they can get to do it, young people, old people, professionals, military, and yet you carry this respect for every other person that puts a chute on their back."

As Scannon returned from his meeting with Belcher on Police Hill, he was beginning to realize two things. The first was that skydivers like Powers, O'Brien, and Major were uniquely qualified to help with his search. Like the Lamberts, they had traveled the world and were accustomed to rugged conditions. They were comfortable with a high level of risk, and used to working together under pressure. Their experience in aerial formations was also surprisingly adaptable to the water—the best way to conduct a grid search in the channel was to canvass the seafloor in a linked formation. Finally, many of the skydivers had learned to jump while serving in the military. They had a bone-deep respect for the missing men.

The other thing Scannon was beginning to realize was that he needed a better organization. If he wanted the recovery lab to see him as a partner, he would need to make his work more palatable to the military command. That meant giving it a name and a stated mission, something that could be written down to show that it wasn't just one man's quixotic obsession. Over the next several months, Scannon began to craft a formal identity for the search. He came up with a name: the BentProp Project. He designed a logo of a battered propeller superimposed above blue and red stripes. He found out where military units printed their challenge coins, and produced one with the BentProp logo on the front. On the back, he printed a line from the Laurence Binyon poem "For the Fallen": "At the going down of the sun and in the morning / We will remember them."

Next, Scannon decided to name his expeditions. A journey to the islands would no longer be "a journey." It was a "PMAN," short for Palau-Marines-Army-Navy, and he gave each PMAN a Roman numeral. He backdated the first to 1999, so it was PMAN-I. That made the trip to Police Hill with Belcher PMAN-III. Then Scannon began to change the way he kept records. When he reached the last page of his fourth artist's notebook in 2002, he didn't buy another. Instead, he bought a small yellow notepad with waterproof pages, which he could stuff in his pocket and bring into the field to fill with diagrams and coordinates. The lyrical reflections that wafted through the huge white pages of his journal disappeared. There would be no more long descriptions of the rain on Iberor, no thoughtful contemplations of the sunset on the golf course overlooking the southern bay. On the small, lined pages of the yellow pads, he assigned formal positions to the friends who joined him. As more skydivers came along in 2002 and 2003, he gave them titles like "Dive Safety Officer" and "Team Navigator" and "Military Liaison."

Watching the BentProp Project emerge, the Lamberts rolled their eyes. They found the stiff formality amusing at best. In less charitable moments, they would say that it was pretentious and unnecessary. The shift from an ad hoc labor of love to a routinized organization felt awkward and stiff, and they were deeply skeptical of all the skydivers showing up. On their own recent missions with Scannon, they had been forced to insist that he take days off, and relax a little, and enjoy the islands. But the skydivers were willing to drill down with Scannon day after day, and it seemed to the Lamberts as if the whole endeavor was becoming uncomfortably militarized. It was as if, in his quest to find the missing men, Scannon had discovered a new side of himself.

In fact, it was just the opposite.

SCANNON'S NEW CONNECTION with the military emerged from a long and conflicted past. He had spent most of his life trying to get away from the US Army, and it was only with reluctance that he now turned back. Born in 1947, he was a product of the war himself. His father, Tony Scannon, had been a captain in Europe, who fought a line through France and then worked for General George Patton in postwar Germany. His mother, Nora Esterházy, came from the other side: born in Romania and raised in Czechoslovakia, she worked for the Nazis during the war.

For Nora, the job was not a choice. As a teenager in eastern Europe, she watched the Nazi ascent with natural suspicion: her family lived in Bratislava, just a short train ride from Vienna, where Hitler's arrival in 1938 brought cheering crowds to the Heldenplatz—but Nora's family had sufficient money and social standing to be wary of any change. She was a well-educated young woman, fluent in German, Hungarian, English, Czech, and Slovak, and she was even proficient in Latin. When the German consulate instructed her to help their embassy with translation, Nora made the journey each morning past barbed wire to transcribe documents in a windowless room. At night, she listened to her parents rail

against the Nazis she was helping—and on the streets of the neighbor-
hood, she found a small community of teens who groused about the Germans. When some of those friends drifted into the Czech resistance,
forming a link to the underground network that stretched across Europe,
Nora began to feed them information from the consulate. Anytime she
translated a document that seemed important, she would carbon an extra
copy and slip it into her purse. Then, to avoid being frisked on the way
out, she would flirt with an embassy officer until he offered her a ride
home. "I don't know exactly how that relationship worked," Scannon said
with a bemused smile. "She never went into detail, and I sure didn't ask."

For Nora, the small subterfuge was an act of faith as much as daring.
Though she would eventually pass along more than a dozen documents,
she never knew how far they made it, or if they went anywhere at all. She
would later confess to her daughter, Harriet, that the only file she could
remember described her homeland, Romania, and its vast oil refineries at
Ploesti.

In 1943, Nora convinced the German government to let her move to
Leipzig and enroll in medical school. But just as classes began, so did the
American bombardment. She spent as many days hiding in a bunker as
she did in class, listening as American bombers turned the city into one
of the most devastated in Europe. Years later, at her condominium in
Florida, she would surprise her children by jumping from a chair and
cowering on the floor as a vintage B-24 bomber passed overhead.

By the time Nora met Tony Scannon, they were both living in postwar Germany. Nora had brought her parents in a harrowing journey by
train, and Tony had a job organizing performances by visiting stars like
Roy Rogers. It was a world apart from where each had been a year
before—Nora ducking bombs in Leipzig, while Tony fought through the
Ardennes—but they found themselves dancing together at the parties
Tony arranged.

It was still illegal for a US soldier to marry a European bride; the abun-
dance of American men in the ruined cities of Europe was a social

tinderbox that the Army was not eager to ignite. Brothels abounded on the streets and dalliances were commonplace, but it would be another year before marriage was formally allowed.

Somehow, Tony and Nora escaped those rules. The story they passed down to their children was that Tony's boss, General Patton, approved the union shortly before his death in December 1945, and lent the couple a Mercedes that had once belonged to Hermann Göring for the reception. Whether or not that story was exactly right, the Scannons did marry in Germany before Patton's death, and afterward they left Europe to live near Tony's birthplace in Georgia.

The move was hard on Nora. Hostility toward European refugees was fierce in the rural South, and as she gave birth to three children in four years—Pat in 1947, Harriet in 1948, and Mike in 1950—the pressure of living in a hostile, alien environment proved too much. When Tony deployed to Korea in 1951, Nora filed for divorce. Two years later, she met another Army officer and tried again.

For the Scannon kids, Harry Walterhouse would prove a different kind of paternal figure. Like Tony Scannon, he was a lieutenant colonel, but where Tony was strict and distant with the children, Walterhouse was warm and attentive; even as a soldier, he was less a warrior than an intellectual, interested in the role that military force could play in postwar development. By the time the Scannon children entered adolescence, his theories on what is now called nation-building had become early benchmarks of the field. In particular, a small, dense book entitled *A Time to Build*, which described the history of "military civic action" from ancient Rome to modern Africa, would be a staple of scholarly studies for decades to come. When the opportunity arose for Walterhouse to spend four years in postwar Germany, he and Nora settled into a large house near Nuremberg.

Like rural Georgia, small-town Germany was still laced with postwar hostilities, and Nora encouraged the kids to stay close to home. They spent most days playing in the forest adjacent to the house, and to keep them occupied, Nora embraced their curiosity. When Mike, at age six, showed an interest in biology, she brought home dead frogs and birds to dissect, using her medical school background to tease apart the musculature in an impromptu biology lesson. "They were always cutting something up," Scannon said. "It was gross."

Pat's interest was chemistry, and Nora brought home liquids, powders, and booklets of experiments. When he finished the written recipes, he would mix concoctions of his own. "Mostly I just burned a lot of things," he said. "I always wanted to make a big explosion."

There was no television in the house, so in the evenings they listened to military broadcasts on the radio or made up stories of their own. Years later, the Scannon kids would look back on their years in Germany as some of the best in their lives, which made the return to the United States all the more difficult. In 1962, Nora and Harry Walterhouse split, and Nora sank into a depression. She sent the children to live with their father, who was back from Korea and living in Georgia with a wife and two daughters.

Tony Scannon was forty-nine years old with a lifetime commanding men, but he had little idea what to do with young kids. He turned to the tools he knew. There were inspections on Saturday morning, harsh penalties for mistakes, and consequences for any hint of insubordination. Even today, the Scannon kids wince at the memory. "There wasn't a lot of joy in the house," Harriet Scannon said.

For Pat, school became an escape. He threw himself into his studies, finding in academic success a solace from the vagaries of life. At sixteen, he graduated from high school and took a year of classes at Augusta College to burnish his résumé before applying to universities. His first choice was Georgia Tech, which had a stellar chemistry program, but at Tony Scannon's insistence, he also sent an application to West Point. Then Tony pulled strings at the military academy, and intercepted the letter of acceptance from Georgia. In the fall of 1967, Scannon drove to New York to attend the only option he believed he had.

Today, West Point is widely celebrated as an academic force, but during the turmoil of the Vietnam years it was somewhat less renowned. Scannon felt listless. His mind disengaged. By the end of his first semester, he was ready to transfer out, but he was terrified that his father would think he'd given up. He decided to finish his freshman year and attend yearling summer camp, including the notorious Recondo week, before announcing plans to drop out.

He finished his undergraduate degree at the University of Georgia, and drove his Mercury Cougar west to begin a doctoral program in chemistry at UC Berkeley. It was 1971. The Bay Area was a notorious cacophony of drugs and protest, but Scannon passed through oblivious. At a party one night, he was surprised to find that a brownie was spiked with marijuana; it would be the only drug experience of his life. Instead, he chased the doctorate at breakneck speed, finishing his coursework in three years and writing his dissertation in two months. Years later, when he gave the commencement speech at Berkeley, he would be introduced as the only person ever to receive a chemistry doctorate in three years. But as he was walking across campus a few months before graduation, he experienced a sensation that he would later describe as an epiphany. "I was literally halfway through a step," he said, "when I realized that I didn't want to become a chemist. I wanted to become a doctor."

Scannon collected his PhD and enrolled in medical school. By the time he graduated in 1976, he was twenty-nine years old, with an MD, a PhD, and a debt to the military still hanging over his head from West Point. He decided to complete his military service with a residency at the Letterman Army Medical Center in San Francisco, where he met a radiologist named Hugh Cregg, whose son was emerging as a popular singer with the stage name Huey Lewis. Cregg was looking for a young partner to join his practice, and he offered to bring Scannon in. Scannon by then was married to his girlfriend from Berkeley, and their daughter, Nell, was three years old, but he declined the offer, telling Cregg that he wanted to start a company of his own. He found financial backers, including technology magnate David Packard, and set out to build a company that would combine his interests in chemistry and medicine. It would be a few years before someone told him that what he was doing was called "biotech."

By the time Scannon connected with Chip Lambert and made his first trip to Palau, he'd spent more than a decade of his life at Xoma. His colleagues had no inkling of his military background, his studies at West Point, or the deep influence those experiences would have on his life. But as Scannon began making journeys to Palau, he realized that his interest in the missing men was linked to his past. It was driven by a sense of duty and the need to sacrifice as his parents had, by a feeling of awe at his father's drive through the Ardennes, and his mother's courage in a Nazi consulate, and his stepfather's unwavering faith in the benevolent potential of military might.

To anyone else, Scannon's spontaneous obsession with the lost men could seem peculiar, even bizarre. He carried no visible tether to his military past. But to Scannon, the work in Palau felt like the solution to a life-long conundrum. It was a way to focus his passion for science on something larger than his own company, and to honor the military tradition in his family without abandoning his sense of self. "I had always wanted to be a civilian, but my history brought me back to the military," he said. "What I've found is that I love working with the military. I just don't want to work for them."

TEN

WASTELAND

As Franklin Roosevelt steamed away from his meeting with Nimitz and MacArthur, the strategy for the war was settled, but it remained top secret. In fact, Roosevelt's trip itself was secret. Though the president had met with reporters on the dock and at the Holmes mansion, the interviews were under embargo until his return to Washington, DC. Other than MacArthur, Nimitz, and a few senior commanders, no one in the US military knew which way the war was turning.

Certainly the men on the ground didn't know. In the Central Pacific, they drove onward through Tinian and Guam, while in the South Pacific, MacArthur pushed across the rim of New Guinea—with the Long Rangers bridging the distance between them. Some days, they flew north to cover Nimitz; others, they zipped west to back MacArthur.

One rainy afternoon at the end of July, Ted Goulding kicked about the

Big Stoop tent aimlessly. It was his day off, and Ted hated those. Every successful mission counted toward the end of his tour, and the day he finished fifty, he would go home. To speed things up, he'd volunteered to fly as a substitute for any crew with a sick man, but so far, no luck. So he was in the tent. Listening to the rain patter on the flysheet, he tried to imagine life in New York, the summer heat fading into autumn's descent, the snow arriving soon to blanket the banks of the Hudson, and he picked up a sheet of paper to write Diane's parents with a request.

"Hey folks," he began. "Here I am at last. How is everything at home? How is Dee and our son Teddy? Please take good care of them for me because I will be home pretty soon. I wish this whole mess was over so that we could all come home. . . . There are only a few more months left of warm weather, then it will get cold. Could you look in a catalogue and find some warm clothing for Dee and Ted? Don't worry about the money because I will send it to you. Get some nice warm little shirts, hats, mittens, and sox for Teddy, and get Dee some warm slacks, shoes, sox, gloves, and undies and such. Send me the list of things and the total amount, and I will send you the money. That way Dee won't have to use up the money she is trying to save. Keep all this to yourself until you get the stuff and then give it to Dee and tell her that I didn't even forget about the weather at home. I want them to be warm and healthy. . . . In other words, please make sure that Dee and Ted have everything they want."

When the sun returned a few days later, Ted pulled his cot outside and stretched out below the tropical glare, baking the cold from his bones, but after a few minutes, Jimmie Doyle rousted him for a swim. They ambled toward the shoreline and tumbled through the rough surf. As evening fell, they returned to their bunks and Jimmie wrote to Myrle, "We sure got dunked a lot, and both of us are a little red!"

Since the mix-up over Crum's girlfriend, Jimmie and Myrle had settled back into an easy rapport. Myrle reported from Lamesa with the weather, the gossip, the progress of crops, and the comings and goings of friends, while Jimmie soaked up each detail, combing through the newspapers she sent for the most arcane trivia. "I have read everything in the paper, even the want ads," he wrote, noting, "Lee Barron has a lot on 4th and Miller for sale. What sort of place is it, and is it worth what he asks? You know the place, just north of the old lady's where I built the fish pond? I think there used to be a couple of houses there. Why not take a look at it, and if it's worth the price, maybe we can arrange for the money. What do you think?"

When Myrle sent a copy of the book *Big Spring*, a collection of folksy tales from the town where her sister lived, Jimmie grew homesick reading lines like "Why, on a clear day, you can stand on top one of these little hills around Big Spring and see to hell and gone, way over to Lamesa." He confessed to Myrle in a letter, "Sorta got the blues in a way. I have been reading the book, and it brought back everyone so plain. I can just see the whole country, and boy, that country sure has a hold on me. Those plains would sure be a welcome sight to Jim."

Always, Jimmie asked about family. Growing up with just his father, he'd taken to calling Myrle's parents "Mother" and "Dad," and he traded letters with each. When Myrle's mother wrote that one of her other daughters, Dorothy, was pregnant and moving to a new farm with her husband, Tracy, Jimmie wrote to Myrle for specifics. "Where is this farm of Tracy's?" he asked. "Mother said they had a pretty nice place, but she didn't give any details." When two weeks passed and he still hadn't heard more, he brought it up again. "I have heard about Tracy and Dorothy's farm," he wrote, "but no one has ever said a word about where it is. Is it close to Sparenberg, or near town? And how are they doing with it?"

Jimmie had a special fondness for Myrle's sister Gladys, whose broad, round face was perpetually lit up with glee. Back in Texas, she and Jimmie were forever prodding and teasing each other, and Jimmie tried to keep the spirit of the relationship alive in his letters. "Tell Gladys it's a good thing that her boyfriend is in Italy instead of here," he wrote to Myrle. "Because she would probably lose him to a native woman. The native women don't wear any clothes from the knees down, nor from the waist up." When Myrle wrote back that Gladys had taken a job in the egg dehy-drating plant, making military rations, he wrote, "Tell Gladys to leave just a little more taste in those eggs when she dries them." But when Myrle replied that she was taking a job alongside Gladys at the plant, he re-sponded with uncharacteristic worry. "Please don't hurt yourself," he wrote, "for the money isn't anything compared to your health. I know you feel better when you are working, and you're awful sweet about it, but please take care of yourself."

While Myrle's letters always seemed to brighten Jimmie's day, Johnny's letters from Katherine often had the opposite effect. Each time he re-ceived one, he would tear it open eagerly, skimming through the pages in search of news that she was pregnant. Nearly three months had passed since they said good-bye, and Johnny could hardly stand waiting for the good news. So far, it hadn't come. In fact, Katherine sent confusing sig-nals, suggesting in one letter that she was pretty sure she was pregnant, then wondering in the next why she wasn't. "She keeps him in a state," Jimmie wrote to Myrle. "He will get a letter saying she is, then the next day, he'll get one saying she isn't, so he is on needles and pins about it. But that is one of their worries we can't do anything about. I talk to him, and try to help him all I can, but I feel sorry for him. I know just how he feels, for I went through the same experience. Remember?"

Johnny also had a tendency to write Katherine when he was lonely. His frustration would bleed onto the pages, and throw Katherine into a panic. Jimmie told Johnny to knock it off. *Put on your best face*, he said. *The letters are for her, not you.* But Johnny seemed incapable of holding the loneli-ness in. "When he gets the blues," Jimmie confided to Myrle, "he sits down and takes it out on her, and it doesn't do a bit of good. It must make her feel worse. The best thing he could do would be to just try to keep from getting low, and when he does, just sweat it out." When Johnny's sister Mary wrote to let him know that Katherine was keeping a secret herself, and had been fighting an infection for several weeks, it only made his depression worse. He wrote to Mary, "Six months ago I got married. Now I'm thousands of miles from my wife. What a life."

The one thing airmen could not discuss in their letters was the war. Each time they pushed an envelope into the postal drop on base, they knew it would be opened and read by a censor, who would use a pair of scissors to snip out any explicit reference to the unit, the islands, the mission, or the enemy. How much else the censor read was anyone's guess; each man was left to imagine for himself which of the officers he encountered on the base knew the most intimate details of his life. "The officers that censor our mail are with us in our same squadron," Ted Goulding wrote to Diane. "They aren't supposed to mention anything they have read, or whose mail they have read, but there is always that feeling in our hearts and minds."

Once in a while, an errant mention of the war would slip past the censors, as when Johnny wrote to his brother-in-law in early August, "You should have seen us bombing yesterday, Gilbert! We really blasted the hell out of things!" Or when Jimmie wrote to Myrle the same day, "I have shot down one Jap ship so far. I can't say where or when," and praised his crew: "All the guys are swell, and I couldn't ask for a better bunch. We have the best pilot of the war." To his sister Mary, Johnny wrote, "Our pilot told us if there was anything on the ship we wanted to learn to do, to tell him. So I told him I wanted to fly it. He's gonna teach me!"

But what Johnny couldn't know as he finished that letter was that hours earlier the news of Roosevelt's trip to Hawaii had broken in the US news. The cover of the *New York Times* that day showed a photo of Roosevelt, MacArthur, and Nimitz sitting on the deck of the USS *Baltimore* in Hawaii, beside the headline "Roosevelt and Leaders Map Plans for Return to the Philippines; A Job for M'Arthur."

For the first time, the path ahead was clear. If the president was sending MacArthur to the Philippines, he would have to get through Palau. That meant the Long Rangers would be packing up soon and leaving

Camp De Luxe for a new base, six hundred miles to the west and right on the front lines of war.

THE ISLAND OF NEW GUINEA stretches across the South Pacific like a lid hovering over Australia. It is the second-largest island on earth, and in 1944, it was one of the most politically fractured. At the western end, it lay deep in Japanese territory, almost to the oil refineries of Balikpapan, while the eastern end was just as firmly in Allied hands, reaching to the doorway of the Solomon Islands. In between, the wild core of the island was a swirl of impenetrable jungle, with soaring mountains, yawning canyons, and verdant forests filled with so many native tribes that some eight hundred languages were spoken.

For months, MacArthur's troops on New Guinea had been fighting their way through the jungle, trying to drive the Japanese west, while Australian forces pressed up from the south. But the jungle did not allow for clean dividing lines. The same folds and pockets that kept native tribes isolated now became sprinkled with Japanese holdouts, some of them so deeply naturalized into the landscape that they lost all contact with the imperial command. A few would remain in hiding for decades, trading gunfire with anyone who approached.

On Los Negros, the Long Rangers had been tucked against the safest part of New Guinea; to reach Palau, they would have to move west to the front line.

The satellite islands of northern New Guinea appeared inconsequential on a map, with exotic names like Numfoor, Biak, Owi, and Wakde. But to the Army Air Forces' command, those islands were the great prize of the New Guinea campaign. They had been seized by MacArthur's forces over three months of fighting, and they offered American fliers some of the only protected airstrips in the region—a place to stop, regroup, refuel, and even repair their ships on long South Pacific missions.

One of the first US pilots to land on those islands was Charles

Lindbergh, whose visits to Wakde Island in particular marked a decisive moment in the war.

Lindbergh had first landed in the Pacific in late April, just as Sadae Inoue reached Palau and the Big Stoop boys finished in Tonopah. At forty-two, Lindbergh was still lean and sinewy with a cocksure smile, and he saw his trip to the Pacific as the culmination of a personal penance. Three years earlier, he'd resigned his officer's commission in the Air Corps to protest the European war, and he'd been trying ever since to regain his military standing—first by petitioning to have his rank as a colonel reinstated, and when that didn't work, traveling to US military bases to test and evaluate new craft. He had accepted an advisory position at Willow Run on the condition that his salary be $666.66 a month, the same amount he would have earned as a colonel in the war, and he'd even volunteered as a human test subject at the Mayo Clinic to examine the effects of altitude on the human brain.

For many Americans, this was still not enough to redeem Lindbergh's reputation. He was widely regarded as a racist, an anti-Semite, and a promoter of eugenics, whom even Franklin Roosevelt considered a "loyal friend of Hitler." Yet to the pilots he visited on US bases, his arrival brought a special kind of joy. War had a way of making ideology seem quaint in the face of survival, and here was the world's most famous pilot, quite possibly its best, ready to offer advice on the very aircraft to which they entrusted their lives each day. The chance to fly alongside Lindbergh, and learn from him, was irresistible. For Lindbergh, it was a way to prove his fealty to the American cause, and to taste the action.

As he traveled through bases in California and Hawaii, then Fiji and Guadalcanal, he began to join Marine and Navy fliers on combat missions. In May 1944, he flew to an active battlefield on the island of Bougainville, crawling on his hands and knees past Japanese bodies to join American troops at the front line. In early June, he joined Marine pilots from VMF-118 and VMF-222 on bombing missions to Kavieng and Rabaul. Then he continued west to visit the Army's 475th Fighter Group in

New Guinea, where he began flying missions on the P-38 Lightning, crossing the very satellite islands that would soon be home to the Long Rangers.

The P-38 was a twin-engine fighter, the first of its kind in the American fleet. Because it was still relatively new, its limits were untested. As Lindbergh racked up missions with the 475th, other pilots in the unit began to notice something unusual. No matter which plane Lindbergh flew, or where he went, he always came back with more fuel than anyone else. Like an experienced scuba diver, he had learned to preserve his tank, mostly by lowering RPM and thinning out the fuel mixture. This became especially clear on a mission from Wakde Island to Waigeo on July 3, when the rest of the formation ran so low on fuel that several of the pilots had to turn back—yet Lindbergh completed the mission and returned to base with 260 gallons to spare.

Two days later, Lindbergh was summoned to MacArthur's headquarters in Brisbane, Australia. The men already shared a history. Fifteen years earlier, at the height of Lindbergh's early fame, his mother, Evangeline, had been on a cruise ship returning from Turkey when a rumor spread in the American press that she was romantically involved with the captain. Evangeline denied the story, but it was titillating enough to cause a minor uproar in the US news, which then reverberated back to the boat. She spent the second half of the voyage hiding in the room of another passenger, Jean Faircloth, and when the ship finally docked in New York, it was Faircloth who strode through a throng of reporters on the dock to bring Lindbergh on board to fetch his mother. Six years later, Faircloth herself fell in love on a big ship. She and Douglas MacArthur had been together ever since.

Lindbergh found MacArthur at his office on the eighth floor of a massive stone building on the city's busiest intersection. MacArthur's staff had chosen the building because it was "the largest and most modern office" in Brisbane, but by coincidence the edifice happened to be inscribed with a fitting slogan for the US-Australian relationship: "Amicus

certus in re incerta," or, "A faithful friend in uncertain times." In anticipation of MacArthur's arrival, the second and third floors of the building
had been fitted with air raid blast walls. Sitting in MacArthur's office, the
two men laughed about their connection, but MacArthur's real purpose
was grave.

Some of his commanders were concerned that Lindbergh was flying
combat missions. It was illegal for a civilian to do so, and they wanted
MacArthur to ground the pilot before he got hurt. MacArthur was not
especially troubled that Lindbergh was flying, but he was intrigued by the
report that Lindbergh could make the planes so efficient. Was it true, he
asked Lindbergh, that he returned to base with hundreds of gallons to
spare? And if so, how far did he think a P-38 could fly?

Lindbergh made a few mental calculations. Officially, the P-38 had a
combat radius of 570 miles, but with the right approach, he guessed it
could travel about 20 percent longer. He told MacArthur that his best
guess was about 700 miles, or roughly the distance from Wakde Island to
Palau.

As Lindbergh spoke, MacArthur's face lit up. He pulled the pilot to a
map and began pointing excitedly at landmarks, explaining his plan to
drive northwest from New Guinea, past Palau, to the Philippines. If
Lindbergh could hit Palau directly from the New Guinea islands, it would
simplify everything. "MacArthur said it would be a gift from heaven,"
Lindbergh wrote in his journal that night. "He asked me if I were in a
position to go back up to New Guinea to instruct the squadrons in the
methods of fuel economy which would make such a radius possible. I told
him there was nothing I would rather do, and that I could go back at once.
He said I would have any plane, and do any kind of flying I wanted to, and
that an increased fighter radius would be of very great importance to his
plans."

As Lindbergh returned to the satellite islands, he began to train other
pilots in his method, and on August 1, he and three other P-38 pilots decided to test the plane's range. At 9:27 a.m., they set off for Palau.

Blazing across the water, Lindbergh watched his fuel gauge inch down. He checked with the other pilots by radio and confirmed that their tanks were holding up as well. Just north of the equator, they entered a storm front, barreling through the streaky gray lines and shooting up through a gap to daylight. A few minutes after noon, the islands came in sight—Angaur, then Peleliu, then Koror, and finally Babeldaob spread out before them.

As the P-38s looped across Babeldaob and began the journey south, Lindbergh spotted a Japanese seaplane racing up from the water. One of the P-38 pilots shot after it as Lindbergh watched. "It banks frantically left—straightens out—the P-38 is in position," he recorded in his journal. "A streak of tracers—a sheet of flame trails out behind the enemy—his plane becomes a comet of fire—rolls over—crashes into the sea—the surface of the ocean flames where it has disappeared. It has been only a matter of seconds."

Glancing in his mirror, Lindbergh saw another Japanese plane racing up behind him. This one was a fighter. Lindbergh swerved to the right and pushed his throttle to the firewall, but the fighter was closing in. "I am not high enough to dive," Lindbergh wrote. "I must depend on speed and armor plate and the other members of my flight. I nose down a little and keep on turning to avoid giving him a no-deflection shot. He must have his guns on me now—in perfect position on my tail. I hunch down in front of the armor plate and wait for the bullets to hit.

"I think of Anne—of the children. My body is braced and tense. There is an eternity of time. The world was never clearer. But there is no sputtering of an engine, no fragments flying off a wing, no shattering of glass on the instrument board in front of me. The Zero is climbing away."

Lindbergh watched in confusion as the fighter fled, then he spotted the other P-38s swooping after it, smothering the Japanese pilot in a stream of bullets. In seconds, the fighter was trailing down in flames.

That night, Lindbergh returned to the base shaken. He had made good on his promise to MacArthur and flown a new course for Palau, yet he'd nearly died in the attempt, and as word spread of his close call, the pressure on MacArthur grew. Within days, the general sent word: Lindbergh was to stop flying and return home.

Lindbergh decided to spend a final night on Wakde Island. Touching down on the airfield, he gazed out the window. The island had been captured from the Japanese three months earlier and the devastation was still overwhelming. "Wrecked planes lined the sides of the runway," he wrote in his journal, marveling at the contrast between what a pilot saw in the clouds and what he found below. "In the lonely beauty of the sky," he wrote, "one seems cleansed of the stench and bedlam of war, free of the suffering, the degradation, and the filth of surface armies."

Even as Lindbergh wrote those words, the advance echelon of the Long Rangers was just a few hundred yards away, scraping out a new campsite on the island's southern peninsula. In the days to come, the rest of the unit would arrive on Wakde to begin their daily flights to Palau along the route that Lindbergh pioneered.

FOR THE BIG STOOP BOYS, Wakde was a shock. If their camp on Los Negros had been one of the most comfortable in unit history, Wakde was among the worst. Most of the trees on the island had been incinerated in the US assault, leaving only cindered trunks that protruded from the sand like burnt matchsticks. Without trees, there was nowhere to take shade, but as the thirst and dehydration set in, there was also no reliable source of clean water. Like Lindbergh, they would be forced to confront on Wakde the true face of war, and the devastation their own planes usually wrought from above.

"Wakde resembles no island I've lived on or visited, and only some I've bombed," one man from the 372nd Squadron wrote on the first night. "The few palm trees still standing wear tattered crowns and shattered trunks; the disused Jap foxholes and slit-trenches gape menacingly on all sides; piles of smashed guns, vehicles, and other equipment—the detritus of war—have still to be bulldozed into the sea . . . meals are eaten from mess kits; drinking water, tepid and tasting of iodine, comes from hanging canvas Lister bags; showers are available only to those who wait in line for the one designated hour a day the precious sun-warmed fresh water is dispensed from a P-38 belly tank on a raised platform."

Even Tent City was a hastily constructed mess. The ground had been cleared in such a hurry that the grading was uneven, and after a storm, pools of water would linger for days, filling with mosquitoes and chiggers. Malaria and scrub typhus spread through the camp, and the flies were so abundant that they formed an instant crust on any scrap of food. In a squadron report at the end of the month, commander Jack Vanderpoel wrote, "Wakde had recently been taken, and the results of the battle were still evident when we moved in. . . . Bomb craters and fox holes pocked the area, ruined Jap equipment, planes, stores, and ammunition were strewn all over the island. The smell of rotting Jap dead pervaded the air."

The Long Rangers' camp also perched on the most dangerous part of the island. While their quarters on Los Negros pointed north toward six hundred miles of open ocean, on Wakde they stared across a narrow strip of water to the bloody hills of New Guinea, where nightly battles echoed with gunfire and the shouts of dying men. It took a few days for the danger of the new camp to sink in. During the first week on Wakde, one adventurous crew decided to slip across the channel for a peek at the front line. As veteran Sam Britt recalled in *The Long Rangers*, the men "donned their steel helmets and strapped on their .45s and hopped a landing barge for the mainland." When they spotted a US military vehicle careening down a dirt road, they flagged it down and asked for directions to a hillside where there had recently been fighting.

"They went to the hill as directed," Britt continued, "and found a considerable number of Japanese bodies scattered around where they had fallen the night before. There were pistols, helmets, map cases, binoculars—a really great untouched store of souvenirs. As they stood there, trying to decide what to pick up first, a whistle was heard coming from down on the road. There was a jeep pulled up just at the edge of the clearing at the foot of the hill. Behind the jeep was a GI, down on his hands and knees, frantically blowing his whistle and yelling for the men to get down the hill immediately, and that was an order. The hunters came down the hill in great spirits, while the GI jumped into the jeep and backed it into the canopy of trees covering the road. The group followed, and clustered around a very tough-looking and equally angry infantry first sergeant, who had in all probability, saved the lives of some, if not all, in the group. The sergeant let them know, in very salty language, that the Japanese had spent the night booby trapping the bodies up on the hill. They were there, and had not shot any of the hunters because they were waiting for them to pick up something and blow up."

While that crew hurried back to Wakde, Jimmie and Johnny were at the Big Stoop tent setting up their gear. The wooden floors they had enjoyed on Los Negros were too big to transport by plane, so most of their belongings sat directly on the ground. They dug a small moat around the tent to divert rainwater, but even so, the floor was always damp. As Jimmie kneeled to write a letter home, he tried to describe the scene for Myrle: "Johnny is making fun of the position I'm in, but it's the only place I can get where I can see. I'm on my knees on the ground, and have a tool box for a desk, with a candle on the end of my bunk. John started to write, but gave it up until tomorrow. But I had to write you a few lines just to say hello and to tell you I love you. And it helps me feel closer to you."

The living conditions on Wakde were crude, but the working conditions were worse. The runway was in such poor shape that it would have been funny if it weren't so terrifying. First constructed by the Japanese, it was intended for much smaller planes. An empty B-24 needed five thousand feet to take off. Fully loaded, it might need seven thousand. The Wakde airstrip was just that long, but it wasn't flat. Like an amusement park ride, it rose and fell as it crossed the island. A plane waiting for takeoff began at the bottom of a hill, climbed a steep incline for about one thousand feet, then descended into a low area known to fliers as "the hol-low," before ascending the final thousand feet in a desperate race to pick up speed before running out of room.

For a crew waiting its turn for takeoff, the view could be disconcert-ing. Through the cockpit window, a pilot and co-pilot watched the plane in front of them lurch up the hill, disappear into the hollow, and reappear on the other side, barreling toward the ocean. When it worked, the plane would lift off just in time for its wheels to skim the breakers. When it didn't work, things got wet. Veterans of the unit recall at least one plane that went in the drink.

Most of the aircrews on Wakde developed a method for the runway. Al Jose, a top-turret gunner in the same squadron as the Big Stoop crew, recalled his pilot's approach. "You had to stick the tail of the plane in the water at one end," he said, "and pour in all the power you could, and Christ it was an uphill climb. Then you'd go down into the hollow and come up the other side, and our pilot would put the yoke down, collapse the hydraulics and the landing gear, and then pull it up and collapse it again, hard—just bouncing the plane off the ground! It was an ass-pucker every time."

If you made it, you were on your way—streaking across the intermi-nable ocean to a fortress of caves, cannons, phosphorus bombs, and twenty-five thousand Japanese troops.

ELEVEN

SECRET POLICE

Sadae Inoue had come to Palau for a heroic defense of the Japanese perimeter, but by August 1944, his mission was looking more heroic than defensible.

A lot had changed in four months. The Japanese defeat on Saipan had shaken Prime Minister Tojo from power, removing the man who sent Inoue to the islands. With Tojo gone, the rest of the military was pulling back to defend the Philippines. That left the garrison at Palau more ex- posed than ever, and as the front line withdrew, so did their supplies. For the soldiers on Koror and Babeldaob, food and fuel were scarce. As the historian Mark Peattie described the situation in *Nan'yō*, "During the summer of 1944, the Japanese high command decided to pull back to the Philippines, making the Palaus expendable. This [decision] fatally imperiled the Fourteenth Division. On the one hand, the Tokyo high command concluded it could not spare more ships, planes, or troops to reinforce the Palaus, since these were now needed to defend the Philippines. On the other, it could not risk losing elements of the division trying to evacuate it by sea, even if shipping were available to transport it. After July 1944, the Palau Sector Group was essentially on its own."

As if all that weren't enough, now that the islands were isolated, the Allied assault was coming. With naval aviators buzzing the islands on photographic recon missions, it didn't take a close reading of Sun Tzu to imagine that an attack was imminent.

Already, the Palauan islanders were evacuating the city. There was little reason to stay. Though the colonial Japanese had been relatively benign in the 1920s, building roads and schools and transforming Koror into a modern city, the relationship between Palau and Japan had been degenerating ever since. Islanders would not soon forget the segregation policies of the 1930s, when their children were taught to reject island customs, mimic Japanese manners, worship photos of the emperor, and celebrate jingoistic holidays like the "Day for Appreciation of the Imperial Flavor." And as the war escalated, indignity gave way to oppression. "All residents of the Palau islands," the historian Wakako Higuchi wrote in *Remembering the Pacific War*, "including both Palauan and Japanese women and children in elementary schools, were made to work on the construction of military facilities."

Faced with such dismal prospects in town, many islanders returned quite literally to their roots. Building camps in the Babeldaob jungle, they learned to subsist on the tubers of the taro plant as their ancestors had. When the war dragged on and the taro ran low, they turned to wild nuts called *keyna*, and when the *keyna* ran out, they scraped by on the poisonous fruit *belloi*, soaking its bumpy brown flesh to remove toxins, then boiling it and choking it down. Life in the jungle camps was hot, wet, dangerous, and dispiriting, but at least it didn't require them to build barracks for the occupying army.

But the Palauan refuge on Babeldaob was not to last. As US planes began to canvass the islands in late July, an increasing number of Japanese soldiers began to settle on the big island. There had been a small detachment of the kempei-tai on Police Hill since the beginning of the year, but according to a journal kept by the commander of the kempei, Colonel Aritsune Miyazaki, the rest of the unit began to arrive on Babeldaob soon after. In fact, on the same day in July that George Bush sank his first enemy ship in the northern atoll, a flight of thirty-one additional American planes laid waste to the kempei facility on the island of Koror. The next day, while Roosevelt, Nimitz, and MacArthur were gathering in Hawaii, another strike demolished several of the Fourteenth Division's buildings downtown. Then, the following day, yet another bombardment left the division headquarters on Koror in shambles. "Bombers attacked. Barracks were burned. Forty soldiers and sixteen natives were killed," Miyazaki scrawled into his journal. Within days, both the kempei and division troops were relocating to Police Hill.

For Palauans, the sight of Japanese officers streaming onto Babeldaob was as ominous as it was unexpected. Peering through a curtain of foliage at the massive construction on Police Hill, they began to whisper that the Japanese had come for them. Soon there were a number of theories and rumors circulating through the Palauan camps, and today the wartime legends of Palau offer a vivid glimpse of the island experience.

One of the most widespread stories that summer involved a bunker that Japanese soldiers were building in the district of Ngatpang. The bunker, islanders believed, was too large to be an air raid shelter. Instead, they guessed that it was part of a secret plan to exterminate them. The Japanese, they whispered, were still angry with the Palauans for abandoning the city, and one day soon, they would come into the jungle to round everyone up. They would lock them all inside the new bunker and detonate a bomb. There was no evidence of such a plan, and none would emerge after the war, but in an atmosphere already rife with resentment, the story quickly gained the currency of fact. Six decades later, many Palauans still spoke of the "extermination plan" as though it were settled history.

At the same time, a countervailing legend formed in the jungle, this one with an American hero. His name was Captain Morikawa and he was ethnically Japanese, but was said to be a spy for the United States who had penetrated Inoue's command. By day, Palauans said, Morikawa walked through the jungle in all-white clothes. When he encountered the islanders, he would offer them food, water, and advice on how to tend their land. A skilled farmer, he helped many families improve their gardens. Then he would return to Inoue's headquarters at night to spread misinformation about the Palauans—tricking the Japanese commander into thinking the islanders were far away. Eventually, the Palauans wrote a song to honor Morikawa, with the lines "They were preparing an air raid shelter at Ngatpang, in an attempt to exterminate us all. Were it not for our rescue by Morikawa, Roosevelt's spy, we would have all perished."

Years later, the historian Wakako Higuchi investigated the Morikawa legend. She found a retired officer named Yoshiyasu Morikawa living in Japan, who had spent two years working for Inoue during the war. Trained as a surveyor, Morikawa confirmed that he often walked through the hills and jungle alone. His assignment, he explained, was to traverse Babeldaob in search of possible US landing sites, but Inoue had asked him to be especially friendly toward the Palauans he met. The Japanese, Morikawa insisted, were nearly as frightened of the islanders as the islanders were of them. "According to Morikawa, one great anxiety the Japanese military had during the war was the civilian unrest that prevailed throughout Babeldaob," Higuchi wrote. "In order to alleviate the food shortages [Morikawa] taught the Palauans how to enlarge their farms, and especially how to cultivate tapioca and sweet potatoes." It was a measure of how deeply Palauans mistrusted the Japanese that they interpreted Morikawa's kindness as proof that he wasn't really Japanese.

"The Pacific War was the turning point in relations between Japanese and Micronesians," Mark Peattie wrote. "It began with the generally passive and sometimes even willing acquiescence of the islanders toward

Japan and its war effort; it ended with the near total abandonment of the Japanese cause by these same people."

But if the war drove a wedge between Japan and Palau, it also brought up divisions within the Japanese army itself.

OFFICIALLY, THE KEMPEI were Japan's military police, but in practice they filled a role more like secret police—tracking down political enemies, real and imagined. Like the Nazi Gestapo, they were widely feared, functionally autonomous, and influential in ways that did not come through on an organizational chart. Often, the leader of a kempei unit answered only to a regional general, and only in an oblique way. In a place like Palau, that meant the kempei commander experienced little oversight from Sadae Inoue, who spent far more time worrying about the gun emplacements on Peleliu, Angaur, and Battery Hill than about the comings and goings of a few kempei men.

That suited Aritsune Miyazaki just fine. As leader of the South Seas Kempei-tai, Miyazaki was in some respects Inoue's opposite. Where Inoue was a battle-hardened general, with such a martial bearing that his own wife described him as "strict," Miyazaki was long-winded and excitable, given to regaling his subordinates with stories of his own valor. As his personal assistant, Keishiro Imaizumi, put it, "The unit commander liked to talk about himself, and when he grew tired of that, he would talk about old times—for example, stories about the time when he was in officer's school, stories about women, stories about the time when he was Kobe detachment commander . . ."

The kempei under Miyazaki were divided into sections, including the Intendance Section, for administrative affairs; the Special Higher Section, to dispense military discipline; and the Criminal Section, to manage the unit's prisoners. Among them, the Criminal Section was by far the most feared among Palauans. It had been the first kempei detachment on Police Hill, and it was the one that might arrest a Palauan and hold him indefinitely for a minor offense.

The commander of the Criminal Section was Kazuo Nakamura, who relished his independence from Miyazaki almost as much as Miyazaki sought distance from Inoue. Born on a farm just west of Hiroshima, Nakamura was skittish, careful, and mistrusting; he found Miyazaki's braggadocious manner offensive. As a child, Nakamura was routinely beaten by an alcoholic father, and he dropped out of school after third grade to work on the family farm. In his teens, he began to follow long days in the field with even longer nights on the town, and by the time he was twenty, he'd contracted a debilitating strain of syphilis, which left his legs permanently unstable, his ears ringing, his vision blurry, his reflexes slow, and his penile urethra glutted with ulcers. After that diagnosis, Nakamura met and married a young girl, Fujiko, who lived near his family—and soon she was ill, too. A year after the wedding, their first child was born with severe intellectual disabilities, and a year later, a second child arrived with gross nervous system malfunction. By the time Nakamura was drafted into the army at age twenty-seven, his assignment to the elite kempei-tai seemed like a rare stroke of luck. Yet he quickly discovered that, in Miyazaki, he would answer to a commander with little sympathy for his health, and whose violent tantrums mirrored his father's.

"If we opposed his intentions," Nakamura said of Miyazaki, "he would scold us and berate us angrily in a thunderous voice, or strike us, or chase us subordinates with his sword, shouting that he would kill us."

In his first months on Police Hill, Nakamura had enjoyed the distance from Miyazaki, but the dank tropical air of Babeldaob worsened his health. His migraines were constant and racking; he felt a strange burning sensation on the skin of his head; and the syphilis began to creep into a large vein by his heart, shunting the flow of oxygen to his brain. At the end of the war, doctors would diagnose him with "paresis of the insane."

Somehow, despite his condition, Nakamura managed to supervise a dozen men in the Criminal Section, many of them with health complications to rival his own. Yoshimori Nagatome was a sergeant from the southern tip of Japan, whose wife, aging parents, five siblings, and nine children all lived together on a three-acre farm, where half of them suffered from a debilitating autoimmune disease. Nagatome had been spared the illness, but contracted yellow fever within weeks of his arrival in Palau, and by summer he was grappling with a persistent case of bronchitis as well.

Sergeant Major Chihiro Kokubo was beset with a case of dengue fever that seemed to recur or flare up every few days, and he had been fighting dysentery since the day he landed on the islands. Kokubo had grown up in extreme isolation. Born to a large family, he'd been sent to live with childless relatives at the age of eight, taking their surname so that he and his parents could inherit their fortune. As part of the arrangement, Kokubo was rarely allowed to see his mother and father. "I always experienced loneliness when I saw my brothers and my own parents," he said later. Drafted at the age of twenty-one, he'd served two years on the home islands, then a year as a civilian, before being drafted back into the kempei and sent to Palau.

As crude as the conditions were on Police Hill, they continually grew worse. While the Long Rangers relocated from Los Negros to Wakde Island in late August, the kempei were in the middle of a move themselves, building a new hideaway in the jungle below Police Hill. In a dark patch of forest, they carved a network of caves and tunnels into the banks above a small stream, and by the time the Long Rangers began their missions to Palau, most of the kempei had taken up residence in the sodden jungle camp. Trudging through the mud between caves, it was easy to wonder how they had sunk so low—from the exalted status of secret police to the crude and primitive conditions of the natives they had come to occupy.

Throughout the spring and summer, the Criminal Section had been arresting dozens of new prisoners, including Palauans who stole bread or failed to avert their eyes, Indian Muslims working on the islands as indentured servants, and the Jesuit missionaries who were suspected of having sympathy for the United States. But as the conditions of the kempei camp devolved, the Criminal Section began making more arrests than ever—patrolling the islands to provoke confrontations and hauling in multiple prisoners each day. "There is no kempei-tai in the whole world," Miyazaki bragged, "that makes as many arrests as we do."

THE BRUTALITY OF Japanese prison camps in World War II is legendary. Like the Nazi machinery of death, it was so dehumanizing that it can be difficult to comprehend. Captured troops were routinely starved, bludgeoned, mutilated, decapitated, and used for bayoneting practice. A US prisoner in the Pacific was ten times as likely to be killed as his counterpart in Europe.

But what makes the Japanese prison camps of World War II even more shocking is the ruthless speed with which they arose. Just a few years earlier, the camps had been the opposite: a model of civility and respect for captured soldiers. In the years leading up to World War I, Japan was allied with Britain, and when the war broke out in 1914, Japanese leaders honored their alliance by seizing German territories throughout the Pacific Rim. The German soldiers stationed in those territories were rounded up and shipped to Japan, where they spent the next several years in large prison camps. Yet as the war crept by, the camps saw little of the abuse that would come to characterize Japanese prisons in the next world war. In fact, many of the camps were so comfortable and accommodating as to seem like small towns.

One of the most famous camps was the Bando facility, spread across fourteen acres on the small southern island of Shikoku. Bando provided spacious housing for its prisoners in a residential district, along with a commercial zone in which they were free to open businesses. Over time, a collection of about forty German shops rose up in the district, which the prisoners called Tapatau, and Japanese citizens would often visit the prison to shop for German wares.

As Charles Burdick and Ursula Moessner recounted in *The German Prisoners of War in Japan, 1914–1920*, "Tapatau had many specialists. Among the craftsmen were several carpenters, painters, mechanics, draftsmen, photographers, watchmakers, instrument makers, bookbinders, locksmiths, blacksmiths, printers, and more. For those individuals interested in their personal appearance, Tapatau provided a barber, a tailor, and a masseur. To please the palate after a long day's work, Tapatau's inhabitants could rush to the 'Sanitas,' a spa-like establishment, open day and night, with a restaurant that served wonderful coffee cake. The coffee cake was obtained from the Geba, Tapatau's bakery, known to everybody as 'delicious, delicious.'"

Some of the German prisoners at Bando also took jobs in town. Each morning, they would walk through the front gates of the prison to spend the day working for pay in Japanese shops. Afterward, they would return to the prison for dinner, which was typically made from the camp's abundant livestock, including some two thousand chickens, thirty pigs, and countless ducks that bobbled freely through the vegetable gardens and onto the game fields, where prisoners passed the evening playing soccer, hockey, and stickball, or else holding gymnastics competitions. There was a prison newspaper at Bando, an orchestra that performed more than one hundred concerts, and two theater companies.

Not all Japanese prison camps in World War I were as lenient as Bando, but many of them tried. In the towns of Asakusa and Hijemi, the camps offered prisoners a similar level of trust, with the option to take long walks outside the prison and to work in local stores. Even the more restrictive camps, like those at Osaka, Matsuyama, and Kurume, were benevolent by any normal standard. According to Burdick and Moessner, after the 1915 crowning of Japanese emperor Taisho, the commander of Kurume announced that "every prisoner should receive a gift of apples and beer to celebrate the joyous occasion." When a handful of German officers declined to celebrate the coronation of their captors' king, the prison commander briefly lost his temper and hit one of the men. The incident led to a formal investigation, and the Japanese commander was forced to apologize to the prisoner.

What caused such a dramatic change in Japanese prison camps over the next thirty years is a matter of some debate. It's a question that invites lazy generalization about the psychology of empire and "the Japanese mind." Certainly, by the onset of World War II, Japanese troops had been at war for an additional three decades, and the drastic expansion of the Japanese empire placed them farther from home than ever, while their training had become a grueling process that sometimes involved physical assault by senior men. These and other factors may have contributed to a shifting attitude toward prisoners, foreigners, and the native population of their territory islands.

However one accounts for the change, it was clearly evident before Pearl Harbor. The Japanese troops raiding the Chinese city of Nanking in 1937 were already committing atrocities that would have been unthinkable to the prison guards at Bando, Asakusa, and Kurume a few years earlier. In her treatise on the Nanking massacre, Iris Chang described the capture of one shoemaker's apprentice, Tang Shunsan, who was found in a trash bin and herded with hundreds of other prisoners toward an open pit. There, Chang wrote, "the Japanese ordered Tang and the other prisoners to line up in rows. . . . Then, to Tang's horror, a competition began among the soldiers—a competition to determine who could kill the fastest. As one soldier stood sentinel with a machine gun, ready to mow down anyone who tried to bolt, the eight other soldiers split up into pairs to form four separate teams. In each team, one soldier beheaded prisoners with a sword while the other picked up heads and tossed them aside in a pile."

As the war with China morphed into a war with the United States, Japanese soldiers turned their attention to Allied prisoners of war, marching some seventy-eight thousand soldiers, including twelve thousand Americans, up the Bataan Peninsula, while beating them, stabbing them, running over them with trucks, and denying them food or clean water. Another sixty thousand Allied troops were forced to construct a railway between Burma and Siam under hellish conditions, later immortalized in the novel *The Bridge Over the River Kwai*. A quarter of those men died.

In many cases, the abuse of Allied prisoners was either tacitly or explicitly condoned by Japanese leaders. Prime Minister Tojo himself had set the terms for prisoner abuse by announcing early in the war that "the present condition of affairs in this country does not permit anyone to lie idle, doing nothing, but eating freely. . . . In dealing with prisoners I hope you will see that they are usefully employed." Tojo was well aware that this was widely interpreted as a "no work, no food" injunction.

Not that American soldiers were immune to the savage impulse. War exacts a price from all men, and many of the American troops who slogged across bloody battlefields like Tarawa and Guadalcanal devolved to a level of grotesque barbarism—mutilating the fallen Japanese to collect scalps, stringing together their ears on necklaces, and digging into their yawning mouths to pry out gold teeth. Even Charles Lindbergh, who denounced the "Asiatic intruder" so vehemently that he called for "a Western wall of race and arms which can hold back either a Genghis Khan or the infiltration of inferior blood," had been horrified during his visit to the Pacific by the brutality of American troops.

"Their desire is to exterminate the Jap ruthlessly, even cruelly," Lindbergh wrote in his journal. "We hold his examples of atrocity screamingly to the heavens, while we cover up our own and condone them as just retribution for his acts. A Japanese soldier who cuts off an American soldier's head is an Oriental barbarian, 'lower than a rat.' An American soldier who slits a Japanese throat 'did it only because he knew the Japs had done it to his buddies.' I do not question that Oriental atrocities are often worse than ours. But, after all, we are constantly telling ourselves, and everyone else who will listen to us, that we are the upholders of all that is 'good' and 'right' and civilized. .... I would have more respect for the character of our people if we could give them a decent burial, instead of kicking in the teeth of their corpses."

For the Japanese kempei huddling in their jungle camp on Babeldaob—sick and wet and hungry and demoralized under the roar of US bombers overhead—the rage and frustration were rising to explosive heights. Unlike the soldiers of the Fourteenth Division, they had no anti-aircraft cannons to fire at the passing planes, no fighters to scramble, and no phosphorus bombs to unload. All they had was a miserable, muddy hideaway, and a prison full of hungry, desperate islanders. They were adding more prisoners to their collection every day, for infractions that were increasingly slight, but one prize loomed over the rest. One day, the kempei told themselves, one of those American planes would come down.

TWELVE

LAST DAYS

Wakde was a wasteland, but the boys made do. Under the tatter of gunfire, the blinding sun, the bursts of rain, and the stench of rotting corpses, they found small joys on the ruined island.

After a few days of settling in, Jimmie and Johnny set about exploring the wide beach just east of the Long Rangers' camp, splashing into the water to wash away the grime. In a report to Thirteenth Air Force headquarters that month, Jack Vanderpoel wrote, "Many discarded P-47 belly tanks were found on the island. Soon a small fleet of boats made from them began appearing off the coral reefs. Some were merely propelled by paddles, others had crude sails, a few had elaborate and expertly rigged sails, and one appeared with a small motor. These boats are very popular and many hours are spent cruising around nearby waters and swimming from them. . . . In spite of the crowded, uncomfortable living conditions, poor food, hot weather, and length of duty overseas of a large portion of the personnel, the morale remains good. Griping and grousing are prevalent, but efficiency and accomplishment are high."

On August 23, Vanderpoel led the unit's first mission to Palau. It would be a photographic survey to identify targets for the coming bombardment. Just after dawn, Vanderpoel climbed into the cockpit of a Liberator called the *Dina Might* with an eleven-man crew that included two photographers, and bounced down the Wakde runway.

The journey north crossed an endless expanse of open ocean. As Vanderpoel streaked forward, he stayed beneath a heavy blanket of cumuli, surveying the water. Following protocol, he pulled up as he drew close to the islands, topping out at twenty-three thousand feet—but when he looked down, he couldn't see the target he'd come to surveil. All he could see were the tops of clouds. Vanderpoel pushed down. Bursting through the bottom of the clouds, he saw the islands stretched out before him. Even in the muted light, they made a breathtaking sight, swaddled in soft green foliage against a wavering expanse of aquamarine, like some half-imagined mélange of tropical color.

The photographers on board were shuttering photos as Vanderpoel sped across Koror. He circled twice over downtown to give them a clear shot. There was a nest of government buildings on the western side of the islands, between a hospital and a long pier. The guns of Battery Hill were silent, but as he turned south to retrace his route, he saw the hillsides erupt. Shells punched into the air and a fighter plane tore down a runway. Vanderpoel watched it race toward him and soar overhead, dropping a pair of phosphorus bombs directly above. Vanderpoel yanked the control yoke to steer away from the white-hot fire, but the Zero was already coming back for another pass. It sprayed the air with bullets, then looped around for a third approach. Eventually, Vanderpoel knew, the fighter would connect. There was only one option, and it wasn't by the book.

He waited for the Zero to pass again, and leaned hard into a turn, banking until his nose was pointed directly at the fighter. He surged forward, chasing it down as fast as the Liberator could travel. The Zero was a lighter and more nimble plane—it swooped and swerved, but Vanderpoel dodged to keep it in front of him. Finally, the Zero raced away in a straight line, shrinking to a small dot on the horizon. Vanderpoel grinned. He turned the Liberator toward Wakde. It was a moment he would relish and retell for the rest of his life.

As Vanderpoel touched down that evening, Jimmie and Johnny were returning to their tent from another afternoon on the beach. As evening fell, rain arrived, and they huddled inside. Jimmie balanced a candle inside his helmet and wrote to Myrle, "Johnny and I went swimming, and we sure had a lot of fun. Have a nice good place, good sandy beach, and the water is really clean." A few feet away, Johnny wrote to Mary, "Sis, if you can send me some camera film, I'll take some pictures and send them to you."

In the morning, a massive cargo ship docked in the deepwater port just west of the Long Rangers' camp. The hulking Liberty Ships took their name from the Patrick Henry dictum "Give me liberty or give me death," but any US organization that raised $2 million in war bonds could name a ship of their own. There was an SS *Jefferson Davis* to honor the Confederate South, and an SS *Wendell Willkie* named for Roosevelt's opponent in the last election. Like the B-24, the ships were tall, boxy, and widely ridiculed. Roosevelt called them "dreadful looking," while *Time* magazine dubbed them "ugly ducklings." But to the Big Stoop boys, the SS *Stanley Matthews* pulling into Wakde that day was a thing of beauty. It carried most of the gear they had been forced to leave behind on Los Negros.

As the ship unloaded, the boys wandered up a dusty road to a makeshift stage. Bob Hope was scheduled to land at any moment for an afternoon performance. A month had passed since his arrival in the South Pacific, and he'd been performing as many as four shows a day, for which he would eventually receive the Congressional Gold Medal in a White House ceremony. According to Hope's biographer, William Robert Faith, after the ceremony Jack Kennedy remarked, "Bob, I was one of those lucky guys who sat in the rain on a Woendi island, watching you and your troupe perform."

Hope's flight landed on Wakde three hours late, and Jimmie and Johnny waited in a crowd of agitated airmen. In film footage taken from the stage that day, the men can be seen clambering for position as bombers rise from the adjoining airstrip. But when Hope appeared, all eyes turned to the stage, and for a few short moments, the war was forgotten. The men swayed to Frances Langford's crooning ballads, wilted at the sight of Patty Thomas prancing across the stage in a blue swimsuit, and laughed uproariously at Jerry Colonna twirling the ends of a muskrat mustache, while Hope himself cracked wise in baggy fatigues and a tilted safari hat, jabbing the air with the tip of a long cane. "I love this beautiful island," he called out, "with its magnificent palms—two of them with tops!" In his next column for American newspapers, he wrote, "We did a show on Wakde the other day. They had a stage set up right near the runway—so we could escape if we laid an egg, I guess. And the show was almost ruined by the planes taking off. Every time you read a straight line, you have to wait until the plane took off before delivering the punch line. It plays havoc with one's timing."

As the show drew down in late afternoon, Hope and his troupe bowed to thundering applause, then marched back toward the airfield to climb aboard a transit plane, lurching down the Wakde runway for the next stop on their tour.

The Long Rangers drifted back to camp. Their gear was unloaded. Their move was complete. Their short reprieve was over. In the morning they would begin their assault on Palau.

THE KEMPEI ON BABELDAOB hated the jungle. The dark hot air bloomed with humidity, the orange clay stuck to their skin, the shrieks of birds flooded the air with a cacophonous din, and each time the American planes came over the horizon, they were forced further into disgrace, racing across the muddy camp through narrow shafts of sunlight to dive headlong into the tunnels they had carved in the wet earth—sergeants and lieutenants and privates and even Colonel Miyazaki himself, all pressed together in the darkness, gasping for air and bracing against the concussive blasts of bombs.

Sometimes they scurried into the tunnels and the bombs never fell. Most of the Allied targets were farther south, and by the time the planes reached Babeldaob their bomb bay doors were open and empty. Then the kempei would crawl from their caves, humiliated and relieved. Other times, the Liberators would swoop down from the north in a surprise attack, raining down munitions that rattled the hills and the men.

After a raid on August 26, Miyazaki gazed over the splattered campsite at the bodies of two men. "23 B-24s attacked," he recorded in his journal. "Sergeant Ikushima and leading private Umasaka were killed." He made a note to send a letter of condolence to the senior man's wife, Tamiko, at their home near Toyama Bay. For Chihiro Kokubo, the loss was more personal. Rikiso Ikushima had been his only friend. Since leaving his parents at the age of eight, Kokubo had struggled to make personal connections. But in the space of only a few months, he and Ikushima had grown close. They traded stories, confided their fears, and even shared supplies. Just a few weeks earlier, Ikushima had given Kokubo a large white handkerchief that he'd stolen from one of the Jesuit missionaries in the prison.

As the rest of the kempei cleaned up from the August 26 attack, Kokubo wandered the parade grounds overcome with grief. He collected Ikushima's remains and burned them over a campfire. Then he scooped up the ashes and placed them in a small wooden box, which he wrapped inside the white handkerchief and began to carry with him, promising that, someday, he would avenge his friend.

Seven hundred miles south, the Liberators were landing. As the airmen stepped onto the tarmac, the Big Stoop boys were not among them. Under the new combat schedule, they had not been assigned to the mission. It was the second day in a row they had been forced to wait on Wakde while other airmen hit Palau. Waiting wasn't easy. No man looked forward to combat, but a wasted day was worse. Each evening the planes came back from Palau shredded by artillery, some of them so badly damaged that it was hard to believe they'd flown. One returned with no hydraulic system and two holes in the wing "as big as a hat," one man recalled. Others didn't return at all. In the fog of anti-aircraft fire, two of the Liberators collided. A third, from the Fifth Bombardment Group, simply disappeared. Every man who had been to Palau said the guns were the worst he'd ever seen. At times, they said, the shells were so thick that it seemed you could step outside and walk across the sky.

After a noisy dinner, the men wandered down to the southern tip of Wakde. A firefight was unfolding on New Guinea and they gazed across the water. Allied tanks were pummeling a Japanese position, and US gunboats had just arrived to pour in a second layer of fire. The horizon glowed yellow against a darkening sky and the Long Rangers cheered. "Watched tanks and boats shell the coast," one man wrote in his journal, adding, "Good show!"

Dawn broke clear on August 28 as the Big Stoop boys gathered at the airstrip for their first mission to Palau. They climbed aboard a shiny new Liberator and rattled down the runway into flight. Speeding north, each man settled into a familiar position. The target was new, but the journey was not. After weeks of flying the long route to Yap, the hours of waiting were automatic and reflexive. As the miles trailed by, they chatted, argued, laughed, and stared forward in silence.

Three hours in, they hit a storm. Lightning cracked and turbulence shook the boxy plane. In the cockpit, Norman Coorssen pulled back on the yoke, climbing into the clouds. He could see the rest of the squadron rising with him as he disappeared into the fog, and a cascade of rain and erratic wind rattled the B-24. Norman held fast. At 11,500 feet, the air began to clear. He leveled the plane and watched through the window as the squadron materialized around him. They were no longer in a tight formation, but at least they were still together. That was more than he could say for the other two squadrons. They were nowhere in sight.

The target was just minutes away, but the mission plan was shot. Their orders were to follow the other two squadrons over Koror, but there was no way to follow planes you couldn't see. As Norman steered across the southern islands of Angaur and Peleliu, the clouds below him cleared. This, he knew, was a mixed blessing. It would give the boys a clear view of the target, but it also gave the Japanese a clear view back. He crossed the islands of Eil Malk and Ngeruktabel and saw Koror ahead. The hills were quiet. They were the first to arrive. He drew closer and the foliage of the dark islands flashed with fire. The shells were coming in 250-round bursts, heavy but bearable. In the bombardier's compartment, Art Schumacher steadied his nerves and counted to bombs away. Three, two, one— he pounded the bomb release button and the payload sailed down. It was a perfect strike on the western end of Koror. Buildings burst into a swirling cloud of black smoke.

Suddenly, the VHF radio crackled. It was a pilot from another squadron. He was just a few miles back and calling his flight leader, William Dixon.

"How far below base are you going to bomb?" the pilot asked.

Norman listened for the reply. It was a risky question. The word "base" referred to a secret number, chosen essentially at random. The idea was to give pilots a way to discuss their altitude. If commanders set "base" at eight thousand feet, a pilot could say that he was flying at "base plus five" or "base minus three" without giving away too much. Still, you had to be careful. It was always better to say nothing, especially near the target. The sound of your voice alone was a clarion call to Japanese gunners.

Many pilots in the unit would have ignored the question, but Dixon was a new arrival. Though he was the most senior man on the mission, he'd spent most of the war in Panama, where the rules of radio discipline were not as strict. After a few seconds, the radio crackled. It was Dixon—not only answering the question, but ignoring the code. "Coming in at 11,500 feet," he called. Then he added that he was flying 157 miles per hour.

There was a moment of stunned silence before a third voice came on, flat and dry: "I hope the Japs didn't hear that."

They did. As the Dixon squadron crossed the southern bay of Koror, they flew into a battery of explosive shells. All six planes reeled in the onslaught, but Dixon took the worst. A large hole opened at the base of his right wing and his fuel tank ruptured, spraying fire into the air. He struggled to control the plane, but it was too late. The wing tore off. The plane corkscrewed down. A man's body shot into the air, plummeting down without a parachute. The fuselage streaked across Koror, smashing into the north shore, while the lone wing fluttered into shallow water beside a small island.

Back on Wakde, the Big Stoop boys retreated to their bunks. They had watched the crash up close and the sight was sickening. "Commanding officer of 372nd got anti-aircraft right up through bomb bay," one man wrote in his journal. "Went down in flames. Landed in target area. No one got out. Never had a chance. Terrible sight." Johnny opened up a letter from Katherine. She mentioned that an older man was flirting with her at work, and he flew briefly into a rage before Jimmie calmed him down. "That boy still doesn't realize how much responsibility he has now," Jimmie wrote to Myrle. "But that is something they will have to work out for themselves."

A LOW MALAISE WAS SETTLING over the camp. As the last days of August crept by, the men began to realize that Palau was unlike any target they had seen. In their first five missions, they lost more than forty men, and privately each man had to confront the shrinking of his own odds—the likelihood that, on missions to come, he would lose good friends, at least.

Increasingly, commanders worried about morale. "This war is beginning to get rough," the adjutant wrote in his action summary. "It will take a hell of a lot more than Bob Hope to improve their poor morale. It has become a critical situation. . . . The men are true Americans and will see the deal through, but there is no question that they are pretty bitter about the whole situation."

For the Big Stoop boys, the final night of August passed slowly. They were scheduled for an early-morning flight to Palau, their first mission since the Dixon crash, but as they shuffled into their tent to lay out gear and write letters home, none could mention their previous mission or the one to come. If they knew they were going to fly with a new pilot, they kept it from their letters as well. As ever, they avoided the subject of the war, giving their last letters home an eerie cheer.

"Dear Folks," Earl Yoh wrote. "How is everyone at home? I am feeling fine. I suppose the boys have started to school and have a grudge against their teachers. How is Dad? Is he still working? How is Grand Pa and Grand Ma? Tell them I said hello. You can also tell George and Anne I said hello. Mom, I increased my allotment yesterday to $75. I don't know if it will come out of September pay or not. Is that other coming through alright? Well, I guess I had better say Good Night for now. Love, Your Son, Earl." At the bottom, he added, "God Bless You."

Jimmie, meanwhile, was deep into a love letter to Myrle. If his writing was occasionally florid, it was nevertheless remarkable from a man with a grade-school education. "Sweet," he wrote, in what would become the last letter in Myrle's collection, "my mind is nearly a blank tonight, for I am all took up with thoughts of you and home. Maybe it won't be too long until the day when I will be home, and we will be together again. With your arms around me, I can forget all this, and settle down to spending years with you. Gee, what a glimpse of you would be worth! I'll have lots of time for just feasting my eyes on you. How I miss you! Sweet Darling, tomorrow is a busy day, and I have to get up early. So I'll stop for tonight, and tomorrow I'll do better. But you know I love you with all my heart, and will for always. Tell the folks hello, and write as often as you can. Good night, Sweetheart. With all my love, Jimmie."

THEY GATHERED AT THE AIRSTRIP before dawn. It was a morning like any other. In film shot by a unit cameraman that day, the sun over Wakde airfield gleams against the silver B-24s while ground crews bustle through familiar routines on the coral runway. A little after 6 a.m., the crowd of airmen began to climb aboard the fleet, each man moving into his position with the burnished confidence of a veteran flier.

Since their arrival three months earlier, the Big Stoop boys had flown nearly a dozen ships, including the *Babes in Arms*, the *Dina Might*, and several with no name, but that morning they were scheduled to fly airplane number 453, the same plane that Norman Coorssen had flown without them on his observation flight to Yap. Now it would be their turn to fly the same plane without him.

The reason for Coorssen's absence that day may never be entirely clear. He was the only man from the Big Stoop crew who wasn't present. A few others were relatively new additions, like flight engineer Robert Stinson, who joined the crew in July, and co-pilot William Simpson, who was the third man to fill that role. Photographers also came and went, depending on the mission. Since their arrival on the islands, the Big Stoop boys had flown with five different combat cameramen on a total of nine missions. Their favorite photographer was Mario Campora, a bulky young man from western Massachusetts with a tangle of brown hair and the delicate features of a child. Campora had only flown with the Big Stoop boys three times, but he fit in so well that they'd invited him to join the crew photo in July. He was scheduled to fly with them again that morning, but he woke up with a throbbing cold and resigned himself to a day of rest. Instead, they got photographer Alexander Vick, another familiar face.

Vick had been with them on their last mission. In fact, every man on the plane had been on the prior flight—except Jack Arnett.

No Army document can explain why Arnett took the helm that morning, and no living veteran of the Long Rangers knows. At least two possibilities remain. If the unit historian Jim Kendall was right, then the Big Stoop boys were not scheduled to fly at all, and they were rushed onto Arnett's plane only after his crew refused to board. But in letters written the night before, the men seemed to know they were scheduled for the mission. Jimmie Doyle referred to a busy day ahead and the need to wake up early—the same language he always used on the night before combat. The other possibility is that the Big Stoop crew was scheduled to fly all along—and it was Coorssen who failed to board the plane, and Arnett who was the replacement.

This much is certain: by September 1, 1944, Jack Arnett had been ejected by at least one crew. Six weeks earlier, the men who trained with him in Tonopah had thrown him off their plane. Only two members of that crew, and the wife of a third, survive. But all three recall the incident in detail. Arnett, they say, was an exceptional pilot, but he could be abrasive and imperious. Where officers like the Big Stoop navigator Frank Arhar followed the advice to "laugh with your men," Arnett was known to bark orders and demand extreme obedience. "He was bossy, and whenever he spoke something, he expected you to do just that," said Jack Pierce, the top-turret gunner who trained with Arnett in Tonopah. "Well, the boys didn't want to do exactly what he said—and they let him know it."

According to Martha Raysor, whose husband, Jim, was on the same crew, the tension between Arnett and the men was apparent even before they left the United States. "He thought he was better than the rest of them," Raysor said. "One time, they were all traveling in California, and gas was at a premium, and Jim says, 'Well, if you want to go by my folks', my dad can probably give you some gas because he works for the oil company.' So they drove there, and the rest of them went in and had something to eat. But Arnett wouldn't get out of the car. He was an officer and my husband was not, and he wouldn't lower himself."

As Pierce recalled it, the tension only grew in combat. Among other problems, Arnett began to drink. "A lot of us were drinkers," he said, "but not on the aircraft. He would go into the airplane with a bottle in his hand. My position on takeoff was to stand between him and the co-pilot, so I got to observe what went on. Many times I saw him with a bottle at the steering apparatus."

By the second week of July, the crew had seen enough. The officers confronted Arnett about his domineering manner, but the conversation did not go well. Arnett threatened to have them punished for insubordination. In desperation, they turned to the enlisted men for support. "The word got to us through the other commanding officers," Jack Pierce said. "He was planning to let them go and keep the enlisted men. Well, they objected to it, and we stuck with them."

Faced with a disintegrating crew, squadron commander Jack Vanderpoel came up with a tidy solution. Another pilot, Charles McRae, had been sidelined for weeks with an ear infection, and was coming back into rotation. Vanderpoel assigned McRae to take over the Arnett crew, and he gave Arnett the crew that had flown with McRae in training.

As Arnett began flying with his new crew, there was no sign of conflict. On the contrary, his record remained stellar. Twice, on missions from Los Negros to Yap, he was forced to turn back when an engine failed, but each time, he managed to bring home his plane and crew safely. By September 1, he had been flying with his second crew for seven weeks—the same amount of time he had spent in combat with his first. Perhaps the second crew had also seen enough of Arnett. Perhaps, in the final days of August, they, too, refused to fly with him. Or perhaps Jim Kendall was mistaken about which Arnett crew "voted him out." There are no surviving members of the second crew to ask.

Nor did Arnett's family have any inkling of his troubles. Like so many other families, all they would know in the years to come was the threadbare agony of a lost child. At their home in Charleston, West Virginia, his parents hung a portrait of Jack above the fireplace, staring at the amber-eyed kid who got in trouble for questioning his teachers—the kid whom even a close cousin, Carolyn, remembered as "private" and "aloof." His brothers, Marvin and Warren, would always remember Jack as their mama's pet, the one who could get away with shooting blossoms off the flowers in the garden, while their mother, Dessie, would always cling to Jack's last letter home, in which he promised that the war had not hardened his heart. "They have not made me hate anyone," he wrote, and she pasted the words into a scrapbook of photos bound in a thick blue cover with the title "A Book without an Ending."

SITTING IN THE COCKPIT of the 453, Arnett watched the first planes in the formation lift off. Anywhere else and it would have been a comical sight. One by one, they rolled to the head of the runway with the languid majesty of a great beast, turning to gaze down the long, white airstrip that stretched across the island, but the moment the pilot leaned on the throttle, the illusion of grace vanished—the plane lurching forward, bobbling and clattering wildly on the uneven surface, disappearing into the hollow, and then charging up the other side toward the water. In Tonopah, the Army had spent a small fortune paving runways for B-24 training, but on Wakde, it was clear that they might as well have trained on the desert floor.

When Arnett's turn came, he guided the 453 through the same gauntlet, gripping the controls and bracing himself in the cockpit as the plane hurtled forward, until at last the pandemonium gave way to the easy vibration of flight. Wakde Island shrank below until it was just a speck fading behind them.

The mission plan called for the usual eighteen-plane formation, with six from the 372nd Squadron in the lead; then six from the 424th, including Arnett's; and finally, six ships from the 371st bringing up the rear.

Together, they would fly northwest to another satellite island, Niroemoar, then they would angle north for the journey to Palau. As they closed in on the archipelago, three planes from the lead squadron would split off, circling north over Babeldaob on a reconnaissance mission, while the remaining fifteen planes would converge into a box formation for the strike. Their target was a string of buildings at the center of Koror—government facilities, a power plant, a sawmill, and a school.

No battle plan survives contact with the enemy, but the plan that day didn't come close. Within twenty minutes of takeoff, one plane in the Big Stoop squadron began losing oil and had to turn back. Then, half-way to Palau, the formation ran into a squall, and as they tried to steer around it, the Big Stoop squadron went one way while the remaining two squadrons went the other. By the time they all emerged on the far side of the storm, the Big Stoop was far behind.

As a tactical matter, this could hardly have been worse. The original plan called for the Big Stoop to cross near the middle of the formation. Now they were so far behind, they weren't in the formation at all. They would reach the islands several minutes late, with every gunner on Koror waiting.

Watching the islands grow on the horizon felt like staring at an on-coming train. Plumes of smoke trailed up from the bomb blasts left by the first two squadrons, and the sky glittered with shrapnel streaming down. The squadron pulled close together. They had learned from expe-rience to make themselves into a small target. "When we first got there," a gunner on the mission, Al Jose, recalled, "we'd tell the guys who came in close to us, 'Get away! Get away!' But after a while, we realized that we wanted it tight, and we were shouting, 'Come on in!'"

From his position in the top turret, Jose stared into the waist window of the 453, where Johnny Moore leaned on a .50 caliber gun, searching the sky for something to shoot. "I was right on top of him," Jose said. "They were to my left, flying forward, and I could look right down in the plane. I saw the whole thing."

As the five-plane squadron pulled over Palau, the sky went dark. Jose would later write in his journal that the shells came in "400-round bursts—heavy, intense, accurate." Explosive shells ripped through the wings, floor, and cockpit of the five planes. "There was just a ton of it coming up at us," Jose said. "There was nothing you could do."

As Jose watched, the first blast struck the 453. It tore into an engine on the left wing and there was a flash of light as shards of metal flew into Jose's plane. "That one just blew the hell out of stuff," he said.

As the left wing of the 453 burst into flames, Art Schumacher reacted—pressing the bomb-release lever to jettison the munitions and reduce weight. In the cockpit, Arnett fought for control, feathering an engine on the right to compensate for damage to the left, and making a long, wide arc to the east.

"He was slipping right to keep the fire away from the fuselage," Jose said. For a moment, it seemed to work, and the 453 eased over Toachel Mid as if it were coming in for a landing on southern Babeldaob. Then the left wing folded back. Then it snapped off.

Al Jose felt a weight in his gut. *Now it's over*, he thought, watching the wing float down as the plane torqued out of balance and tumbled toward the water. A parachute popped out. Then another. Then the fuselage snapped in half, and there were two great splashes below. Al Jose gritted his teeth. The squadron stayed close. They passed through the worst of the anti-aircraft fire and made a wide loop. When they returned to the crash site, they descended to four thousand feet. The anti-aircraft artillery in the hills blasted fire in their direction. Some of Jose's crewmen were already injured. One was bleeding from the gut. Another plane in the squadron was riddled with more than one hundred holes, and had lost its hydraulic system, navigator's telescope, intercom, and left gas tank, while in the back, the waist gunner had flak from two seventy-five-millimeter projectiles lodged in his stomach. Still, the squadron stayed low over the wreckage. They circled for ninety minutes, looking for survivors.

"It was crazy," Jose acknowledged. "They don't even make movies like that."

But the only thing they would see was a lone Japanese patrol boat speeding away from the wreckage toward the shore. There was no way to know for sure whether a captured airman was on board.

Back on Wakde that night, one man wrote in his journal, "Went to Palau today. One of the planes was hit and broke into flames. Two men jump out and Jap speed boat pick them up. Hope they get along okay. Palau is hell."

THIRTEEN

BREAKTHROUGH

BentProp was growing. After ten years on the islands, both the team and the mission were changing. Scannon had begun the search with a list of three B-24s. Now he knew of at least four others, plus a medley of smaller planes. He no longer traveled with the Lamberts and Bailey, but came with the skydivers each year—and each year, they drifted farther from the Arnett channel.

On their first day, they would stop at the Palau Historic Preservation Office, a low concrete building on Koror, where the national archaeologist, Rita Olsudong, would issue them a permit to search for wartime wrecks. Scannon had first reached out to Olsudong at Bill Belcher's request. Having the permit gave BentProp the sheen of legitimacy, and once his papers were in order each year, Olsudong would pass along the coordinates of any newly discovered wrecks. With her endorsement, he was also welcome at the highest levels of Palauan politics. From time to time, the president of Palau, Tommy Remengesau, would summon Scannon to the capitol for a personal update on the search.

At the same time, Scannon's relationship with the military lab was deepening. Each year he delivered a typed report on his latest mission, including maps and photos and archival documents to explain what he'd found. With two wars brewing, in Afghanistan and Iraq, the reports sometimes traveled far beyond the lab. For a man heading to Mazar-e Sharif or Kunduz, to Basra or Fallujah, the knowledge that someone, somewhere, would never let him disappear made the daily face of combat a whisper less grim. In 2002, the commandant of the US Marine Corps, Jim Jones, wrote Scannon a personal note:

"I want to express my sincere gratitude to the BentProp Project for your altruistic quest to locate the servicemen who fought in World War II and have been declared missing in action in the jungles and waters surrounding the Republic of Palau. For more than half a century, the fates of hundreds of these men have remained concealed beneath sand and silt, encrusted in coral, or shrouded by leaves and vines while loved ones have lived with the pain of not knowing. Through your tireless efforts, the families and friends of many of these brave airmen have finally achieved closure."

By the fall of 2003, Belcher and the recovery lab were planning a large-scale return to the islands. They would arrive on a C-17 filled with equipment for a monthlong dig of three sites that Scannon had found. First they would excavate the mass grave site on Police Hill, then they'd move to the wreckage of a Corsair in a harbor near Koror, and finally, to the ruins of an Avenger scattered over a hilltop on Peleliu.

For Scannon, the prospect that the lab might finally bring home the lost men of Palau was a source of exhilaration and deep regret. After hundreds of hours on Toachel Mid, he had all but given up on the Arnett plane, and the decision to focus on smaller craft seemed a necessary step. But the B-24 would always hold a special place for Scannon. No other plane came close to the time and energy he had spent looking for the Arnett Liberator, and no other airmen haunted his imagination like the Arnett crew. The sight of Tommy Doyle's powerful frame shaking at the Long Ranger reunion as he described the painful rumor that his father had abandoned him would forever be a reminder to Scannon of why he came back to the islands. Now that he had the full support of the US military and the island government, his failure to locate Arnett seemed all the more glaring.

There was a photo of Jimmie Doyle and the crew taken two months before the crash. They were lined up before the *Babes in Arms* on Los Negros airfield. Many of the men in that picture were still a mystery to Scannon. He had never been contacted by the families of Yoh, Price, Stinson, Moore, or Coorssen, and he had promised the military that he wouldn't contact them. Thirty years of MIA recovery had made the lab cautious. Johnie Webb and the staff knew how explosive a situation could become if a family's hopes were raised and nothing was found. The lab never revealed details of an investigation until it was complete. For Scannon, it was a frustrating way to work. He would have liked to keep families informed, and to hear back from them. There were times when he found himself staring at the picture of Jimmie and his crew, searching each man's face for some clue to who he was. There was Johnny Moore, like a young Elvis with a single lock of dark hair dangling over his eyes. There was Ted Goulding, his face grave, with an odd satchel attached to his hip. There was Earl Yoh, his skin as soft and pure as a young girl's, his belt buckle as shiny as the day he got it. Scannon wanted to call their families and learn more about those men. He would have liked to draw on their hope to keep his own alive. Instead, he felt himself turning away from the photo, and losing faith that he would find the men.

At the same time, another BentProp member was beginning to fixate on a different kind of photo. Flip Colmer was a former Navy fighter pilot and an avid skydiver. He'd first met Scannon through the SkyDance school in 2001, and joined the missions to Palau every year since. Colmer was an inexhaustible presence on the islands. Whether standing in mud up to his hips or snorkeling through a pounding rain, he seemed happiest when the conditions around him were worst, and he was content to subsist for weeks at a time on a diet of Spam and Oreo cookies.

Colmer's experience as a fighter pilot got him thinking about mission photos. During his years in the Navy, it was common to send a second plane after a bomb run to shoot pictures of the damage. Those photos were known as bomb damage assessments, or BDAs, and they were often taken a day or two later. In fact, they were sometimes taken by another unit, and would not appear in the original mission report. To find them, a researcher would have to guess that they existed, and then sort through a second set of records. "The bulb went off," Colmer recalled. "Even if there weren't photos in the mission report, there could be photos in the BDAs."

With just four months left before the 2004 mission, Colmer called the National Archives in College Park, Maryland. He couldn't be sure that World War II pilots had done bomb damage assessments, or that they would have been called by that name, but he tried to explain to a researcher what he meant. "Do you have anything like that?" he asked.

"Sure," the archivist said. "Come on down." There was a warehouse full of aerial photographs in Valley Forge, Pennsylvania. If Colmer put in a request for them at the front deck, the archival staff would retrieve as many canisters as he wanted to see. Colmer called Scannon right away with the news. By the time they hung up, they were ready to book the flight to Maryland.

Scannon had been to the archive in College Park many times, but he wasn't surprised to learn that he'd missed something important. It was the largest archival building in the world, with two million cubic feet of records, and it was still relatively new. The facility had been completed in 1993, and many of the World War II documents in places like Maxwell Air Force Base were still being transferred in. Along the way, there were inevitable glitches in the system. For an obscure place like Palau, you might find records filed under "Peleliu," "Micronesia," "Western Caro-lines," or even "Philippines."

The lobby of the archive was a soaring modernist space filled with light, and Scannon hurried toward the elevators for the photography floor. Colmer had flown in to join him, along with a man named Reid Joyce, who had first joined Scannon on the Arnett channel in 2000. A small, gentle figure with glasses, Joyce had recently retired as a psycholo-gist after working with the military's human-engineering labs, and he brought to BentProp an organizational sensibility that surpassed even Scannon's. He was building an online database to digitize the team's re-search files.

As the three men gathered in the archives, they sifted through a byz-antine catalog of photos, ordering every canister that seemed to have a marginal relationship to Palau. By the end of the day, they had filled out dozens of orders for overnight delivery. They spent the night in a nearby hotel, and returned early in the morning to wait anxiously as the staff wheeled out a cart stacked with tall, black canisters marked with details like "Intelligence, Photographic Division."

Scannon, Colmer, and Joyce slipped on cotton gloves. They each re-moved a canister and cracked open the lid. The stench of developing chemicals flooded into the room, and it dawned on Scannon that the film had not been viewed since the end of the war. He carefully removed a translucent sheet and rested it on a light box. It was a massive twelve-by-twelve negative with the shapes of islands and coral heads clearly visible against the water. In the foreground, there was a huge white silhouette of a bomb falling toward the ground. Scannon worked his way through the images in the canister, then a second canister, then a third, when suddenly Colmer called out, "Here's the reel from September first!"

Scannon and Joyce spun around. They stared for a moment in silence. They had come to find bomb damage assessments taken after the mis-sion, but these were photos taken the same day. All three men gathered around Colmer's light box to examine the film.

There were only ten negatives in the series, all taken from plane number 101. It was the plane that had suffered the most damage that day, and it was a miracle to think that the photographer on board, with shells ricocheting through his plane and slicing into the stomach of a waist gunner just a few feet away, had the presence of mind to stand by the window taking photos of the mayhem below. There were no obvious signs of the Arnett plane in the pictures. They showed the southwestern coast of Babeldaob, a few coral heads offshore, and a pair of tiny white dots near the waterline.

"What do you think these are?" Scannon asked, pointing at the dots.

Colmer and Joyce shook their heads. There weren't any buildings in the photo, so it wasn't a bomb damage assessment. But the specks were too small to be the plane.

Then the realization hit Scannon. It *was* the plane. In the frantic moments over Koror, the cameraman must have taken a few extra seconds to get the shot. By the time he began shuttering images, Arnett was nearly down. Those tiny white dots were the wing and the fuselage, but they were thousands of feet below.

Scannon looked at the last two photos in the series. The spots were in different places, moving in a line across Babeldaob toward water. In fact, they were heading toward the place where he and Susan had seen the propeller on their first day of diving, ten years earlier, right after they left the Dixon wing. Scannon had been back to that propeller countless times. It was old and weathered, and he'd never been able to measure the blades precisely. Without the measurements, he couldn't be sure what kind of plane it came from, but he'd always wondered if it was a B-24.

Suddenly Scannon remembered a Graves Registration Service report written in 1947. It described a B-24 crash in the same area. He had dismissed that possibility years earlier, when he learned that the airplane listed in that report had been found somewhere else. Now he realized that the GRS was right: there was a B-24 in that area, just not the one they thought. It was the 453.

The memories kept coming. He thought of an interview two years earlier with a Palauan elder named Ricky Speis, who said he'd seen a bomber go down in the same position. At the time, Scannon had gone directly to the site and spent a few days diving. But when he found nothing, he returned to the channel.

Staring at the new photos, Scannon's heart leaped and sank. Two things were clear. After ten years of searching for Arnett, he had just come across the most promising clue yet. And for ten years, he had been searching in the wrong place.

THE JOURNEY TO PALAU was always tinged with magic for Scannon. As the trip drew closer, he began to dream of the warm tropical air, the fusty familiar aroma of the jungle, and he would find himself closing his eyes to imagine the moment he would step down from the plane onto the islands. But the 2004 mission would be unlike any other. For one thing, Scannon knew he was closer to Arnett than ever before. For another, he knew that BentProp wouldn't be the only team searching the islands. The military lab was scheduled to begin a full-scale excavation of Police Hill that year: even as Scannon dove for Arnett, Belcher would be two miles away, digging for evidence of the mass grave.

For weeks, Scannon spent his nights preparing. He packed and repacked his bags, ordered and reordered equipment, and by the time he boarded a flight from San Francisco International, with an apple pie from Susan tucked into his carry-on bag, his check-in luggage was stuffed with 120 pounds of photographic equipment, computer drives, and an endless array of scuba gear, and he'd mailed himself two large boxes with a printer, history books, research files, an old machete, and videotapes of earlier missions.

Settling into his seat on the flight, Scannon tried to calm his mind. He ordered his usual tomato juice without ice and dropped a CD by the Hawaiian band HAPA into his portable player. Then he opened his yellow waterproof notepad and, for the first time in years, let his thoughts and hopes pour out.

"1100—Now on Pacific," he began. "I cannot but think of men shipping out 60 years ago, with uncertainty, in the same direction. Many had time to think about it, zig-zagging their way from San Francisco or San Diego. Others flew their bombers and had less time to think, a lot less. Now I am peacefully making my way in a much less circuitous direction to Palau—where a few men found and never left. Do they know we are coming or that we are there? Are their spirits waiting to be remembered, or at least not forgotten? Or do their spirits live through their families, embedded in the DNA they left behind? To whom does this matter? In the end, it matters to me, and it matters to a few folks—incredible folks crazy in their own right—who sacrifice their time/money to get beat up in the jungles, in the waters, on the coral, by the sun—to freeze in the rain."

At Honolulu International Airport, he met up with Reid Joyce, who had been traveling since 3 a.m. After a quick hello, they found their seats and settled in for the seven-hour flight to Guam, each man retreating to his thoughts. They were briefly interrupted when a passenger two rows up had a seizure and Scannon helped stabilize and monitor him. Then he was back in his seat, the cabin lights dimmed, gazing through the window to the eternity of night.

The airport on Babeldaob was a single runway that stretched toward the water in darkness, but inside the terminal, Scannon and Joyce found three Palauan friends waiting. Joe Maldangesang (*mal-dang'-uh-sang*) was a scuba guide at the local dive company Neco Marine. He'd first met Scannon in 1996, on the mission with Chip and Pam Lambert and Scannon's daughter, Nell. With a limited English vocabulary, Maldangesang had spent the week wondering what kind of crackpot Scannon was. "I'm thinking, 'Maybe this guy is crazy,'" Maldangesang recalled. "Why does he want to dive here? It's so ugly!"

But Scannon had taken an instant liking to Maldangesang. Unlike some of his earlier guides, Maldangesang was never in a rush, and he projected a quiet joy on the water, throwing in a line to yank out fish or chomping on betel nut until his grin was brilliant orange. Scannon had hired him as a boat driver each year since.

Like many islanders, Maldangesang had a deep affection for the American fliers of World War II. The relationship between Palau and Japan had grown strong since the war, but many Palauans still regarded the US victory in the Pacific as their moment of liberation. As Maldangesang returned to the waterways with Scannon each year, he witnessed the discovery of Corsairs and Avengers, and soon he began to join the search himself—taking a position in the underwater grid, humping through the jungle, and interviewing tribal elders about their wartime memories. His wife, Esther, was a princess in Palau's matrilineal society, which only added to the value of his support. Some of the islanders who had once scratched their heads at Scannon, wondering if he was just another treasure hunter looking for Yamashita's gold, began to pass him information through Maldangesang. By 2004, Maldangesang had become central to Scannon's project. Scannon presented him with a BentProp coin, and named him in reports to the lab as a team member.

Now Maldangesang was at the airport with Esther and a Palauan friend. They exchanged hugs and handshakes and Esther draped a floral lei over Scannon's head. Then they piled into a car out front and sped toward Koror. Along the way, Scannon and Joyce explained about the photos.

As Scannon awoke the next morning, he resisted the urge to rush to the water. There was equipment to unpack, gear to set up, and paperwork to submit at the Historic Preservation Office. He also wanted to review his plans with Maldangesang, view the new search area from a small plane, and track down Ricky Speis, the Palauan elder who had first pointed to the site two years earlier. In between, he and Joyce would pick up the other team members at the airport, including Jennifer Powers, who was filming a documentary about BentProp with SkyDance founder Dan O'Brien and a videographer they had asked to join them on the islands, Pete Galli.

Over the next three days, while the rest of the team coordinated permits and equipment, Galli showed Scannon a trick with the program Photoshop. He imported the new archival photos and superimposed them over a current map of Palau, stretching and angling the images to see where the white specks fell on the modern landscape. With a line-drawing tool, he could extend the trajectory of the dots to predict exactly where they were heading. Scannon had never seen Photoshop before, and he was amazed at the possibilities. On the fourth day, he and Galli went to the airport to lease a private plane. The pilot who had once flown Scannon over the channel, Spike Nasmyth, was no longer on the islands. But a pilot named Matt Harris agreed to remove the back door of his twin-engine Islander plane so that Galli could lean out and shoot photos of the water. Then Galli and Scannon retreated to the hotel, huddling over Galli's laptop to add the new images to the Photoshop overlay.

On the fifth day, Scannon brought the team to meet Ricky Speis. He was a short, squat man with a light dust of gray hair and deep copper skin. At his home on southern Babeldaob, he welcomed the group to sit on his front porch below a sign that said "God Bless Our Home." With a peach-colored polo shirt and loose khaki shorts, Speis was hardly the conventional image of a tribal elder, but his memory stretched across sixty years to the day in 1944 when, as a seventeen-year-old student on his way to visit his parents, he saw the 453 cross the sky.

"I was on the hill at Aimeliik," he said, gesturing west with a weary frown. "I was on my way home but it became hard from the Japanese shooting up and the planes bombing Koror. Koror was smoking, and then all of a sudden, I saw the plane being hit and losing part of its tail, then spinning down and impacting on the reef." He paused, and Scannon asked if he would show them where the plane landed. Speis nodded. Sure, he said. Come back in the morning.

On the water, Maldangesang motored expertly through narrow passages that cut between the coral heads. One wrong turn, and the boat would run aground in water just inches deep. About a mile offshore, they passed the propeller that Scannon had first seen in 1993. After all the years of seeing the propeller, it suddenly looked different to Scannon. The possibility that it might have come from the 453 chilled him. Speis gazed past the propeller to a spot just a few yards north. That, he said, pointing, was where the plane went down.

Everything was beginning to converge on a single region. Scannon and Galli spent another two days mapping the area for a search. Using the Photoshop overlay, they drew a grid on the coral heads, noting the boundaries of each square and the best way to reach it. While they plotted the approach, Maldangesang chased down yet another lead. Speis had mentioned a fisherman who knew the area well, and Maldangesang wanted to ask if he'd ever seen anything strange in the water. To his surprise, the fisherman was tight-lipped. He didn't want to get involved, he said, or spend hours motoring around the coral on a boat filled with Americans. But when Maldangesang promised to keep his identity secret, the fisherman said yes: he'd seen a huge jumble of metal embedded in one of the coral heads. Using a verbal shorthand, he explained to Maldangesang where it was. When Maldangesang returned to Scannon's hotel, he pointed to the spot on a map. It was right near the center of the grid that Scannon and Galli were mapping.

Finally, on the morning of January 26, the BentProp team boarded a boat for their first dive. It had taken ten days, but between the Photoshop overlay, the tip from Speis, and the fisherman's advice to Maldangesang, they had collected enough information to launch a systematic search. They would begin with the fisherman's directions.

When they reached the site, Maldangesang handed the wheel of the boat to Galli. Two pairs of divers would make the first sweep: Scannon with Maldangesang, and Joyce with Powers. They would descend together and move across the coral as a group. But when Scannon reached the bottom, he looked around and saw only Maldangesang. After a few minutes, he raised his hands in a gesture of questioning annoyance. Maldangesang returned the gesture. They waited, dangling in the translucent blue to the sound of their own breathing, but Joyce and Powers did not come back. Finally, Scannon pointed up. Maldangesang nodded. They surfaced to the sound of Pete Galli shouting.

"They found something!" he called. "Reid just came up for his camera! He's heading back down!"

Scannon and Maldangesang glanced across the water to where Joyce's air bubbles were rising, and they dove back under, following the trail through a column of deepening blue, descending farther into the void until the surface no longer shimmered above them and the shapes of two figures began to materialize gently in the darkness. The first was Joyce, floating at the side of a steep rise of coral. The second was Powers, holding on to something tall and thin. It was a propeller. As Scannon approached, he could see that she had both arms wrapped around the blade, her eyes wide, bubbles streaming up from the edges of a grin she couldn't contain.

"I was not letting go!" Powers said later. "I dropped right onto it and I said to myself, 'I'm staying here until someone finds me.'"

Scannon felt his heart drum against his chest as the rhythmic whoosh of his regulator rose and fell. He drifted close to Powers in a daze. With trembling hands, he reached out for the chalkboard attached to her waist, writing in large, blocky letters: ARNETT.

Powers nodded. She pointed down the sloping coral to a tangled mass of metal resting by the seafloor. It was an engine, with a second propeller attached to it, and below that, the unmistakable profile of a B-24 wing. The whole front half of the plane stretched out before him.

Scannon drifted down. He passed through the wreckage of the Liberator in awe. He saw the nose-turret bracket resting on a ledge, surrounded by hoses and wires and warped aluminum skin, and he paused to study a small metal box. There were four thin rods protruding from it, with a knob on the end of each. It was a throttle. The throttle. Jack Arnett's throttle. Each of the sticks controlled one engine, and they were all stuck in position by the growth of coral. Two of the sticks were pushed forward, and two pulled back, and it occurred to Scannon that this might be exactly the movement a pilot would make to compensate quickly for the loss of power on one side. He stared at the quadrant as a flood of emotion coursed through him. In ten years of searching, he had experienced many sensations at the wreckage of lost craft—the excitement of discovery, the chill of mortality, the overpowering sense of debt and duty to the missing. But as he gazed at the throttle he felt overcome with the low ache of loss. It was as if, in that final position of the throttle, Arnett's will to survive was recorded forever. "It was the last correction Arnett made," Scannon said later. "I can't explain why, but that was the thing that struck me the hardest."

As the BentProp team rose to the surface and climbed aboard the boat, there were hugs and shouts, then Scannon asked for a moment of silence. From his backpack, he pulled out a small American flag, and then a Palauan flag, asking Joyce, Powers, and Maldangesang to help stretch them over the foredeck. He quietly recited two stanzas of the Laurence Binyon poem etched on the BentProp coin:

> *They went with songs to the battle, they were young,*
> *Straight of limb, true of eye, steady and aglow.*
> *They were staunch to the end against odds uncounted;*
> *They fell with their faces to the foe.*
>
> *They shall grow not old, as we that are left grow old:*
> *Age shall not weary them, nor the years condemn.*

At the going down of the sun and in the morning,
We will remember them.

In the hotel that evening, Reid Joyce fought back tears as he tried to capture the experience in his journal. "When you're part of a group that spends time searching like this," he wrote, "you tend to tell and re-tell the stories of the people for whom you're searching. And you begin to be pulled back in time, in your mind, to the events that led to the disappearance of these brave souls. You see and hear anti-aircraft fire exploding around you. You feel the aircraft bucking. You feel the adrenaline rush as the deadly explosions get closer. You feel at least a shadow of the terror that must have followed, as the aircraft was hit and the left wing came off, and those eight men who weren't able to get out knew in their hearts that there's no way they'd survive the violent, spinning plunge toward the water, in this beautiful corner of the world so far from home. That's pretty intense, personal stuff, and you find yourself talking to these guys. Many times, aloud or just to myself, I've said, 'Hey, guys—we're here. We want to find you. Where are you? How about a sign? Something? Anything? Is this latest magnetometer anomaly the one that's going to lead us to you? Are we really about to close the circle?' I finally got the answer today."

BELCHER. THAT'S WHAT Scannon was thinking as he returned to the hotel. Bill Belcher was on the islands. The recovery team was *already there*. With a few phone calls, he tracked the anthropologist down and raced through the day's events. Listening, Belcher tried to process the jumble of information hurtling through Scannon's grin. "It was pure joy," he recalled later with a laugh.

For Belcher, the B-24 did raise complications. It was the first time he had been on the islands at the moment of discovery, which brought a host of new responsibilities. Though he wasn't an underwater archaeologist himself, he was fiercely protective of any archaeological site, and the lab would expect him to monitor BentProp and ensure that they didn't tamper with the wreckage. It had taken three years for Belcher to get permission for the dig on Police Hill, and one wrong move on the B-24 could jeopardize the lab's support for both. Belcher also had to make sure that Scannon didn't contact families with the news. That part, he knew, would be the hardest for Scannon to resist.

For Belcher, diving on the 453 wasn't negotiable. It was the best way to confirm that the wreckage was really a B-24, and to see if there were any signs of human remains on board. It was also the best way to make sure that Scannon had not gone inside the fuselage or, in the thrill of discovery, handled any pieces. Finally, it was a virgin wreck—unseen by human eyes since the day it plunged from the sky. There was no way Belcher was going home without a look.

On the morning of January 30, he motored to the site with Scannon. As they approached the coral, he was struck by the color of the water. The outgoing tide pulled sedimentary debris from the mangrove swamps nearby, creating an opaque swirl of mud and silt. "It's just murky," Belcher recalled, "and you can't see anything from the surface, but then you drop in and it's just amazing. About thirty feet down—*boom*—there's a big propeller stuck in the side of the coral. And then down some more—*boom*—there's the rest."

Belcher began to explore the site, making a mental inventory of the wreckage. He noted each fragment buried in the coral—the turret guns, the cockpit seats, the engine blocks, the flight deck pedestal, the shattered pieces of aluminum tumbling down the underwater hillside toward the sandy flats below. But underneath his scientific detachment, he felt the pure rush of discovery. Nothing, not even the mile-long underwater caves he had traversed or the experience of breathing trimix gas at four hundred feet, compared to the B-24. It was the whole front end of a World War II bomber separated into a dozen large pieces, and resting unseen, untouched, on the seafloor since the day it disappeared—every strut of steel, every scrap of fabric, every .50 caliber shell a testimony to the presence of the men inside.

"It was," Bill Belcher said, "the most spectacular thing I'd ever seen."

While Belcher examined the wreckage with Scannon and the Bent-Prop team, Maldangesang drifted off alone. A lifelong diver, he had mastered the art of conserving air, and long after the rest of the team had surfaced, he was still underwater. When he finally came up, he shouted, "What a lucky day!"

Scannon turned and saw on Maldangesang's face a grin that he would never forget.

"I thought it was a rock!" Maldangesang shouted. "It's huge and long! It's the tail and the body!"

Powers gasped. Joyce felt the hair stand up on his arms. Belcher and Scannon scrambled back into their gear to drop in, swimming around the coral head with Maldangesang and plunging to the bottom, where the fifty-foot tail of the plane lay perfectly preserved, leaning against the sloping hill with debris spilling from the windows—camera lenses from the aerial photographer, oxygen bottles, wires and tubing, and piles of .50 caliber ammunition. On the side, the waist gunner's window yawned open, and Scannon swam over to peek inside. In the shadows, he could just make out a flicker of movement and he strained his eyes for a better look. Long, thin streamers fluttered in the water, but what could they be? Dock lines abandoned by a passing ship? Wire so old that it had become loose as twine? Then he realized: Parachute shrouds. Not the tiny, synthetic lines he'd used at SkyDance. The old, heavy kind from the war.

Scannon swam around the plane and pushed his head through an opening on the bottom. He strained his eyes for a closer look at the lines rippling in the darkness. He traced them back to a common point deep in the fuselage, where a single deployed parachute fluttered in the water. But there was no harness. If it had been attached to a man, the man was gone.

That night, Scannon fought the urge to call Tommy Doyle. He had promised Belcher and the lab that he would keep his distance from the families, but every instinct in his body pushed him to pick up the phone. On the other side of Koror, Belcher was struggling, too. His supervisors in Hawaii were furious that he'd been down to see the plane without approval, and they were even more irate that BentProp had posted news of the discovery online—describing Belcher's visit, Arnett's name, and the tail number 453.

In the days to come, Belcher and Scannon would commiserate about the stringent military rules, as Belcher wrestled with the disapproval of his command, threatening at one point to quit. But in the end, each man would acquiesce to the protocol of the lab. The most important thing for each of them was to see the lost airmen brought home. It would be a massive undertaking for Eric Emery's new underwater program. A small fighter in shallow water would have made an easier target. For the B-24, a complete recovery might cost more than $1 million, and might require dozens of men to work for months, even years. To convince the command that the project was worth it, they would have to apply just the right mix of deference and pressure.

Scannon quietly removed the references to Arnett and Belcher from the BentProp website, leaving only a vague mention of the "four-engine bomber." As he returned to California, he watched the phone, wondering if the Doyles had seen the earlier version. But the phone didn't ring, and Scannon had promised not to call the Doyles himself. He returned to his office at Xoma, while in Hawaii, Bill Belcher resumed his duties at the lab—determined to pull every string, and push every button, until Eric Emery went to Palau.

FOURTEEN

FALLOUT

The loss of any crew cast a pall on the Long Rangers, but the casualties in Palau were stunning. In a single week of missions, the unit had lost more than fifty men. It was the third-bloodiest week since the start of the war, and for the new commander of the 424th Squadron, Jack Vanderpoel, the first combat losses.

For all his exuberance and bravado, Vanderpoel took those losses hard. Those who knew the young captain say that he retreated to his private quarters to anguish over the letters home. It was one thing to face the artillery in his own cockpit, or even to watch a plane go down in the adrenalized rush of combat. It was something else to linger on the loss during a quiet moment, and to contemplate in writing the devastation it would mean at home. The vanishing of a single plane in the Pacific sent ripples to the far side of the world, and for Vanderpoel it was important to recognize each lost man as a man. When he didn't know the crew members well, he would circulate through the camp, asking questions about their backgrounds and their interests before he sat down to write. "My father didn't talk much about the war, but the one thing he talked about was the difficulty of those letters," his son, Eric Vanderpoel, recalled. "He said it was easier to write the officers' families, because he knew who they were. But he couldn't know all the enlisted men, and that bothered him. He said he worked hard going to the tents and talking to the mates of the guys who were lost, so he would have something meaningful to write."

As September passed, Vanderpoel composed his first letters to the Big Stoop families. "Dear Mrs. Moore," he wrote to Johnny's wife, Katherine. "It is my regrettable duty to inform you that your husband has been reported as 'Missing in Action' on 1 September 1944. On a scheduled combat strike mission in the Southwest Pacific Area, the plane of which your husband was Assistant Radio Operator/Gunner was hit in the left wing by two direct heavy anti-aircraft bursts while over the target, causing one of the engines to burst into flames. Two men parachuted out, and then the airplane snapped in two and crashed into the water. Planes flying with the ship dropped down to a low level and searched the area without results. Your husband was a new member in our squadron, but his friendly manner won him many friends and his loss is deeply regretted by the entire squadron."

While Vanderpoel wrote the other families, Mario Campora walked the camp on Wakde in a daze. As a photographer, he was not formally a member of any crew, but he thought of himself as one of the Big Stoop boys. They had invited him to join their crew photo, and he kept a copy of it in his tent. Now the photo served only as a reminder that his best friends on the island were gone, and that, if he hadn't been sidelined by a fever, he would be gone as well. He promised himself that when the war was over and he was back home in western Massachusetts, he'd save money for as long as it took to visit their families around the country.

The Big Stoop tent on Wakde sat empty until the mortuary men came to collect belongings—sorting through duffel bags to gather combs and brushes and souvenirs, deciding what to save, send home, or destroy. There were no hard rules for those decisions, and the packages that began to arrive in Ohio, Texas, Arkansas, and New York said as much about the man who mailed them as the man whose belongings were inside. There was no way to know, for example, the special meaning that Jimmie and Johnny attached to the matching shells they had collected on Los Negros six weeks earlier at low tide. Nor was there any way for Myrle and Katherine to know that the shells were missing. Like so many things, the shells had meaning only to the boys who found them, and the meaning, with the boys, was gone.

At home in Marlboro, New York, Diane Goulding was coming back from a picnic with Ted Junior when the telegram arrived. She read it once and stumbled into her room, where she stayed for weeks, raging and crying while the family tended little Ted. "I won't say she abandoned the baby," her brother, Paul Graziosi, said. "But she stayed in that room, it seemed, forever. She never smiled, she never laughed, she didn't even wear her glasses if she came out of the room and went to the bathroom, which was an outhouse. I think she didn't want to see the world. We took care of the baby."

In her room, Diane was struck by how little she knew of Ted, how little time she'd had to get to know him. She knew his father had come to the United States from England in about 1910, and two years later, had sent for his mother and siblings to travel aboard the *Titanic*, and she knew that when the ship went down, he wore a black armband for weeks before a letter came to let him know they'd booked a different ship. She knew that, by the time Ted was born a decade later, the home was drowning in conflict, as his father drank and fought with his mother and took out his anger on the kids. But Diane scarcely knew Ted's parents herself. She knew none of the Goulding family in England, and had no idea whether any of them would want to be part of Ted Junior's life. Now it was too late to ask—that, or anything else.

Or was it? Secretly Diane had a nagging feeling that Ted wasn't really gone. It was crazy, she knew, but there it was. Some combination of instinct and faith told her that he was alive. Lost, maybe, or captured, or sick, or perhaps it was amnesia. Over the next three decades, she followed every scrap of news from the Pacific for a sign of Ted. Each time a Japanese soldier emerged from a jungle hideaway in the 1950s and '60s, she would picture Ted coming out from his own cave one day, or being released by his captors, and part of her grieved at the thought that he might be in trouble, while another part smiled at the thought that he might come home. In the years to come, she would remarry and begin a new family with three daughters, but when that marriage grew rocky, Ted Junior left home and rarely came back to Marlboro. Then Diane's second husband died, and she was alone again, alone with the undying faith that Ted was still alive. Late in life, she would say, with tears streaming down her face, "I always thought he might come home. I thought he had amnesia. I thought he was going to remember who he was."

At night, Diane wrote to the other families of the crew, like Jack Arnett's mother, Dessie, and Jimmie's and Johnny's wives. She wrote to the Yoh family in Ohio, and the Schumacher family in Minnesota. To Myrle Doyle, she wrote, "I thought I'd just offer my sympathies and I know how you must feel. Everything is so uncertain, one doesn't know what to think. All we can do is to hope and pray we'll hear good news soon of our loved ones."

Diane's letters became a kind of a life raft for Katherine Moore as the autumn rains in Arkansas gave way to winter and a spring flood. "I got another letter from Diane," Katherine wrote to Myrle. "She writes often. I don't know what I'd do without you and your letters. They have helped me over some rough spots."

In their letters, the families searched one another for hope, asking what the lost men had said about the war, what news the Army had sent, and what personal effects they'd received. Katherine had opened the package to find just two bundles of her own letters to Johnny, his fountain pen, his pipe, and a pair of swimming trunks. When Myrle wrote to say that she'd received Jimmie's hat and clothes and assorted trinkets, Katherine wrote back, "I should say, you did get more of Jimmie's things back than I got of Johnny's. I know Johnny must have surely had other things. I guess though, they have so many things to attend to like that, that they couldn't possibly keep everything straight." Even Katherine's copy of the crew photo was beginning to rip and disintegrate from her tears. "If you have any copies made from yours," she wrote to Myrle, "please have an extra one made for me and tell me how much it costs." When the photos and letters weren't enough, Katherine drove to Texas to spend a week with Myrle and Tommy. Then she decided to stay for good.

Back in Arkansas, Johnny's sister Melba moved in with their parents. Her mother had called in desperation, saying, "Melba, your dad's gone crazy," and when Melba arrived at the house she found John Senior in a catatonic state, crouched up in his chair as if bracing for impact. After eighteen years of fishing and hunting with Johnny, the thought of a lifetime without his son was too much to bear. As the weeks passed, he refused to eat, couldn't sleep, and his body began to fail. A doctor prescribed anxiety medicine, but it made little difference. Finally his eyes did what his heart could not, and John Moore went blind. "Mama said she lost them both," Melba recalled. Every time Melba closed her own eyes, she saw Johnny standing on the porch with that wild fear, whispering, "I don't think I'm ever going to see you again."

In the South Pacific, Jack Arnett's brother Marvin struggled with the news. He was a pilot like Jack, but in the Navy's Air Transport Service, flying a route between island bases. One day, on a flight through the Caroline Islands, he made a detour over Palau, swooping low to look down for a sign of Jack on the islands. Crazy, he thought. But he couldn't help it. A few weeks later, he did it again. Then Marvin Arnett was making detours all the time.

As the years passed, Mario Campora returned to western Massachusetts—with a burgeoning family, and a job running a gas station, and a life that left little time or money for cross-country trips. Near the end of his life in 2007, he confided to his family that he had always been haunted by the loss of the Big Stoop crew, and by his own broken promise to offer comfort to their families. "That was his biggest regret," his daughter, Cindy, said, her own voice breaking. "He always thought he should have found a way." And a few miles east, in the hills of Amesbury, Norman Coorssen tried to return to the life he'd left behind. But nothing, including Coorssen, was the same.

He'd waited a month after the crash to fly again, boarding a plane on October 3 to attack the oil refineries at Balikpapan. It was one of the most heavily defended Japanese positions in the South Pacific, and every man on the mission expected heavy losses. "It is doubtful that a more dangerous, grueling, and heart-breaking mission was ever flown in any theater of the war than the October 3, 1944, raid by the 307th to Balikpapan," the historian Sam Britt wrote. By the end of that day, the Long Rangers would return with seventy airmen missing and their fleet in tatters.

For Coorssen, the mission also had a personal resonance: he was scheduled to fly with Jack Arnett's most recent crew. Whatever had brought on the crew change of September 1, it was echoed a month later on the mission to Balikpapan: the pilot who had lost his men, with the men who'd lost their pilot.

Yet they never finished the mission. A few minutes after takeoff Coorssen turned back. "This turn back," the mission report explained, "was made due to pilot illness and failure of the auto-pilot." Squadron commander Jack Vanderpoel never believed that explanation. Sixty years later, he was still fuming. At a Long Ranger reunion in August 2004, just six months after Scannon's discovery of the wreckage, Vanderpoel sat down with Greg Babinski, whose father had flown with Arnett that summer and with Coorssen on the October 3 mission. Babinski knew little about his father's war, and even less about Arnett or Coorssen. But he was compiling interviews to piece together his father's story. As he and Vanderpoel sat together in a booth at Rachel's restaurant in Nashville, Babinski handed Vanderpoel a list of names he'd seen on mission rosters with his father. Vanderpoel scrolled down the list, noting the names he remembered. When he got to Coorssen's name, Vanderpoel stopped and his face darkened. "His opinion," Babinski said later, "was that Coorssen turned back, not because of mechanical problems, but because he lost his nerve." In his notes, Babinski wrote, "Coorssen was a coward." They were Vanderpoel's exact words.

For Coorssen's family in Amesbury, the man who returned home from the war was unmistakably changed. The carefree kid who had laughed his way through college was gone, replaced by a grim figure who rarely smiled. He would live out the next forty years of his life in a routine so exacting that even his close relatives found it baffling. "He wore the same outfit every day," his nephew, Gary Coorssen, said. "A gray suit, white shirt, and a maroon tie and socks." He also drove the same car, buying a new model every year. "Always blue, always a Pontiac, always a sedan," his sister-in-law, Helen Coorssen, said. Each morning, he would disappear into his office at the family business, whiling away the afternoon on Marlboros and nips of scotch. In the evening, Helen said, "you could tell what time of day it was when he would drive through town on his way home." At home, "the house was so meticulous, you could eat off the basement floor," Gary added. But Norman Coorssen seemed to take little joy from his ritual existence. "I don't recall him ever laughing," Gary said. "I can't even picture him with a smile." Once in a while, a family member would press for an explanation. "Norman," his brother George would say, "tell me what happened in the war." Norman would only frown and mutter, "I don't want to talk about it." In forty years, he never did.

"Norman just refused," Helen Coorssen said. "Absolutely refused to discuss it. It's one of the mysteries that I shall carry to my grave."

Many of Coorssen's relatives wondered if he'd done something wrong.

They never knew about the crew change, never heard the name Jack Arnett, and never found out about his final, aborted mission until after he was gone. All they knew was what they saw in Norman himself. By the time he died of heart failure, in 1983, it was as though he'd been gone a long time. He'd vanished somewhere in the South Pacific, the last casualty of the Big Stoop crew.

FIFTEEN

RECOVERY

Tommy and Nancy rarely left Texas. They rarely saw the point. Once in a while they might slip across the border with New Mexico for a weekend getaway or pop into Arkansas for a visit with Tommy's family, but most of the time it suited them better to stay home and save the money. Nancy was frugal by nature, and Tommy by experience. After you'd lost everything, you learned to hang on to what you had.

On cold winter evenings, Nancy liked to fire up the computer after dinner to check on friends. When the BentProp team was in Palau, that meant a stop by their website to read the latest news. Nancy no longer expected a breakthrough on Tommy's dad but she enjoyed the daily updates all the same. It seemed like every year the team uncovered three or four new fighter planes, and when Colmer and Joyce would post photos on the website with a short description of what they'd found, Nancy would lean close to the screen to study every detail, marveling at the infinite variety of colors in the coral and the jungle, and the way the gnarled wreckage of a plane disappeared into the landscape. There was something mesmerizing about Scannon's transformation, too. On the islands, he abandoned his usual uniform of khakis and blazers and pressed oxford shirts, and in the photos of him crawling through woven mangrove roots in a mud-splattered T-shirt and cargo pants with a machete strapped to his back he was almost unrecognizable. Even his face looked different on the islands, with the whites of his eyes and his snow-white beard gleaming against tan, weathered skin.

Yet when the BentProp team began to post photographs of the Arnett wreckage in early 2004, Nancy didn't see them. She and Tommy were farther from home than they'd ever been. Their son, Casey, had emerged from his childhood health problems and become a US Marine. He was about to graduate from officer candidate school in Quantico, Virginia. Between planning, packing, traveling, and then finally settling home after the 1,300-mile trip, Nancy and Tommy forgot all about the BentProp mission. By the time they remembered and Nancy pulled up the website to catch up on the daily reports, all the references to "Jack Arnett" and "the 453" had been wiped clean. Instead, she found herself staring at the vague, redacted language approved by the military lab. "All it really said," she recalled, "was that there was a four-engine bomber, it was in the water, and they'd been looking for it a long time. I just read that, and read it again, three or four times, and I thought, 'I'm not reading what I'm reading.'"

Nancy shouted for Tommy to come into the room. When he loped through the door, she jabbed a finger at the computer screen and said, "Tommy, you read that. Tell me if I'm going crazy.'"

Tommy didn't spend much time on computers, but he squinted his eyes and read through the post. Then he read it again. It sure sounded like his daddy's plane. But wouldn't somebody have told him? While he scrolled through photos of the wreckage, a blur of brown and gray shapes in a haze of blue-green water, Nancy picked up the phone and punched in Scannon's number. When he picked up, she blurted out, "You found the plane!?"

Scannon didn't answer. His mind raced to find the words. After months of wondering if the Doyles knew about the discovery, it was a relief to know they did—but he still couldn't confirm the details. The military was adamant: only they could verify the identity of the plane, and only they could notify the families. It was just the kind of bureaucratic red tape that had turned Scannon off to the military as a younger man, but if he wanted to stay in the good graces of the lab—if he wanted them to trust him, and work with him, and investigate the sunken plane, and bring home the lost crew—then he would have to play by their rules. If he wanted to give real answers to the Doyles, he couldn't answer their questions now.

"I can't tell you it's Jimmie's plane," he said finally. "Here's what I can tell you: it's a four-engine bomber, it's in the water, and it's near Koror. The only four-engine bomber that flew over there was the B-24, and there were only three that went down near Koror. We've found the other two. So you have to decide for yourselves."

Tommy had picked up a second handset and he exchanged a quizzical look with Nancy. "Can you tell me what it looked like?" he asked.

Scannon exhaled. "I can describe the site," he said, explaining that the coral head was small and round, barely a mile from shore, with the front of the plane scattered across one side and the tail resting on the other. He described swimming through the debris and recognizing parts—the nose-turret bracket embedded in coral on the western slope; the pilot controls just below that, fused in position; the shell casings on the sand beside the tail; and inside the fuselage, the parachute shrouds billowing in the current. The end of the tail, he said quietly, was pushed into the sea-floor, which made it impossible to see the tail turret.

Tommy felt a knot in his gut. It was clearly his dad's plane, Scannon didn't have to spell that out. But the image of his father's tail turret buried in sixty years of muck and debris filled him with dread. If his daddy was in that turret, it meant he'd experienced a brutal death, trapped inside the plexiglass bubble with a clear view of the sky as the plane spun and tumbled toward the water, then smashed into the surface and drifted toward the bottom of the lagoon while water poured in through the cracks. Yet finding his daddy in the tail would also mean that the rumors weren't true, that Jimmie hadn't abandoned him, that he could let go of the great torment of his life.

"I want to see it," Tommy said quietly.

"We're going back in a few months," Scannon replied.

"If I go," Tommy said, "I want to go down."

"You get certified, and I'll take you."

LEARNING TO DIVE in West Texas is a study in chlorine and mud. Tommy signed up for a winter class and spent his weekends blowing bubbles in the shallow end of a pool, then he survived a half-hour dunk in the cold brown mess of an inland lake, and he was a licensed diver. Of course, he'd never actually been deeper than twenty-five feet, hadn't touched a single flipper into salt water, and the only thing he knew for sure about diving was that he didn't plan to make a habit of it. But he figured he could get down to the plane at least once, and whatever happened after that was worth it.

Tickets to Palau were $4,000 per person, which was about as much money as Tommy and Nancy had ever spent on anything. The flight was so long that it took a whole day of traveling each way. Then there was the day that disappeared over the international date line, and the day you lost trying to get the fuzz out of your head. Tommy and Nancy swallowed their disbelief, and in March 2005, they drove to Dallas to begin their journey to the far side of the world. Tommy wore jeans and a plaid shirt, with a belt buckle the size of Texas. Nancy wore a slim white blouse and sea-green slacks. She'd lost forty pounds for the trip.

As the Doyles made their way west, Scannon was on the islands with Chip and Pam Lambert. It had been four years since their last expedition together, and the Lamberts were still skeptical of the direction Scannon was heading. They had no love for the skydivers or the new rituals of BentProp—the logo, the coins, the embroidered hats, and the quasi-official leadership titles might have helped with the military brass, but to the Lamberts it felt contrived and off-putting, especially Scannon's title of "Team Leader."

Yet the Lamberts still felt deeply connected to the Arnett plane and crew. They had helped Scannon begin the search in 1993, when he returned from their mission to the Bush trawler; then they joined him on the channel in 1996, and again in 1999, and once more in 2000, logging hundreds of hours in the quest to find the plane. Now the president of Palau had declared the wreckage protected. Both the Palauan and US governments resolved to keep its coordinates secret, but the Lamberts were still listed as members of BentProp, which gave them special dispensation.

Scannon was equally conflicted about his split with the Lamberts. At a certain level, he would always regard them as superior explorers. They had a wealth of diving experience that he would never match, and although they hadn't found Yamashita's gold, they continued to make staggering discoveries, like the wreckage of the USS *Mississinewa* on a nearby Pacific atoll. Chip had also begun to appear in a television series about wreck diving on the History Channel, and some of the most famous divers in the world counted them as friends.

But in other regards, Scannon believed he was better off without the Lamberts. When they joined him on missions, they always wanted to take days off for fun, splitting their time between the channel and recreational dive sites on the reef. Scannon had no interest in those things. He didn't even particularly like to dive. Gliding between sharks and giant clams and bursts of neon coral was, to him, only a half step removed from sitting on the sofa and watching television, and in the skydivers he'd found a team that was focused entirely on the search.

As the Lamberts joined Scannon for three days of diving, they agreed to leave the past behind, swimming through the Arnett wreckage, examining tiny details, and dissecting everything they'd seen over cocktails at the Palau Pacific Resort.

By the time the Doyles reached Palau, the Lamberts were on their way home, and the BentProp team was beginning to arrive for the 2005 mission. As Tommy and Nancy stepped into the terminal after the thirty-hour journey from Texas, they found Scannon and Colmer and Joyce cheering, while Joe and Esther Maldangesang draped pink floral leis across their shoulders and crowned them with wreaths. Then they all stepped outside into the warm tropical night, piled into a van, and sped to a hotel in Koror, where Tommy and Nancy collapsed into bed.

Nine hours later they were back in motion.

At 7:00 a.m., Tommy and Nancy reported to the large hotel room that BentProp always used as a hub, and they studied a map with Scannon while Joyce organized camera equipment and Colmer whipped up bacon and eggs. By 7:30, they were on their way to the waterfront at the Neco Marine dive shop; by 8:00, they were racing through the impossibly blue water on their way to dive.

As the boat ripped between islands, Tommy and Nancy stared over the foredeck in a dreamlike state. Many of the islands were so small they looked like sculptures floating on the water, with rocky walls that shot straight up and small holes bored into the sides.

Tommy and Nancy exchanged a wary glance. "We both had the same thought," Tommy said later. Every wartime document that Scannon had given the Doyles made mention of the parachutes. If some of the Big Stoop crew escaped, Jimmie might have been among them. Maybe it was madness to believe he could have survived and hidden until the end of the war. But looking at those tiny caves, it didn't seem like madness at all.

"You're looking up at those islands," Nancy said, "and you see a cave here and a cave there, and you realize how close it is—you're within swimming distance of the crash. You could hide. Run into the water, get on a coral head, duck down. It would be possible. You hear stories about how many Palauans lived in those caves. They were born in the caves. And in the sixties and seventies, some of the Japanese finally came out of a cave on Guam! Now, if they could live in a cave for twenty-five years . . ."

"And then the other side of it is," Tommy said, "where did the stories come from?" Tommy still couldn't imagine a reason that his dad would have left his mom, but he also couldn't imagine why his uncles were so sure he did. Why did they go looking for Jimmie in California? Why did they try to get the TV show *Unsolved Mysteries* to look into the case? And why did Tommy's mother live the rest of her life in a state of emotional limbo, refusing even to talk about Jimmie, and keeping his letters secret? The easiest explanation for the rumor was still the most shocking one. What if it was true?

When Maldangesang reached the dive site, he shut off the engine and dropped anchor. Scannon grinned at Tommy: "Ready?"

"I guess I am," Tommy said.

They stretched into neoprene suits and scuba vests while Nancy peered over the edge at the shimmering blue water. It seemed to flutter from turquoise to indigo to ghostly white, and she strained her eyes for a glimpse of what lay below, but it was impossible to see, impossible even to believe that the plane could be so near. The nose was only forty feet down, closer than the tips of the live oak tree in her yard, and the tail turret would be just seventy feet away, the length of her house.

After a routine buddy check, Scannon gave Tommy the nod to splash in, and he felt the warm sea swish around him as he began to drop through darkening water. As Tommy drifted down, he saw Joe Maldangesang drop in, swimming to his side to take his elbow and guide him to the bottom. Tommy glanced up at the pinprick of sunlight on the surface. He was already deeper than he'd ever been in Texas, with nothing but a veil of blue above, below, and all around. The only familiar sight was Maldangesang; even the other divers were too far away to see. Tommy pinched his nose to blow the pressure from his ears and tried to steady himself in the water. He fixed his gaze on Maldangesang, who stared back as they fell toward the bottom. Suddenly, in the corner of his eye, Tommy saw a shadow. He turned and the water lifted like a shade to reveal the massive underwater mountain of coral littered with mangled metal. Tommy felt his pulse shoot up. Maldangesang gestured for him to follow, and they swam around a bend in the coral, past fragments of aluminum dancing with fish, until all at once through the faint blue haze the fuselage came into view. It was as long as a five-story building and still mostly intact, a wide tube of airplane leaning against the coral.

Tommy kicked his fins to get closer and Maldangesang gave him room. There was a rectangular opening on the top and Tommy recognized it as the waist gunner's door. Johnny's door. His dad's best friend. The husband of the woman, Katherine, who'd come to live with Tommy and his mom after the crash. Johnny had always been a ghost to Tommy, like his father. Now, staring at the window and the machine-gun shells spilling onto the seafloor, he wondered if Johnny was near.

Emotions crashed through Tommy like cymbals. He reached out and touched the plane, then pushed his head through the opening. He peered down the long, shadowy interior to where the end of the fuselage plunged into the sand. The tail turret would be down there, just a few feet away. A strange sensation washed over him, and he realized that for the first time in sixty years, he might be close to his father. Sixty years of waiting, wondering, doubting, and in moments he dared not acknowledge, seething at the injustice of his father's disappearance, and now he felt a wave of release. There was still no way to know if his daddy's bones were there. They might be in a cave nearby, or the jungle, or a cemetery in California. But for the first time Tommy could remember, there was a chance that Jimmie was with him. He closed his eyes and held on to the plane and let the feeling overtake him.

_____

As TOMMY AND NANCY RETURNED to Texas, Eric Emery was on his way to Palau. Four years of building the underwater program and it all came down to one plane. For Emery, it wasn't that the plane itself had special meaning. In most respects, it was no different from any other wreck, and part of his job was to maintain critical distance. He hadn't learned much about Arnett or his crew, their mission, or even the islands, and he'd never met Pat Scannon or the Doyles, and he didn't expect to.

But the wreckage was underwater, and that made all the difference. It would finally allow him to test the underwater program, and in doing so, it marked a crossroads in his life, bringing together the disparate threads of a twenty-year journey: the early infatuation with scuba, the academic studies in history, the unexpected fusion of those interests in underwater archaeology, and the sense of purpose he felt on his first expedition to the Mount Independence bridge; then the loss of that feeling as he sank into the Andean lake, and the temptation to abandon his work; and finally, the renewed sense of purpose he felt at the lab, developing an underwater program to bring home men who had gone through a similar fate.

As Emery sped toward the islands on a C-17 transport filled with forensic specialists, ordnance disposal experts, and Navy divers, he felt the weight of the mission bearing down. All of the lab's usual methods had to be adapted for water, but nothing required more adaptation than the team itself. A Navy deep-sea diver hit the water with a skill set that was unmatched in the world. Most of the divers around him were so physically fit that they looked like action figures, but that was only the surface. A Navy diver spent more time underwater than almost anyone alive. Day in and out, he lived there—fixing ships' hulls and clearing channels and setting underwater communication lines. Some of them deployed with SEAL teams to augment combat missions; others helped ordnance units dismantle bombs in the Persian Gulf. Wherever he worked, a Navy diver could expect to spend hundreds of hours underwater, often at depths so

extreme that his body took weeks to recover. In the water, every 33 verti-
cal feet added as much pressure as the atmosphere of the earth. At 66 feet,
a man's body was under three atmospheres of pressure. At 165 feet, he was
under six. At 231 feet, eight. Yet in the Navy dive program, eight atmospheres was just a start. Some of the divers traveling with Emery had been
to 800 feet of pressure, and at the Navy's Experimental Diving Unit in
Florida, a few had breached 2,000 feet—sixty atmospheres of pressure closing in.

To do his job on the bottom of the ocean, a diver sometimes had to
spend days in a compression chamber. When the pressure was high
enough, the chamber could be lowered from the deck of a ship and cracked
open at the proper depth. The diver might spend hours there, working to
repair a beacon or splice a communication line. Then it might be weeks
more in the chamber to depressurize. Along the way, any problem he
encountered—an air bubble lodging in his brain, gas boiling from his
blood, or the dizzying effects of nitrogen narcosis—would throw his life
in jeopardy. He couldn't be sprung to the surface for treatment, and a
doctor couldn't be pressurized in time to save him. He was stuck in the
darkness with only the other divers to help. Each time a diver's fins hit
the water, he faced an irreducible risk. Even in training, it was common
for a man to succumb to a biological glitch and black out, only to be
resuscitated on the deck of the pool by his friends. Over time, the divers developed an insular camaraderie, a closeness of necessity and mutual
advantage that resembled the brotherhood of men at war.

Emery knew the divers on his team were stronger, faster, and more
accustomed to the depths than he would ever be, but he also knew that
they had been conditioned in one problematic way. They were trained to
emphasize speed and power, to accomplish as much as possible on every
dive. The more quickly a diver could wrench off a bolt, snap an old
propeller, or move a rusty flange, the more valuable he was to the Navy.
Speed and power were not just habits, they were essential to the job.

Archaeology was the opposite. It was tentative and cautious and by its very nature embraced the arc of time. A Neolithic vase embedded in the bottom of a Chinese lake could wait another century to be recovered— but it only took one careless instant to destroy the piece forever. To prepare a Navy diver for archaeological work involved more than a new set of tools; it meant trying to impart, in a few days of training, a new conceptual framework. "We're trying to take these guys who are rewarded for speed, and put all these restrictions on them," Emery said. "When you get down there and you've never done it before, you want to just go crazy. You want to dig everything up. And that's like doing brain surgery with a chain saw."

Luckily, the lead diver on the mission was among the most decorated in the Navy. Dave Gove was only thirty-three years old, but he was rated as a master diver, the highest distinction a diver could attain. To reach the rating, a man not only had to excel in the water. He also had to possess a variety of intangibles, like the ability to discern the strengths and abilities of the men around him, and to command their respect, loyalty, and subordination through the innate gift of leadership. In his fifteen-year Navy career, Gove had been honored with a litany of awards for exactly those talents, including the Navy and Marine Corps Commendation Medal, three Navy and Marine Corps Achievement Medals, and seven Letters of Commendation for "excellence under pressure." Four years earlier, he'd been named "Sailor of the Year" by the chief of naval operations in Washington, DC. He was the first Navy diver ever to receive the honor.

As Gove and the divers hauled their equipment to a large metal barge on Koror, then towed it to the crash site, Emery used a scuba tank to explore the wreckage. First he swam around the coral, trying to orient himself. Then he studied the positions of key pieces in the nose and cockpit along the western slope, before moving to the long tail slumped down the other side. It made sense to begin with the tail, he thought. It was a large, clearly defined space, and there might be skeletons inside.

The procedure Emery had developed for the operation was deliberately plodding. There would be no flash of insight, no moments of inspiration. The divers would simply divide the landscape into one-meter squares and excavate one square at a time. Working in pairs, they would descend to the site in hard-hat diving suits, with each diver carrying a large vacuum hose known as a Venturi dredge. The dredge would pump all the sand and debris into a large steel basket on the seafloor. When a basket was full, it could be lifted by a crane to the deck of the barge, where all the other divers would fill buckets of sediment and carry them to a screening station nearby. As they sifted through every grain in search of metal or bone, divers below would fill another basket.

As the first divers headed down, Emery took a seat behind a small desk inside a shipping container. There was a monitor on the desk, streaming a live feed from cameras mounted on the divers' helmets, but the images were fuzzy and Emery strained his eyes to make out the details. It was frustrating to feel so removed from the site, but he wasn't qualified to use hard-hat gear. The Navy certification process was so extreme that many recruits, fresh from competitive high school swimming programs, failed to get through. Emery was two decades older and hadn't even tried. So he was stuck at the monitor, watching and waiting while other men worked his site.

When the first basket was full, the divers hooked metal cables to the corners and a crane operator raised it gently until, with a loud swish, it burst into the air, draining a brownish gray slurry of sediment and debris back into the water. Once the basket was safely resting on the deck, Emery signaled for the rest of the team to approach, all filling buckets of sand and mud to haul toward the screening station. Soon there was a shout. They'd found a boot. Then they found another. Then a zipper with fragments of cloth. Then a button. Then a quarter. Then a couple of pennies. Then another basket was rising to the surface with a .50 caliber machine gun inside. Emery studied the weapon and found pieces of coral growing near the trigger, and mixed in with the coral, human bone, as though a man's hand were still holding on. He placed each item in a bucket of clean salt water to protect it from the air, pacing between the monitor and the screening station as the divers worked their way down the tail. But when they reached the part buried in sand, Emery saw a change come over Dave Gove.

"We were having a great year," Emery said later. "I knew we had remains. But when we got about three-quarters of the way through, the master diver came up to me and he said, 'You know what? With all the sediment we're taking from under this plane, I'm afraid she's going to slip and pin somebody.'"

Emery winced and nodded. There was only one thing he could do. His own protocol forbade him to excavate a new square until this one was complete. But if the dig was destabilizing the plane, there was no way to move forward. He told Gove to bring up the dredges and prepare for the journey home. "It was frustrating," Emery said, "but it was a question of safety. We couldn't take any more sediment from the aft fuselage because that was actually holding the aircraft in place. So we had to stop the mission. I said, 'Look, I need you to shift gears. We'll finish processing all the artifacts and getting the archaeology side of the house closed down. What I need you to do is gather up all your guys and dive them one after another to take notes on this wreck—its position, what it's in contact with, and what it would take to get it up and support it, so we can come in here at a later date and dig it out.'"

Then Emery packed his belongings for the long flight to Hawaii, never imagining that it would be two years before he returned.

EVERY DAY THE WORLD seemed bigger to the Doyles. After a lifetime in Texas, they had been to the far side of the world, and now that they had, they began to travel more often. There was a network of MIA families that reached into every corner of the country, and they met periodically to share their stories and search for answers. For Tommy, the discovery of other sons and daughters with a history like his own was an unexpected source of comfort. The more MIA families he met, the more clear it became that the strange story that haunted his family also haunted theirs. "You go to these meetings," he said, "and everybody has a story like mine. You know, somehow the guy survived. He's still going to come home. You hear that from people who lost somebody in the Pacific, in Europe, in Africa, all parts of the world. As soon as they start talking, there's something along that line. It's a mistake. It's not right. There's something funny about it. Every time."

Even among the Big Stoop families, those stories crept in. There was Diane Goulding in New York, struggling with a lifelong suspicion that Ted was still alive. There was her younger brother, Paul, gripped by the same faith, but so embarrassed by it that he'd never told Diane. "You feel like it's a juvenile thing to be fifty years old and still think your brother-in-law is stranded on some island," he said. "You're expecting somebody to say, 'Are you stupid? He's gone, and he's never coming back.' But I was well past my fiftieth birthday and I was still having recurring dreams. I would say I probably had hundreds of dreams over a fifty-year period." The dreams were always the same. As a child, he had been the first to see Ted coming up the long driveway on his final visit home, and in the dream, he saw Ted there again, older now but still carrying the duffel bag on his shoulder. In an unpublished memoir, he recalled the trauma of the recurring dream. "It would play over and over," he wrote, "and ause me to imagine that my brother-in-law was marooned on a deserted island in the South Pacific. As I grew, my theory remained steadfast. I hid my secret well, but in times of deep thought, I, approaching fifty years old, would see a smiling Ted walking up the road with his baggage. I never shared with anyone the unending recycling of a dream that had overtaken me decades before."

In Charleston, West Virginia, Jack Arnett's mother struggled with her own suspicions. Though she didn't know that during the war Jack's brother Marvin had flown over Palau to look for him, she, too, had always believed that he was still alive. After the war, she and her husband, B.B., would relocate to Florida, where they kept a painting of Jack above the fireplace for the rest of their lives, and in the strangest moments, Dessie would look up at the painting and wonder what Jack looked like now. When she received a telegram from the War Department that still listed him as "Missing in Action," she took the words as a hopeful sign, writing to Myrle Doyle, "I am thankful for that thread of hope. Do you still hope our boys are alive? I am sitting here by my window, looking through the darkness of the night to the stars overhead. The darker the night, the brighter they shine." When Dessie saw a newsreel at the local movie theater, showing footage from a Japanese prison camp, she jumped from her seat and raced into the projection booth to demand that the operator rewind the film. One of the men in the footage, she was certain, was Jack. "She believed he was alive for the rest of her life," a niece, Carolyn Arnett Rocchio, said. "She never really believed he was gone."

As Tommy spoke with other Big Stoop families, he learned about Johnny Moore's father, gone blind and mute from grief, and he called Johnny's wife, Katherine, in the final years of her life, and the brothers of Earl Yoh in Ohio. For the first time, Tommy found himself offering answers, rather than questions. In the summer of 2006, he flew to another Long Ranger reunion in Bellevue, Washington, where he met Diane Goulding in person for the first time. Sitting at the dinner table with Diane, her son, Ted Junior, and his wife, Bev, the Doyles handed an envelope to Diane. Inside was a letter she had written to Tommy's mom six decades earlier.

Diane opened the envelope and removed two pages of yellow paper covered with her own handwriting. "Dear Mrs. Doyle," it began, "I received a letter from the War Department saying your husband has been missing since September 1st with my husband, and I thought I'd just write to you to offer my sympathies, as I know how you must feel. We have an 18-month-old son who is named for his dad. Do you have any children? [Ted] has only seen him for seven days, over a year ago. I hope it will be real soon when he sees his son again. We must pray and have faith, and I know we will find all our prayers and dreams answered and coming true. Hoping we get good news soon, I remain, very sincerely, Diane M. Goulding."

Reading the letter, Diane Goulding's face crumpled, and she sobbed quietly. Then she folded the pages back into the envelope and pushed it across the table to Nancy, who whispered, "No, no, that letter is yours," as Diane's eyes flooded again.

Autumn descended, and Tommy and Nancy checked in regularly with the recovery lab. More than a year had passed since the mission to Palau, and Emery had not been back. The divers were still manufacturing a metal cradle to stabilize the wreckage. Nancy wanted to know how it was coming and when it would be complete. She never had trouble reaching Johnie Webb and she knew he held a lofty position at the lab, but she also knew that Webb hadn't been to Palau himself. Whenever she hung up with him, she felt a step removed from the operation. What she wanted more than anything was to reach the leader of the recovery team. One day in the fall of 2006, she asked Webb if she could.

Eric Emery had to read the email a few times to be sure he understood. It was the public affairs officer wanting to know if he would speak with a relative of the B-24 crew. As far as Emery knew, that was a pointless question. He'd never been allowed to speak with a family member before, and he'd always believed it was forbidden. At a personal level, he was happy to speak with a family. The reason he'd come into the unit was to provide answers for them. But he knew family contact was Johnie Webb's domain, and the rules were strict. He sent the email up the chain of command, asking how he should respond. To his surprise, he got an email from the lab's scientific director saying it was okay to speak with the Doyles.

Emery called Tommy and Nancy in Snyder, but he found himself mostly listening. There was so much he didn't know. He'd never heard about their trip to Palau, just days before the recovery began, and he was stunned to hear the rumors about Tommy's dad. The one part of the plane he couldn't reach, Emery explained, was the tail turret. It was the whole reason he'd called off the recovery, and the reason he was building the cradle. Now the cradle was nearly finished, and he was heading back in a few weeks. The next part of the plane he planned to explore was the tail turret. If Tommy's dad was in there, Emery would find him.

Emery watched the cargo plane unload on Babeldaob with the Doyles on his mind. "Once you make that connection," he said, "you know these people are waiting and hoping, and you start to wait and hope as well." But as the divers put the stabilizers in place, the hope faded fast. They pulled back a layer of sand, then another, and another, but all they found was more sand. Where the tail turret should have been mounted on the plane, all that remained were two bolt holes. The turret was missing.

Emery was no longer confined to the monitor. He had used the two-year break to enroll at hard-hat dive school. To train, he awoke at 5 a.m. each day and spent two hours running and lifting weights. Then he worked out another hour each night, watching his diet and losing weight, building cardiovascular and muscular strength. He'd graduated from the school with kids half his age, and now he could join the hard-hat divers working below the barge. He made daily, sometimes hourly, trips down, excavating deep into the sediment, but the turret was simply gone. "We cleaned that sucker from top to bottom," Emery said. "It just wasn't there."

Near the end of the tail, Emery spotted something odd. There were small wrinkles in the aluminum skin, almost as though the turret had twisted off. From the direction of the wrinkles, it seemed most likely that it would have landed on the far side of the coral with the nose and cockpit. "It was twisted counterclockwise," Emery said, "so I'm thinking that will put me straight over to the other side, which is where the forward section of the airplane is." But as the divers moved to the other side, filling baskets of debris from the nose and cockpit, they found everything but the tail turret. "We were digging and digging, and finding great stuff," Emery said—arm and leg bones, shoes and buttons, coins, and even a pair of aviator sunglasses.

Emery extended the trip. Then he extended it again. In total, he would spend three months on the site, finding bones until the end. "We were removing remains and diagnostic material evidence up until the day we left," he said. Yet as he climbed aboard a transport jet for the flight to Hawaii, Emery felt a certain emptiness hanging over him. He had once asked Jon Faucher why, on that day in the Andes, he dove into the icy water with his back broken in two places, to pull Emery's body from the sunken chopper, and Faucher told him, "I didn't want to face your parents and tell them I did nothing." For Emery, the fear had become his own. As he watched the islands drop away from the plane, he dreaded his next conversation with Tommy Doyle.

"There was a lot riding on this," he said later. "By the time I left, I was placing personal pressure on myself to produce results for the Doyles."

SIXTEEN

TRAPPED

Pat Scannon couldn't stop thinking about the parachutes. Since finding the plane underwater, he'd only become more determined to locate the men who weren't on it. Yet trying to track down individual airmen was even more daunting than trying to find the plane. For one thing, a man's body made an awfully small target. For another, Scannon couldn't be sure how many of those men there were. Most wartime records—including the consolidated mission report, the squadron report, and the missing aircrew report—described two parachutes in the sky. Scannon had also spoken with a gunner on the mission who recalled seeing two parachutes, and who produced a tiny journal in which he'd written: "Plane in B-1 got shot down over target. Two guys bailed out."

Then again, the Palauan witnesses to the crash weren't so sure. It was either two or three parachutes, they said, and Scannon took both possibilities seriously. After fifteen years on the islands, he knew that the first-hand account of a Palauan witness could be more accurate than the official reports. Sure, those reports were written right after the crash, while the memory was sixty years old, but you had to consider the context. The mission reports were based on the testimony of terrified airmen who had been fighting to stay alive. A Palauan like Ricky Speis, by contrast, had seen the crash from a familiar patch of jungle, overlooking islands and waterways he'd known all his life. In hindsight, Scannon wished he had given more credence to Speis in 2002, when he pointed at the crash site, instead of spending another two years on the channel. It wasn't a mistake he was likely to make again.

Scannon's research at the National Archives also suggested the likelihood of three survivors. Internal Japanese documents seized after the war listed Art Schumacher, Alexander Vick, and Johnny Moore as prisoners. According to those documents, all three had been captured, detained, and then shipped to a prison in Davao, Philippines, on a ship called the *Nanshin Maru*. That story was repeated in an Army Casualty Message from December 22, 1945, which even reproduced the Japanese spelling mistakes: "1st Lt. Arthur Schumaker and Sergeants John Moore and Alexander Bick all US Army bailed out B-24 over Koror 1 September 1944, captured, and on 5 September placed aboard *Nanshin Maru*." And a later report by the commander of the Marianas cited the same document. But when the Graves Registration Service was unable to confirm that the *Nanshin Maru* had landed in Davao, the lead investigator simply closed the case.

Scannon found it hard to imagine why the Japanese would exaggerate the number. There was no incentive to claim that they had lost track of more American men than they really had, and there was also no way to explain how else they would have learned the names of all three men. But Scannon didn't buy the story about the *Nanshin Maru*. Shipping prisoners to the Philippines in September 1944 didn't make sense. The islands were under daily assault, commanders were bracing for a ground invasion, and the flow of cargo to and from the islands had long since tapered off. "All the sea lanes were mined, and aircraft patrols were in place," Scannon said. "It just didn't sound right."

The more likely explanation, Scannon believed, was that the men had been executed. Ever since he'd learned of the mass grave on Police Hill, he wondered how many Americans might be there. He knew that, by September 1944, the kempei were killing their prisoners routinely. There was no reason to think they would have spared American prisoners the same treatment they dispensed to Jesuit priests.

As Eric Emery returned from the 2007 mission with a cache of bones and artifacts, Scannon turned his attention back to the mass grave. Bill Belcher's monthlong dig had found nothing, and now they weren't even sure they had been looking in the right area.

Each year, Scannon received dozens of calls from volunteers who wanted to join the effort, and two of the newest team members specialized in archival research. He was struck by how often such people appeared just as he was beginning to need them. Dan O'Brien and the skydivers materialized just in time to bring a new level of focus to the team. Flip Colmer brought his command experience from the Navy to help manage the growing roster—allowing Scannon to step aside, as he had at Xoma, and become part of the organization he'd built. And as the team discovered a raft of new planes, including the Avengers and Corsairs, Reid Joyce swept in to build an online database for archival materials.

Now there were two new volunteers who lived near the National Archives, and whose talents intersected neatly.

Katie Rasdorf was a former Marine who loved nothing more than to scour the archives for documents that no one else could find. Where the rest of the BentProp team would often return from the archives with a stack of documents that another member had already seen, Rasdorf had a way of locating records that nobody knew existed. She came back to the archives week after week, befriending the staff, learning the intricacies of the file structure, and photographing hundreds of documents, which she uploaded to the team website for Mark Swank to read.

Swank was a wry, compact man with mischievous eyes and an alarm-
ing memory. Most of his friends in suburban Maryland knew him as the
owner of a dive bar called the Crofton Cantina, which was plopped alongside a highway. Most nights, Swank could be found at the bar with his
wife, Dreama, either watching Nascar on television or beating his cus-
tomers at pool and darts. But Swank also had a second job that was less
apparent. By day, he worked for the Defense Intelligence Agency in a job
he would only describe as "boring" and "technical" before quickly changing the subject. Whether or not the job was boring, it was clearly important. Over the next few years, he would disappear for months at a time to
do classified work on military bases in Afghanistan. Wherever he went,
Swank brought a personal laptop filled with BentProp files. A visitor who
found him in the cantina on any given Thursday would notice that, somewhere around midnight, he would put down his pool cue and settle into a
corner to read, his face lit up by the digital images of mission documents
and bomb-run photography.

One day, nosing through Rasdorf's files, Swank noticed a series of
documents he'd never seen before. Like the files Don Shuster discovered
in 1999, they were transcripts and statements from the war crimes
tribunals—but there were hundreds of new ones and they included star-
tling details. In page after page, the Japanese kempei described their
crimes against civilians, islanders, and the Jesuit priests. Some of them
drew maps of the mass grave with ominous phrases like "place where
prisoners squatted down" and "where we buried the bones."

Sitting in the corner of his bar, Swank opened a new word processing
file and began to take notes on the new files. Then he overlaid the new
maps with satellite imagery of Babeldaob, trying to discern where Sadae
Inoue had placed his division headquarters, and where the kempei-tai
would have hidden their jungle camp. Swank had never been to Palau, and
he knew little about the Pacific Islands. But he began to develop a close
familiarity with the Japanese soldiers who had lived there. He memorized

their names and military backgrounds, studied their medical histories, and in some cases, even discovered psychiatric evaluations by Allied doctors.

Next, Swank began to compare each soldier's depositions and testimony over a period of months, to see whose story was consistent and who he should believe. The officers, he realized, were the least reliable sources. From month to month, major details of their stories would change. Swank believed this was because they knew they would be held accountable for what happened under their command. The enlisted men confessed more freely, offering the same details again and again. They described a rash of executions through the summer of 1944, peaking in September, when a B-24 crashed in the water and three airmen were captured. The airmen had been taken to division headquarters, kept in isolation, and interrogated for several days by division guards. In 2008, Swank called Scannon with a theory about what happened next.

EVEN THE MOST CONSISTENT KEMPEI had a hard time remembering dates. After three years in Allied custody, some of them placed the B-24 crash in mid-August, while others believed it was mid-September. But there was one Japanese soldier who remembered everything in detail.

In a series of interviews at Sugamo prison during 1947 and 1948, Fourteenth Division guard Toshio Watanabe offered dates, times, and descriptions that Swank, sixty years later, could verify with US Army documents. The three captured airmen, Watanabe said, were stationed with "the Wakde American Air Forces Unit" and reached Palau at "about 1100 on the first of September." This was only six minutes earlier than the time listed in Army records. After the crash, Watanabe continued, "three aviators came down in parachutes." They landed in the water "southwest of Babeldaob island," and were scooped up by Japanese troops. After being paraded through military stations on Koror, they arrived at division headquarters on Babeldaob, where Watanabe watched them arrive. He even remembered their positions. "One was an officer," he said, "one was a photographer, and one was a machine gunner."

The first evening, Watanabe went on, the guards locked them inside an empty barracks. Night was falling, and the full moon glowed through an open window as the airmen huddled together on the floor. Another Japanese soldier who visited the prisoners that night recalled them "sitting in a room at the end of the long barracks with their hands tied together and they were wearing blindfolds. There were three sentries standing guard, and the sentries seemed to be giving the prisoners water and cigarettes. Food was given to them which consisted principally of dry bread."

As night passed, the sentries traded one-hour shifts. During one shift, a private named Sekio Seki noticed small cuts and lacerations on the men. "There was a burn on the back of the head of one," he said, and because there was no medic or first-aid equipment, Seki "dampened a towel with my mouth and wiped that area gently. As there were small wounds on the hands and arms beside that one, I treated those places in the same way. When this was finished, the prisoner said, 'Thank you,' in a low voice."

In the morning, Watanabe returned to the barracks with the head of Inoue's interrogation program, Toshihiko Yajima, and a Japanese civilian who worked at the Palau Girls' School and spoke English. Over the next three days, Watanabe and Yajima interrogated Schumacher, Moore, and Vick. The airmen made no effort to withhold information. Just two weeks earlier, a special liaison had flown to Los Negros from Washington, DC, expressly to advise the Long Rangers on what to do if they were captured. After the presentation, one pilot described the instructions like this: "If we are lucky enough to survive a parachute jump into the jungle, or a ditching at sea, and unlucky enough to be captured by the Japanese, we will live longer if, (a) we tell our interrogators everything they want to know that we are entitled to know in our particular jobs, because they probably already know all about that sort of thing; and, (b) can string together a sweaty and lengthy account of our real or imagined sexual prowess, a subject that presumably fascinates the Japanese. A uniformed emissary of rank came all the way from Washington to tell us this."

Schumacher, Moore, and Vick followed the instructions. The chief interrogator would later recall that the men knew little of strategic value, but shared what they did know about Wakde and the targets they were instructed to hit on Koror. "I learned about the organization of their airport," Yajima recalled, "and also the intention of their bombing forces." After three days of questioning and little to show for it, Yajima called off the interrogation. He left the airmen in the division barracks for another two days before, on September 6, he came back with a handful of senior officers, including Inoue's chief of staff, Tokuchi Tada, and the leader of the kempei, Aritsune Miyazaki.

The group arrived at 1:30 p.m. and strode to the end of the building where Schumacher, Moore, and Vick were still crouched together on the floor with their hands tied behind their backs. No sooner had the Japanese commanders arrived than they were interrupted by the shouts of a junior officer, who raced into the building with news that US bombers were coming.

With only seconds to react, the officers raced to the building's air raid shelter, while the guards scurried behind them, pushing with Schumacher, Moore, and Vick. There was a long, tense wait in the shelter as a formation of B-24s laid waste to the surrounding camp. Yajima, Tada, and Miyazaki squeezed against the wounded, filthy American prisoners inside the bunker. Finally, when the raid was over, everyone spilled out. A disgusted Tada barked to Yajima, "Suspend the investigation of the three aviators and deliver them to the kempei-tai." Then he turned to Miyazaki: "I request the three prisoners be executed."

"I acknowledge," Miyazaki replied.

To deliver the prisoners to the kempei, Yajima assembled a small detail of division soldiers. They piled into the back of a truck and followed a winding dirt road to the jungle camp. Miyazaki was already there, assembling an execution team. According to one kempei soldier, Giichi Sano, Miyazaki had come back from the air raid shelter with blunt orders. "Miyazaki said to me, 'The division headquarters has asked us to dispose, meaning execute, the three American aviators,'" Sano recalled.

To lead the execution party, Miyazaki appointed the head of the Criminal Section, Kazuo Nakamura. As with most kempei, Nakamura's health was declining on the islands. His syphilis was so debilitating that he'd been confined to bed for several weeks, but he strapped on his sword and called out for several of his men to join him.

One of those men, a sergeant named Yoshimori Nagatome, was outside in the garden. "I was slowly beginning to recover from yellow jaundice," he recalled, "and went for a walk in the garden in front of the barracks with my coat off. At this time, First Lieutenant Nakamura said, 'Oi, Nagatome, put on your coat and shoes and come immediately.' Therefore I put on those clothes and went out. Then as he said, 'Put on your belt and come on,' I went back to the barracks again, went out with my belt, and thinking that we were going somewhere, went out to the road in front of the kempei-tai to see." At the road, Nagatome found Miyazaki waiting in a car. The division truck idled nearby. "The prisoners were sitting with their backs against the cab of the truck," Nagatome said, "and between them were the soldiers of the division headquarters holding on to the rope and standing up between them." As Nagatome climbed into the bed of the truck, he sat down facing the prisoners. Another kempei, Chihiro Kokubo, sat beside him, carrying the small wooden box with the ashes of his friend, Ikushima.

Dusk was falling as the execution party rolled down the narrow road from the jungle barracks. The enlisted men sat silently in the back of the truck. The sky was clear and the moon huge on the horizon, casting shadows in the silver light. Miyazaki's car led the way, turning left onto the main road and heading north for a mile before turning right to climb Police Hill. At the summit, Miyazaki crept down the ridge road and stopped at the edge of a clearing. He stepped from the car and motioned for the enlisted men to join him.

"We came to a wide grassy field and got out," one of the division guards recalled.

"All personnel got off the truck," Nagatome added.

Miyazaki ordered the men to follow and walked to the edge of the jungle, stepping forward into darkness. The kempei soldiers trailed behind, followed by the division guards dragging the blindfolded prisoners. Several yards in, Miyazaki stopped. "A hole three meters long, and one and half meters wide, had been dug," Nagatome said. Miyazaki ordered the division soldiers to release the prisoners and turn away. When they had, he commanded Nagatome to bring forward the American officer, Art Schumacher. Nagatome pushed Schumacher to the edge of the hole and forced him to kneel. Miyazaki stepped close to Schumacher. "The unit commander lit a cigarette," Nagatome recalled. He took a long draft, then placed the cigarette in Schumacher's mouth. "He had him smoke in front of the hole," Nagatome said, "and when he had taken two or three puffs, the unit commander shot him in the neck from behind."

Schumacher fell. Miyazaki turned. He called for a second prisoner—none of the kempei knew which of the enlisted airmen was Moore and which was Vick—and he ordered Nagatome to force the prisoner to his knees. Then Miyazaki turned to the syphilis-ridden Kazuo Nakamura. "Behead him!" Miyazaki shouted, and Nakamura raised his service sword high, lashing it down on the airman's neck and slicing through the soft tissue and bone in a fatal stroke.

Miyazaki watched the man fall into the hole, then ordered the final airman brought forward. This time, he turned to Chihiro Kokubo, who was standing several yards away, clutching his friend's ashes. "Miyazaki gave orders to me, 'Sgt. Major Kokubo, do it!'" Kokubo said later. "I handed the remains of Ikushima to Sgt. Hongama and placed myself in position. As I hesitated, Lt. Nakamura scolded me, saying, 'Do it quickly.'" Kokubo drew his sword. He held it high, as Nakamura had. "To give myself courage, I shouted, 'This is for Ikushima!'" he recalled. He slammed the sword into the airman's neck, but not hard enough. "The depth of the wound," another kempei said later, "was about the width of the sword blade . . . one third of the neck. Miyazaki said, 'It is not cut,' and fired one or two shots and killed him with his pistol."

It was done. Miyazaki barked, "Bury the bodies," and marched back to his car, where he lit another cigarette and waited for the men to emerge. "When we got out of the jungle," a division guard recalled, "the CO of the kempei-tai said, 'You may return now. When you return, tell Chief of Staff Tada that the execution was done.' We went back together in the automobile. Upon returning to headquarters, I relayed what I was told by Colonel Miyazaki to Colonel Tada. Colonel Tada didn't say anything, but just nodded."

WHILE MARK SWANK sorted through the war crimes documents, Eric Emery prepared for his third trip to Palau. This time he would have six weeks on the site, but he knew they would be his last. Underwater recovery was too expensive to justify more than three years of work.

As Emery's transport jet unloaded on Babeldaob, he watched the Navy divers piling their equipment on trucks. A few of them had been with him the year before, but they knew Emery was a distant figure and merely nodded hello or stopped briefly for a quick handshake. There were nearly three dozen men in total, and they had been traveling ten hours in the gaping cargo hold of the KC-135, where a deafening roar and wildly fluctuating temperatures kept them from sleeping. Now that they were on the ground, they would begin a full day of work.

The lead diver on the mission this time was a man named Rod Atherton, who had been assigned to the job at the last minute and knew virtually none of the men under his command. Atherton was a huge, roguish figure, given to blunt assessments. Like any master diver, he could recite long swaths of diving literature, including lengthy passages from the

Navy dive manual, though he was quick to admit that he believed some parts were mistaken, outdated, and dumb. He was also, in the manner of any good leader, somewhat fluid with the rules.

To begin the mission, Atherton wanted to get a sense of his men, and he gathered a handful of the most experienced divers onto a small boat, guiding it to the coordinates of the wreck. When he had positioned the boat, he stood to face the men. "Here's what I want to do," he said. "I'm gonna stand back and let you dive." He pointed to a man in his thirties named Paul Wotus, whose rank was just a notch below his own. "I want the chief to supervise. I'm gonna see how you do."

Atherton sat down and Wotus stood.

"Chief Wotus has the side," Atherton shouted.

"Chief Wotus has the side," the men called back.

"Okay," Wotus said, pulling a spiral diving handbook from his pocket. He flipped to a pre-dive checklist and began working his way through the items. Had anyone dived that day? Did everyone feel okay? Had they brought all their equipment? Were their tanks and regulators attached? When Wotus had completed the checklist, he instructed two divers to suit up and he inspected their gear, then gave them the okay to splash in.

Atherton stood again. "Now," he said, sounding irritated. "How long did that take you?"

Wotus looked surprised.

"It took you twenty-two minutes," Atherton said. "It should take you seven." He grabbed the spiral notebook from Wotus. "This is you," he said, burying his nose in the pages. "*Mah mah mah wah wah.* Reading into the book. Next time I'm gonna take the book."

"Okay," Wotus said.

"It doesn't matter what the book says," Atherton continued. "You have to know which part is important."

Wotus stared down.

"What was the weather forecast this afternoon?" Atherton asked.

Wotus shook his head.

"It's supposed to rain," Atherton said. "When is high tide?"

Silence.

"Is it coming in or out?"

Nothing.

"I'm not trying to bust your balls," Atherton said finally. "It's the first dive and all that. But I'm gonna get you sharp on this trip. We're gonna work it out."

Atherton sat down and the boat was quiet until one of the divers emerged from the water and climbed on board. Atherton checked the volume of air in his tank and splashed in to see the wreck for himself. He was gone for only a few minutes, but by the time he returned, all the other divers had agreed: being supervised by a hard-ass like Atherton for six weeks, having every move second-guessed, and being untaught the rules of the Navy dive book, was purely a stroke of good luck. There was no greater currency in the Navy diving program than hard, fast experience, and Atherton was the embodiment of it.

When the barge arrived at the site, Atherton climbed aboard, pacing the deck to help his men set up their gear in designated areas. One region would serve as a medical station for the unit physician, Andy Baldwin. Just a few months earlier, Baldwin had completed a season as "the bachelor" on ABC's reality program of that name, but among the divers this was regarded as little more than folly, and Baldwin showed no more sign of his television experience than he did of his status as an officer. After he had set up his medical equipment, he grabbed a broom and began sweeping rainwater from the deck into the sea. Nearby, another group of divers was organizing a container with wetsuits, masks, and fins, while at the far end of the barge, Emery's friend Rich Wills, who had first told him about the lab a decade earlier, assembled a small group of divers to inspect the mooring lines. Emery himself moved easily among the men, pitching in periodically to help, but every few minutes he would return to the edge of the barge and stare down into the water with his face drawn and tight.

When at last all the equipment was ready, he called for the men to join him, pulling a folded scrap of paper from his pocket.

"Before I left I got an email," he said. "I'm going to read part of it to you, so you understand what you're doing here. This is from a football coach whose father was on this plane." Emery unfolded the paper and began to read. "Eric, looks like this is going to be the year that you will finish the excavation. Whatever we find out, we will always be grateful to you. Of course, our first concern is for your safety and for that of your team of divers. You are, and will continue to be, in our thoughts and prayers. Please give our best to your team. Tell your parents that we are thankful to them for raising such fine men."

As Emery refolded the paper, the deck was hushed. Most of the men studied their feet and Emery let the moment linger. Finally, Atherton broke the spell. "Okay," he snapped, "let's bring these boys home!"

And soon the baskets were rising, buckets pouring into the wet-screen station to be sifted.

In the days ahead, as divers moved through the cockpit and nose turret, they would pull up a handgun, a necklace, a gold ring, and a dog tag stamped with the unmistakable word: DOYLE.

SEVENTEEN

CLOSURE

The rolling hills of Arlington National Cemetery sweep above the Potomac River overlooking Washington, DC. On a cool, clear morning in April 2010, the families of the Big Stoop crew gathered at the end of a long grassy field to bury the remains of their dead.

After two years of extensive DNA testing, the lab in Hawaii had found a match for five men: Jimmie Doyle, Jack Arnett, Earl Yoh, Robert Stinson, and Frank "Big Stoop" Arhar. The remains of those five had been returned to their families and buried in local cemeteries. In Ohio, Earl Yoh's brothers laid him to rest in a grave site their parents had chosen six decades earlier, while Earl's childhood friend, the Reverend Paul Miller, presided over a ceremony of twenty-one guns. In Florida, the Arnetts came together in the courtyard of a small church where Jack's brother Marvin, who had flown over the islands in search of his brother, sat in a wheelchair without expression. His mind was fading and he no longer recognized most of his family, but Scannon had arranged for a vintage bomber to fly overhead, and when it roared across, Marvin Arnett snapped upright, pulling his arm into a crisp salute. In Texas, the plane carrying Jimmie Doyle also brought Casey, serving as the formal military escort for his grandfather's final flight. After a short service in Snyder the next morning, the Doyles spilled outside for the thirty-minute drive to Jimmie's grave site in Lamesa, only to discover that the streets were lined all the way: men and women who'd read about Jimmie in the newspaper, waving flags with their children, and girl scouts standing with hand on heart, and the men of the VFW at attention.

Now those families and the other three were gathering at Arlington. This time they would bury all the bones that could not be identified. They would all be laid to rest together under a large gray headstone marked with all eight of their names, and on the green fields of the national cemetery their families would come together for the first time.

They drew in close around a small opening in the ground as bagpipes played against a light wind. In the distance, six white horses pulled a flag-draped casket up the winding road. When the caisson reached the edge of the field, military pallbearers lifted the casket and marched toward the grave. The sun was high and glaring as they lowered the casket into the ground, then turned to face the families. Tommy and Nancy Doyle were there, squinting into the light, and the nieces of Johnny Moore and Jack Arnett, and the president of Palau, Johnson Toribiong, who sat motionless in a tailored gray suit beside the High Chiefs of the islands. Master Diver Rod Atherton had flown in from San Diego, standing shoulder to shoulder with Dr. Andy Baldwin. In the front row, Diane Goulding perched in a small chair, her soft white hair gleaming above an uncertain smile.

They had come to bury not only the dead, but the mystery and wonder. They had come to lay down the stories, rumors, and fear. Some of their mysteries were still unanswered, but that was just the point. They would never know why Tommy's uncles believed his father survived, and they would never know why Jack Arnett led the men on their final mission. Maybe he'd been ejected by his crew, or maybe he'd come forward to volunteer when Norman Coorssen couldn't fly. What the families finally understood was that it didn't matter. It had only mattered for so long because there was nothing else to grasp. Without answers, the mind searched for patterns and clues, for constellations in the stars.

No man's fixation on the plane was more emblematic than Eric Emery's. He had no personal connection to the airmen, and was still unknown to most of the families. Since delivering the final round of remains, he had even withdrawn from the Doyles. Yet his attachment to the plane was deeply also personal. It represented the fulfillment of his quest to build an underwater program, and to deliver for other men and their families what Jon Faucher had given him. Emery saw his personal commitment to the plane as a kind of weakness. He had been trained to keep emotional distance from his work, and he took pride in his ability to do so. Now that that the operation was complete, his professional impulse pulled him back. He would never speak with another family connected to one of his sites; he had not come to Arlington, citing a previous obligation; and within a year, he would no longer work for the military lab—taking a job instead at the National Transportation Safety Board, where he spent most days behind a desk. He had found his own kind of closure in the 453.

As the Arlington ceremony drew to a close, a bugler played taps. The families stared forward in silence at the edge of the grave. Only Pat Scannon stood back. He watched from across a long expanse of grass, in a neat black suit. His hands were clasped behind him, holding a weather-beaten BentProp hat. The 453 would always be with him. It was the plane that launched his search, and that, for years, brought him back to the islands. But he was already leaving it behind.

He had just been to Palau with Mark Swank. For three weeks, they rooted through the underbrush with a team of nine volunteers, searching for a sign of the kempei jungle camp. Finally, as they tromped through ankle-deep mud one afternoon, along the bank of a small stream, they spotted a fragment of white porcelain near the top of a tree, and, recognizing it as a wire insulator, followed it to a second, then a third, chasing the trail downstream until they reached a clearing pitted with foxholes.

The clay of Babeldaob, as always, had preserved the Japanese trenches, and as Swank scrambled between them, he was flooded with recognition. Each contour of the earth aligned with the maps the kempei had drawn. It was the same camp where Allied bombs killed Chihiro Kokubo's friend, and where Kokubo burned his remains and tucked the ashes in a wooden box. It was the camp where, a few days after that, division soldiers arrived with Schumacher, Moore, and Vick, and where the execution party piled into the truck. Swank and Scannon had traced the route the convoy followed, and in a few months Scannon would return to continue looking for the mass grave. In his mind, he was already drifting back to the islands and the low, moldering aroma, the poison trees, the bats and caves, the gleaming turquoise water.

There was a spot on the water just north of Peleliu that always caught his eye. It was a tiny splash of brilliant green that glowed against the cerulean sea, and it sometimes seemed to Scannon like an eye that gazed back at him from the water. He hoped to have his ashes scattered there one day. His friends could throw them into the air and watch them settle upon the surface, lingering briefly before drifting down through filtering sunlight. When they reached the bottom they would blanket the sand and merge with the coral seafloor, so that in his final place he would be one with the islands, forming a bed to cradle the men that he had never found.

BIBLIOGRAPHY

Alexander, Joseph H. *Utmost Savagery: The Three Days of Tarawa.* Annapolis, MD: Naval Institute Press, 1995.

Alexander, R. McNeill. *Bones: The Unity of Form and Function.* New York: Macmillan, 1994.

———. *Human Bones: A Scientific and Pictorial Investigation.* New York: Pi, 2005.

Arakaki, Leatrice R., and John R. Kuborn. *7 December 1941: The Air Force Story.* Hickam Air Force Base, HI: Pacific Air Forces, Office of History, 1991.

Bahn, Paul, ed. *Written in Bones: How Human Remains Unlock the Secrets of the Dead.* Buffalo, NY: Firefly Books, 2003.

Bailey, Dan E. *WWII Wrecks of Palau.* Redding, CA: North Valley Diver Publications, 1991.

Barnes, Robert C. "Point: Hyperbaric Oxygen Is Beneficial for Diabetic Foot Wounds." *Clinical Infectious Diseases* 43, no. 2 (July 15, 2006): 188–92.

Berg, A. Scott. *Lindbergh.* New York: G. P. Putnam's Sons, 1998.

Bergerud, Eric M. *Fire in the Sky: The Air War in the South Pacific.* Boulder, CO: Westview, 2000.

Biddiscombe, Perry. "Dangerous Liaisons: The Anti-fraternization Movement in the U.S. Occupation Zones of Germany and Austria, 1945–1948." *Journal of Social History* 34, no. 3 (spring 2001): 611–47.

Birdsall, Steve. *Log of the Liberators: An Illustrated History of the B-24.* Garden City, NY: Doubleday, 1973.

Bobrow, Davis B. "The Civic Role of the Military: Some Critical Hypotheses." *The Western Political Quarterly* 19, no. 1 (March 1966): 101–11.

Boesen, Victor. *Navy Diver: The Incredible Undersea Adventures of a Master Diver.* Lincoln, NE: iUniverse, 2001. First published 1962 by Putnam.

Boss, Pauline. *Ambiguous Loss: Learning to Live with Unresolved Grief.* Cambridge, MA: Harvard University Press, 1999.

———. "A Clarification of the Concept of Psychological Father Presence in Families Experiencing Ambiguity of Boundary." *Journal of Marriage and the Family,* February 1977: 141–51.

———. *Loss, Trauma, and Resilience: Therapeutic Work with Ambiguous Loss.* New York: W. W. Norton, 2006.

———. "The Relationship of Psychological Father Presence, Wife's Personal Qualities, and Wife/Family Dysfunction in Families of Missing Fathers." *Journal of Marriage and the Family,* August 1980: 541–49.

Bowman, Martin W. *Consolidated B-24 Liberator.* Ramsbury, UK: Crowood, 1998.

Britt, Sam S. Jr. *The Long Rangers: A Diary of the 307th Bombardment Group.* Spartanburg, SC: The Reprint Company, 1990.

Browne, Courtney. *Tojo: The Last Banzai.* New York: Holt, Rinehart, and Winston, 1967.

Burdick, Charles, and Ursula Moessner. *The German Prisoners of War in Japan, 1914–1920.* Lanham, MD: University Press of America, 1984.

Campbell, Cathy L., and Alice S. Demi. "Adult Children of Fathers Missing in Action (MIA): An Examination of Emotional Distress, Grief, and Family Hardiness." *Family Relations* 49, no. 3 (2000): 267–76.

Chang, Iris. *The Rape of Nanking: The Forgotten Holocaust of World War II.* New York: Penguin, 1998. First published 1997 by Basic Books.

Clancy, Paul. *Ironclad: The Epic Battle, Calamitous Loss, and Historic Recovery of the USS Monitor.* New York: McGraw-Hill, 2006.

Costello, John. *The Pacific War: 1941–1945.* New York: HarperCollins, 2002. First published 1981 by Rawson, Wade.

Dale, Paul W. *The Discovery of the Palau Islands; or, The Wreck of the* Antelope, *June 1783 to December 1784.* Pittsburgh: RoseDog Books, 2004.

Daws, Gavan. *Prisoners of the Japanese: POWs of World War II in the Pacific.* New York: William Morrow, 1994.

Dawson, Michael N. "Five New Subspecies of *Mastigias* (Scyphozoa: Rhizostomeae: Mastigiidae) from Marine Lakes, Palau, Micronesia." *Journal of the Marine Biological Association of the United Kingdom* 85, no. 3 (June 2005): 679–94.

Detroit News. "Willow Run and the Arsenal of Democracy." January 27, 1997.

D'Olier, Franklin. *Air Campaigns of the Pacific War.* Washington, DC: United States Bombing Survey, 1947.

Elphick, Peter. *Liberty: The Ships That Won the War.* Annapolis, MD: Naval Institute Press, 2001.

Energy Oil Committee, Western Axis Subcommittee. "Estimated Refinery Output in Axis Europe—1943." Fischer-Tropsch Archive.

Escobar, S. J., J. B. Slade Jr., T. K. Hunt, and P. E. Cianci. "Adjuvant Hyperbaric Oxygen Therapy (HBO2) for Treatment of Necrotizing Fasciitis Reduces Mortality and Amputation Rate." *Undersea and Hyperbaric Medicine Journal* 32, no. 6 (2005): 437–43.

Etpison, Mandy T. *Palau: Cultural History*. Koror, Palau: Tkel, 2004.

———. *Palau: Natural History*. Koror, Palau: Tkel, 2004.

Evening Independent (Saint Petersburg, FL). "Beautiful Estate Is Headquarters of Chief Executive." August 11, 1944.

Faith, William Robert. *Bob Hope: A Life in Comedy*. Cambridge, MA: Da Capo, 2003. First published 1982 by Putnam.

Faram, Mark D. "The Best of the Best: Sailors of the Year." *Navy Times*, October 10, 2001.

Fast, Charles, ed. *Havilook Yearbook*. Haviland, OH: Haviland-Scott High School, 1943.

Faust, Drew Gilpin. *This Republic of Suffering: Death and the American Civil War*. New York: Alfred A. Knopf, 2008.

Fausto-Sterling, Anne. "The Bare Bones of Race." *Social Studies of Science* 38, no. 5 (October 2008): 657–94.

Ferguson, Niall. "Prisoner Taking and Prisoner Killing in the Age of Total War: Towards a Political Economy of Military Defeat." *War in History* 11, no. 2 (April 2004): 148–92.

Franklin, H. Bruce. *M.I.A.; or, Mythmaking in America: How and Why Belief in Live POWs Has Possessed a Nation*. Expanded and updated ed. New Brunswick, NJ: Rutgers University Press, 1993.

Gutiérrez, Orlando M. "Recent Insights into Racial Differences in Bone and Mineral Metabolism." *Current Opinion in Endocrinology, Diabetes, and Obesity* 18, no. 6 (December 2011): 347–51.

Hales, Dianne. "I'm Filling in a Page of History." *Parade*, May 28, 2000.

Hallas, James H. *The Devil's Anvil: The Assault on Peleliu*. Westport, CT: Praeger, 1994.

Harvey, Bernard Eugene. "US Military Civic Action in Honduras, 1982–1985: Tactical Success, Strategic Uncertainty." *CLIC Papers*, October 1988: 6–60.

Harvey, Gordon K., and Eugene K. Hamilton. *We'll Say Goodbye: Story of the 307th Bombardment Group*. Sydney, Australia: F. H. Johnston Publishing, 1945.

Hastings, Max. *Retribution: The Battle for Japan, 1944–45*. New York: Vintage, 2009. First published as *Nemesis: The Battle for Japan, 1944–45*. London: Harper Press, 2007.

Hertsgaard, Mark. "The Question Bush Never Got Asked." *Harper's*, September 1993: 44–45.

High, Stanley. "Nimitz Fires When He Is Ready." *The Rotarian*, April 1943: 29–30.

Higuchi, Wakako. "War in Palau, Morikawa and the Palauans." Chap. 13 in *Remembering the Pacific War*, edited by Geoffrey M. White. Honolulu, HI: Center for Pacific Island Studies, University of Hawai'i at Manoa, 1991.

Hochberg, Marc C. "Racial Differences in Bone Strength." *Transactions of the American Clinical and Climatological Association* 118 (2007): 305–15.

Hope, Bob. "Bob Hope's Communique." *Saint Petersburg Times*, September 14, 1944: A6.

Hunter-King, Edna J.. "Children of Military Personnel Missing in Action in Southeast Asia." Chap. 15 in *International Handbook of Multigenerational Legacies of Trauma*, edited by Yael Danieli. New York: Plenum, 1998.

James, Philip B. "Hyperbaric Oxygenation for Cerebral Palsy." *The Lancet* 357, no. 9273 (June 23, 2001): 2052–53.

Johnsen, Frederick A. *Weapons of the Eighth Air Force*. Saint Paul, MN: MBI, 2003.

Johnson, Paul. *Modern Times: The World from the Twenties to the Eighties*. Rev. ed. New York: Perennial Classics, 2001. First published 1983 by Harper & Row. Rev. ed. first published 1991 by HarperCollins.

Keate, George, and Henry Wilson. *An Account of the Pelew Islands*. London: G. Nicol, 1788.

Kidder, Warren Benjamin. *Willow Run: Colossus of American Industry*. Lansing, MI: W. B. Kidder, 1995.

Kobayashi, Kazuo. "Origin of the Palau and Yap Trench-Arc Systems." *Geophysical Journal International* 157, no. 3 (June 2004): 1303–15.

Kratoska, Paul H., ed. *The Thailand-Burma Railway, 1942–1946: Documents and Selected Writings*. London: Routledge, 2006.

LaVoie, Christopher P. *Starkey's Boys: The U.S. Salvage Navy and Navy Deep Sea Diving in the Hawaiian Islands*. Bloomington, IN: AuthorHouse, 2006.

Lindbergh, Charles A. "Aviation, Geography, and Race." *Reader's Digest*, November 1939: 64–67.

———. *The Wartime Journals of Charles A. Lindbergh*. New York: Harcourt Brace Jovanovich, 1970.

Lippincott, Benjamin E. *From Fiji through the Philippines with the Thirteenth Air Force*. San Angelo, TX: Newsfoto Publishing, 1948.

Lonsdale, Mark V. *United States Navy Diver: Performance under Pressure*. Flagstaff, AZ: Best Publishing, 2005.

Looker, Anne C. "The Skeleton, Race, and Ethnicity." *The Journal of Clinical Endocrinology & Metabolism* 87, no. 7 (July 1, 2002): 3047–50.

MacArthur, Douglas. *Reminiscences*. New York: McGraw-Hill, 1964.

MacKenzie, Emmett G. *Ten Men, a "Flying Boxcar," and a War: A Journal of B-24 Crew 313, 1944 to 1945*. Lincoln, NE: iUniverse, 2005.

Manchester, William. *American Caesar: Douglas MacArthur, 1880–1964*. Boston: Little, Brown, 1978.

Mankiller, Wilma Pearl, and Michael Wallis. *Mankiller: A Chief and Her People*. New York: St. Martin's, 1993.

Mann, Robert W., and Miryam Ehrlich Williamson. *Forensic Detective: How I Cracked the World's Toughest Cases*. New York: Ballantine Books, 2006.

Marck, Jeff. "Proto Oceanic Society Was Matrilineal." *The Journal of the Polynesian Society* 117, no. 4 (2008): 345–82.

Moore, Raymond A., Jr. "The Peaceful Uses of Military Forces in Underdeveloped Areas." *The Journal of Developing Areas*, October 1969: 112–19.

Moran, Jim, and Gordon L. Rottman. *Peleliu 1944: The Forgotten Corner of Hell*. Westminster, MD: Osprey, 2002.

Nasmyth, Spike. *2355 Days: A POW's Story*. New York: Orion Books, 1991.

New York Times. "Flood in Arkansas as Big Levee Breaks." January 31, 1927.

———. "Overdose of Pills Kills C. R. Holmes." February 6, 1944.

———. "Pacific War Talks; Roosevelt and Leaders Map Plans for Return to Philippines; A Job for M'Arthur; President Makes Trip in Cruiser, 'Amazed' at Hawaii Change." August 11, 1944: A1.

Norman, Michael, and Elizabeth M. Norman. *Tears in the Darkness: The Story of the Bataan Death March and Its Aftermath*. New York: Farrar, Straus, and Giroux, 2009.

Now You Are an Officer Navigator. Selman Field, Monroe, LA: Army Air Forces Navigation School, 1943.

Odenweller, Dan B. "Known Losses of B-24 Aircraft and Personnel." 307th Bombardment Group archive, 2008.

Parrott, Lindesay. "Yap Attacks Aided Landing on Guam." *New York Times*, July 23, 1944.

Peacock, Daniel J. *Lee Boo of Belau: A Prince in London*. Honolulu: University of Hawai'i Press, 1987.

Peattie, Mark R. *Nan'yō: The Rise and Fall of the Japanese in Micronesia, 1885–1945*. Honolulu: University of Hawai'i Press, 1988.

Perret, Geoffrey. *Old Soldiers Never Die: The Life of Douglas MacArthur*. New York: Random House, 1996.

Petersen, Glenn. *Traditional Micronesian Societies: Adaptation, Integration, and Political Organization*. Honolulu: University of Hawai'i Press, 2009.

Philips, Shine. *Big Spring: The Casual Biography of a Prairie Town*. New York: Prentice-Hall, 1942.

Potter, E. B. *Bull Halsey*. Annapolis, MD: Naval Institute Press, 1985.

Raymer, Edward C. *Descent into Darkness: Pearl Harbor, 1941; A Navy Diver's Memoir*. Novato, CA: Presidio, 1996.

Rosenman, Samuel I. *Working with Roosevelt*. New York: Harper, 1952.

Ross, Bill D. *Peleliu: Tragic Triumph: The Untold Story of the Pacific War's Forgotten Battle*. New York: Random House, 1991.

Sherrod, Robert Lee. *On to Westward: War in the Central Pacific*. New York: Duell, Sloan and Pearce, 1945.

Sledge, E. B. *With the Old Breed: At Peleliu and Okinawa*. Novato, CA: Presidio, 1981.

Sloan, Bill. *Brotherhood of Heroes: The Marines at Peleliu, 1944; The Bloodiest Battle of the Pacific War*. New York: Simon & Schuster, 2005.

Steere, Edward. *The Graves Registration Service in World War II*. Washington, DC: Historical Section, Office of the Quartermaster General, 1951.

Stinnett, Robert B. *George Bush: His World War II Years*. McLean, VA: Brassey's, 1992.

St. John, Philip A. *B-24: The Plane—The People*. Paducah, KY: Turner Publishing, 1990.

Telmetang, Marciana, and Faustina K. Rehuher. *Bai*. Koror, Palau: Belau National Museum, 1993.

Tillman, Barrett. *Whirlwind: The Air War against Japan, 1942–1945*. New York: Simon & Schuster, 2010.

Trefalt, Beatrice. *Japanese Army Stragglers and Memories of the War in Japan, 1950–75*. London: RoutledgeCurzon, 2003.

Tugwell, Rexford G. *The Democratic Roosevelt: A Biography of Franklin D. Roosevelt*. Garden City, NY: Doubleday, 1957.

Walterhouse, Harry F. *A Time to Build: Military Civic Action: Medium for Economic Development and Social Reform*. Columbia: University of South Carolina Press, 1964.

Weber, Austin. "A Historical Perspective." *Assembly Magazine*, August 1, 2001.

White, T. D., and Pieter A. Folkens. *The Human Bone Manual*. Amsterdam: Elsevier Academic Press, 2005.

Wiarda, Howard J. "The Latin American Development Process and the New Developmental Alternatives: Military 'Nasserism' and 'Dictatorship with Popular Support.'" *The Western Political Quarterly* 25, no. 3 (September 1972): 464–90.

Wilson, Peter. *Aku! The History of Tuna Fishing in Hawaii and the Western Pacific*. Bloomington, IN: Xlibris, 2011.

Witts, David A. *Forgotten War, Forgiven Guilt*. Las Cruces, NM: Yucca Tree, 2003.

Wright, Derrick. *To the Far Side of Hell: The Battle for Peleliu, 1944*. Tuscaloosa: University of Alabama Press, 2005. First published 2002 by Crowood.

Zellmer, David. *The Spectator: A World War II Bomber Pilot's Journal of the Artist as Warrior*. Westport, CT: Praeger, 1999.

Zuckoff, Mitchell. *Robert Altman: The Oral Biography*. New York: Vintage Books, 2010. First published 2009 by Alfred A. Knopf.

NOTES

The list of sources for this book could fill several volumes. In the interest of concision, I have refrained from listing in the bibliography every letter, interview, trial transcript, and mission report, which number in the thousands. Instead, I cite here those documents on which the book draws most directly. To avoid redundancy, I note the interview date for each person who is quoted at their first appearance in every chapter. Subsequent quotes in the same chapter are drawn from the same interview, unless otherwise noted. In a few cases, as with Pat Scannon, a scene or description may come from dozens of conversations over many years, and the dates cited in such passages refer specifically to the quoted material. Researchers who are interested in learning more about this story should begin at the BentProp website, bentprop.org, and that of the Long Rangers, 307bg.net. However, there is no substitute for the experience of sifting through the reels of footage, stacks of photographs, and mountains of mission documents at the National Archives, their fading yellow pages a last, best glimpse into the world from which our own emerged.

PROLOGUE

Page 1: *a rumpled archaeologist*: From observation. I joined Emery in Palau for the 2008 recovery mission.

Page 2: *they would marvel*: Interviews with divers, including Andy Baldwin, Rod Atherton, Randy Duncan, Totch Mabry, Paul Wotus, PJ O'Dell, Woody Woodburn, Julius

McManus, Jericho Diego, Cameran Cox, Kenny Bontempo, Nick Zaborski, Josh Lamb, and Mariano Lorde. January–March 2008.

Page 2: *the depths were considered secret*: Navy divers are careful not to discuss recent depth records. However, since at least the 1970s, the Experimental Diving Unit in Panama City, Florida, has conducted extensive tests on the limit of human endurance. One record, set in 1972, pushed a man to 1,000 feet; another, in 1979, sent a team of divers in a simulation tank to the depth equivalent of 1,800 feet. These dives required two and three weeks of decompression, respectively.

Page 2: *Air Force historians trained to identify*: Life-support investigators play a critical role in crash identification. Often, by the time the military locates a missing airplane, the wreckage has been salvaged by locals for scrap metal, and what remains is difficult even to recognize as a plane.

Page 3: *sometimes even the gender or ethnicity*: The skeletal variation by gender, region, and ethnicity is widely documented but still open to some debate. Orlando M. Gutiérrez has shown that these differences are apparent at a young age, suggesting a hereditary basis, while Anne Fausto-Sterling has argued that such discrepancies are mostly a product of environmental conditions. Gutiérrez, 347; Fausto-Sterling, 657.

Page 3: *healing properties of superoxygenated fields*: The subdiscipline of hyperbaric medicine was first developed to address decompression sickness among divers. In recent years, studies have suggested a wider range of applications, including the treatment of diabetic foot wounds, cerebral palsy, and infection by flesh-eating bacteria. Barnes, 188; James, 2052; Escobar, 437.

Page 3: *rose ten thousand feet from the seafloor*: This is a conservative figure. The shallow, western side of the archipelago averages about ten thousand feet, but water to the east, in the Palau trench, is much deeper—approaching twenty-six thousand feet in some areas. Kobayashi, 1303.

Page 4: *The people did not have a creation story; they had many*: The first legend described here is that of Chuab; the second is that of Miladeldil. There is also a creation story about a giant exploding clam, and another about a woman who formed the northern islands with a hibiscus stick and a coconut shell.

Page 4: *Many of the island myths featured women*: Such as the legend of the old woman who caught fish in her breadfruit tree, the woman who taught the islanders about natural childbirth, and the women who turned into mermaids. The Japanese occupation of Palau in the early twentieth century diminished some matrilineal tradition, but women continue to elect tribal chiefs and inherit family titles and land. Petersen, 68; Marck, 345.

Page 4: *a special breed of jellyfish*: The lake, Ongeim'l Tketau, is home to a unique subspecies of the spotted jellyfish, which biologist Michael Dawson has proposed to name *Mastigias papua etpisoni*, after former Palauan president Ngiratkel Etpison. Dawson, 689.

CHAPTER ONE: RUMORS

Page 7: *"it seemed like he never would"*: Interview with Nancy Doyle, March 17, 2008.

Page 9: *From the first day of practice*: According to records at Texas Tech, Tommy Doyle and Dave Parks each made four touchdown receptions in the 1963 season. The three that Tommy caught against Kansas State are listed as both a school and a conference record. Parks became the first overall selection in the 1964 draft, chosen by the 49ers; the following year, Anderson was the seventh overall selection—his $600,000 contract the largest in football history.

Page 10: *"I was just born crooked"*: Interview with Casey Doyle, April 25, 2009.

Page 13: *"At last I can write a few lines"*: Letter from Jimmie Doyle to Myrle Doyle, May 28, 1944.

Page 13: *"My Precious, sure am ready for bed tonight"*: Letter from Jimmie Doyle to Myrle Doyle, May 30, 1944.

Page 14: *"Darling . . . there aren't any words"*: Letter from Jimmie Doyle to Myrle Doyle, May 31, 1944.

Page 14: *"It gives me a feeling of serenity"*: Letter from Jimmie Doyle to Myrle Doyle, July 2, 1944.

Page 14: *"I just couldn't look at them"*: Interview with Tommy Doyle, March 17, 2008.

Pages 14–15: *"I was against my mother bringing all this up"*: Interview with Casey Doyle, April 25, 2009.

Page 15: *a fire in Saint Louis*: The fire, on July 12, 1973, at the National Personnel Records Center in Saint Louis, burned for more than four days and took forty-two fire districts to extinguish. Some sixteen million to eighteen million military personnel records were destroyed.

Page 15: *"I can't tell you any details"*: Letter from Jimmie Doyle to Myrle Doyle, June 25, 1944.

Pages 15–16: *"I have talked to some of the fellows"*: Letter from Lloyd Waits to Myrle Doyle, December 11, 1944.

Page 16: *"the Indiana Jones of military archaeology"*: *Parade* magazine, May 28, 2000: 6.

CHAPTER TWO: WRECKAGE

Page 17: *his wife, Susan, had long since*: Interview with Susan Scannon, July 14, 2011.

Page 18: *working for the king's hospital*: Lambert conducted clinical research at the King Faisal hospital in Riyadh until 1983, when he accepted a position at a World Health Organization laboratory in Lebanon. "The day I was to get on the plane to train for the Lebanon job, the Marine barracks was blown up in Beirut. So they canceled that. Then they wanted me to go to Mogadishu, to run a microbiology clinical lab for the UN. Mogadishu was not a very attractive place, and it was getting worse, so I opted out and took a job at Xoma." Interview with Chip Lambert, August 12, 2012.

Page 19: *There was gold on the islands*: The story of Yamashita's gold is debated everywhere it is discussed, but this much is certain. In 1988, Rogelio Roxas filed suit against Ferdinand and Imelda Marcos in Hawaii state court, claiming that he'd found the gold in 1971 and the Marcos family had, in legal jargon, "converted" the treasure to themselves. In 1996, a jury found in favor of Roxas, awarding him $22 billion, the largest judgment of its kind in history. In 1998, the Hawaii Supreme Court affirmed the verdict, concluding "there was sufficient evidence to support the jury's determination that Roxas found the treasure" and "there was sufficient evidence to support the jury's special finding that Ferdinand converted the treasure that Roxas found." In 2006, the conclusion was affirmed yet again by the United States Court of Appeals for the Ninth Circuit, which wrote, "The Yamashita Treasure was discovered by Roxas and stolen from Roxas by Marcos's men." How much of the Yamashita treasure is still buried, and where, no one knows. *Roxas and the Golden Budha Corporation v. Ferdinand E. Marcos and Imelda Marcos*, Supreme Court of Hawaii: 89 Hawaii 91, 969 P.2d 1209, filed November 17, 1998; *Merrill Lynch, Pierce, Fenner, and Smith, Inc. v. ENC Corporation*, United States Court of Appeals, Ninth Circuit: 464 F. 3d 885, filed May 9, 2006.

Page 19: *Lambert's team had come across photos*: Dan Bailey obtained the photos at a booksigning event in Davis, California, where he happened to have a table near Bush's biographer, Robert Stinnett. "He's looking over at my book, and I'm looking over at his book, and he said, 'You know, I have some information you might find interesting—have you seen these photos before?'" Interview with Dan Bailey, August 15, 2012.

Page 20: *"What we wanted to do"*: Interview with Chip Lambert, August 12, 2012.

Page 20: *scouring the continental shelf for abalone*: Snail diving preoccupies a small but fervent community, among whom Buller is considered one of the best. He has recovered more than two hundred abalone larger than ten inches.

Page 20: *the gear shaft of a sunken destroyer*: Bailey and the Lamberts discovered the Japanese destroyer *Samidare* beside the Ngaruangel reef in 1990. Bailey, 194.

Page 21: *"strong circumstantial evidence"*: The article relied heavily on such innuendo, acknowledging at one point, "The document, as incriminating as it appears to be, doesn't constitute irrefutable proof of guilt. Bush may have a convincing explanation." Hertsgaard, 44.

Page 21: *"the trawler sank within five minutes"*: Mission Report, VT-51, Air Group 51, Task Force 58, July 25, 1944.

Page 22: *a gunner on the mission, who said he couldn't remember*: By 2011, the author of the *Harper's* story took a similar position himself. When asked if the abundant munitions on the ship changed his reading of the mission report, he replied, "I don't recall the details well enough to offer any opinion that could be helpful." Written exchange with Mark Hertsgaard, June 2, 2011.

Page 23: *"If Chip wanted him along"*: Interview with Chip Lambert, August 12, 2012.

Page 23: *"He didn't really contribute"*: Interview with Dave Buller, August 29, 2011.

Page 24: *"Hey!" he cried out to Buller*: Interview with Chip Lambert, August 12, 2012; interview with Dave Buller, August 29, 2011.

Page 25: *None of them doubted*: Interview with Pat Scannon, December 1, 2009; interview with Dave Buller, August 29, 2011; interview with Chip and Pam Lambert, August 12, 2012; interview with Dan Bailey, August 15, 2012.

Page 27: *"This was a four-engine plane"*: Drawn from numerous interviews with Pat and Susan Scannon, as well as Scannon Logs, Book 1.

Page 29: *there wasn't much record of the air campaign*: There still isn't. Although a handful of books have appeared over the last decade, few of them mention the Thirteenth Air Force, which flew the longest missions of the campaign and wrought the most damage on Palau. For example, the 2010 book *Whirlwind: The Air War against Japan, 1942–1945*, refers to the Thirteenth only once, as the "least known of all the air forces that fought Japan." Tillman, 237.

Page 30: *"The bloody, grinding warfare"*: Costello, 497.

Page 31: *"the majority of above-ground buildings"*: Bailey, 117.

Page 32: *"All of a sudden, he's calling all these old guys"*: Interview with Susan Scannon, July 14, 2011.

Page 32: *Everything Scannon could find out*: In time, he would discover four additional B-24 crashes within a thirty-mile radius. See Chapter 13.

Page 33: *"This is the opening of my log"*: Scannon Logs, Book 1, 3.

Page 34: *"Plane down here"*: Missing Air Crew Report #8641, September 2, 1944.

CHAPTER THREE: AIRMEN

Page 37: *"Will the B-24 Ever Replace the Airplane"*: Bowman, 113.

Page 37: *one B-24 . . . on a secret photographic mission*: Two crew members died in the attack, and have been memorialized by the World War II Valor in the Pacific National Monument. "These airmen," the text notes, "arrived in Hawaii two days prior to the attack to outfit their plane for a secret photo mission. They were killed on the ground and their B-24 was destroyed near Hangar 15." The wreckage of that plane is also pictured in Arakaki and Kuborn, 67.

Page 37: *"the armament and armor of the B-24 were inadequate"*: Letter from Jimmy Doolittle to Lieutenant General Barney M. Giles, Army Air Forces chief of air staff, January 25, 1945. Johnsen, 54.

Page 38: *"no curtailment"*: Estimated Refinery Output Analysis, Energy Oil Committee, Western Axis Subcommittee, September 10, 1943.

Page 38: *one of the largest imperia*: The size of an empire can be measured many ways. By population, Japan's empire was about the fifth largest in history, with 135 million subjects. By area, it was the thirteenth largest, with 2.8 million square miles—or twice the territory of Nazi Germany at its peak.

Pages 38–39: *The American conquest of the West*: See, for example, the Indian Removal Act and the Trail of Tears, about which President Martin Van Buren remarked, "No state can achieve proper culture, civilization, and progress in safety as along as Indians are permitted to remain." Mankiller, 93.

Page 39: *more than four hundred people per square mile*: With sixty million people spread across 142,270 square miles, Japan's population density was about twelve times that of the United States. US Census Bureau, 1930. Johnson, 189.

Page 39: *"China was twentieth-century Japan's manifest destiny"*: Chang, 27.

Pages 40–41: *the largest factory in the world*: Willow Run figures compiled from Bowman, Kidder, St. John, and Weber.

Page 41: *"Asiatic intruder"*: Lindbergh had famously argued in 1939, "These wars in Europe are not wars in which our civilization is defending itself against some Asiatic intruder." Berg, 396; Lindbergh, *Reader's Digest*, 65.

Page 41: *"The Willow Run factory is a stupendous thing"*: Lindbergh, *Wartime Journals*, 613.

Page 41: *18,000 models were built*: The precise figure varies by source. St. John explains why: "There were so many modifications of existing aircraft one can easily be trapped into counting one airplane twice (or more times). If we can add up all the B-24 type aircraft built of all models . . . we arrive at a number quite close to 18,500." St. John, 10.

Page 42: *"Relentless. Unceasing. On time"*: The newsreel is posted at http://www.youtube.com/watch?v=SYAEBIywGtg.

Page 44: *"He was my pet"*: Interview with Melba Moore, July 15, 2008.

Page 44: *breached the pages of the* New York Times: *New York Times*, January 31, 1927.

Page 46: *"Earl Yoh leaves his way with women"*: Fast, 17.

Page 46: *"I've been on two gunnery missions"*: Letter from Johnny Moore to Mary Harvey, March 26, 1944.

Pages 46–47: *"If you do not have a sense of humor"*: *Now You Are an Officer Navigator*, 32.

Page 48: *"a broadcasting of resources"*: Hastings, 31.

Page 49: *without a single bag of luggage*: Zuckoff, 50.

Page 50: *"strict, but actually quite warm-hearted"*: Testimony of Michi Inoue, Guam War Crimes Trials, August 5, 1948.

Chapter Four: Discovery

Page 52: *"4:30 pm, over Pacific"*: Scannon Logs, Book 1, 22.

Page 53: *"Travel—Overnight—Ugh—Jet lag"*: Scannon Logs, Book 1, 22.

Page 54: *"I can help you," Mad said*: I have based the scenes and dialogue in this chapter on repeated interviews with Scannon and on his log, Book 1, 22–70.

Page 56: *"It was almost too much"*: Scannon Logs, Book 1, 67.

Page 60: *"On both the Custer and Dixon sites"*: Scannon Logs, Book 1, 69.

Page 61: *"a secret voyage to China"*: Peacock, 13.

Page 64: *"I tried to hear the anti-aircraft rapid fire"*: Scannon Logs, Book 1, 61.

Page 64: *"Arnett—needs to be found"*: Scannon Logs, Book 1, 136.

CHAPTER FIVE: LANDFALL

Page 66: *By the end of May*: The description of Los Negros is drawn from letters, journals, unit history reports, and published accounts, including Zellmer, 76–87.

Page 66: *"the South Pacific island I dreamed of"*: Zellmer, 67.

Page 67: *beer and cigarettes made up roughly 70 percent*: The adjutant reported the value of the unit's full inventory at $32,000. "However, all we turned over to the island was $9,000 worth of stock. The rest of the stock was in beer and cigarettes which they would not take. At the liquidation we had the second-largest inventory on the island. The beer, cigarettes, and tobacco that the island PX could not buy, will be rationed out to the enlisted men free." Monthly History Report for June 1944, 307th Bombardment Group, Major Saul C. Weislow, adjutant.

Page 67: *"they'd sell wounded parrots"*: Interview with Al Jose, April 23, 2009.

Page 67: *"one of those big lizards"*: Letter from Jimmie Doyle to Myrle Doyle, June 8, 1944.

Page 68: *a studious air that belied a limited education*: Interviews with Diane Corrado, August 26–27, 2008.

Page 71: *"Do you remember when"*: Letter from Jimmie Doyle to Myrle Doyle, May 31, 1944.

Page 71: *"I go to the show about three times a week"*: Letter from Jimmie Doyle to Myrle Doyle, June 15, 1944.

Page 71: *"Now that," he said, "is real service"*: Letter from Jimmie Doyle to Myrle Doyle, June 16, 1944.

Page 72: *"The attack on the Palaus"*: Peattie, 290.

Pages 72–73: *"With operational control"*: Lippincott, 97.

Page 73: *"This move seemed to symbolize"*: Harvey and Hamilton, 64.

Page 73: *"the most important single target"*: Parrott, July 23, 1944.

Page 74: *"These men are men"*: Faith, 165.

Page 75: *"It was almost a caste system"*: Interview with Helen Coorssen, April 23, 2009.

Page 76: *"'Gee, that's the front line'"*: Interview with Gary Coorssen, April 22, 2009.

CHAPTER SIX: ARNETT

Page 81: *laughing at bombs away*: In a pinch, the men took a more direct approach, opening the bomb bay doors, squatting on the catwalk, and relieving themselves directly into the wind. Occasionally this got messy. Zellmer, 78.

Pages 82–83: *"Crew voted him out"*: Scannon Logs, Book 1, 82.

Page 83: *"The Pacific isn't exotic to me"*: Interview with Susan Scannon, July 14, 2011.

Page 84: *"I want you to take the door off"*: Interview with Pat Scannon, November 14, 2011.

Page 85: *"like we had gone into prehistoric times"*: This scene is drawn primarily from an interview with Pat Scannon, December 3, 2008, and an interview with Chip and Pam Lambert, August 12, 2012.

Page 86: *"I learned from ninety-six"*: Interview with Pat Scannon, August 18, 2011.

Page 87: *"It was skydiving for the sake of skydiving"*: Interview with Pat Scannon, September 22, 2011.

Page 87: *He cracked open the front*: Scannon Logs, Book 2, inside cover.

Page 89: *"there's an empty chair at the dinner table"*: Interview with Pat Scannon, December 5, 2009.

Page 90: *"'We have data on this, but no theory'"*: Interview with Pauline Boss, July 9, 2012.

Page 91: *"Unlike the Holocaust"*: Hunter-King (ed. Danieli), 254.

Page 92: *"I learned more about my dad"*: Interview with Tommy Doyle, March 17, 2008.

Page 93: *"flirting with the wives and daughters"*: Interview with Pat Scannon, September 10, 2011.

Chapter Seven: Pledge

Page 96: *"thrown by the hundreds"*: Faust, 102.

Page 96: *"When he asked, 'Any scars'"*: Sledge, 5.

Page 98: *"I said, 'Well, I'm not interested'"*: Interview with Johnie Webb, December 8, 2008.

Page 102: *"you didn't need to be certified"*: Interview with Eric Emery, March 14, 2008.

Page 106: *"He was gray . . . and his eyes were open and fixed"*: Interview with Jon Faucher, April 10, 2008.

Chapter Eight: Combat

Page 110: *Early on the morning of June 24*: Mission Report, 424th Bomb Squadron, 307th Bombardment Group, June 24, 1944.

Page 113: *"First time I was ever away"*: Letter from Johnny Moore to Mary Harvey, July 11, 1944.

Page 114: *"The only thing that saves boys out here"*: Hope, A6.

Pages 114–15: *"Darling . . . you know how very glad"*: Letter from Jimmie Doyle to Myrle Doyle, July 5, 1944.

Page 115: *"He had too much time"*: Browne, 184.

Page 117: *"The Joint Chiefs reflected the general confusion"*: Manchester, 148.

Pages 117–18: *"increasingly spoke of himself"*: Manchester, 145.

Page 118: *a small fortune acquired illegally*: Perret, 271.

Page 118: *The Blackfeet Indians*: Manchester, 311.

Page 118: *"the humiliation of forcing me"*: Manchester, 363.

Page 119: *"Nimitz conceived of war as something"*: Sherrod, 234.

Page 119: *"a cross between a Jules Verne fantasy and a whale"*: High, 30.

Page 119: *"a mean little dog which growled"*: Hastings, 28.

Page 120: *"one lone figure—MacArthur"*: Rosenman, 456.

Page 120: *"to keep him occupied"*: Wilson, 50.

Page 120: *hosting stars and starlets like Amelia Earhart and Shirley Temple*: The description of Holmes and his mansion is drawn mostly from the *New York Times* and the *Evening Independent*. The *Times* wrote in Holmes's obituary, "Mr. Holmes had one of the most beautiful estates in Hawaii, built on a small island off the windward shore of Oahu. There he gave elaborate parties, outdoing even the famous luaus of the former Polynesian rulers of Hawaii. In recent years, however, he had become somewhat of a recluse. He kept a fleet of speed boats in which he dashed about Hawaiian waters at all hours of the day and night, dressed unconventionally in a loin cloth or wrap-around skirt." *New York Times*, February 6, 1944.

Page 121: *"did not believe that if Mr. Roosevelt"*: Lahey added, "I am putting this on record, I am asking that it be witnessed, sealed, and placed in safe keeping. It is to be opened and utilized only in the event that there might be criticism of me should this later eventuate and the criticism be directed at me for not having made this public." Memorandum by Dr. Frank Lahey, July 10, 1944.

Page 121: *"Physically he was just a shell"*: MacArthur, 199.

Page 121: *"Where do we go from here?"*: Details of the Hawaii conference were recalled differently by various participants. I have tried to avoid details in dispute, but when a choice must be made, I rely on the great William Manchester biography *American Caesar*. Manchester, 368.

Page 121: *"Nimitz put forth the Navy plan"*: MacArthur, 197.

Pages 121–22: *"All of my American forces"*: MacArthur, 197.

Page 122: *"I felt that to sacrifice the Philippines"*: MacArthur, 197.

Page 122: *arguing since early summer*: Halsey's fierce objection to the Palau invasion peaked in September, but it first took shape in June, when, according to biographer E. B. Potter, he argued presciently that "US carrier aircraft could readily neutralize the Palaus" and "the advantages of capturing them . . . would not offset the cost." Potter, 272.

Page 122: *"key point"*: Unlike Halsey, commanders in the Army Air Forces would continue to describe Palau as a vital territory until the end of the war. It was only in later years that conventional wisdom came to support Halsey. "Thirteenth Air Force Command History," January 1945.

Page 122: *Roosevelt announced in the morning*: Exactly when and how Roosevelt told his commanders is unclear. The decision had yet to be ratified by the Joint Chiefs in

Washington, but most evidence suggests that Roosevelt gave MacArthur the go-ahead before he left Hawaii. Just hours after MacArthur's plane took off, Manchester writes, the president announced to reporters, "We are going to get the Philippines back." Tugwell reports that when MacArthur returned to general headquarters in Australia, he "electrified the GHQ staff by telling them that Roosevelt was backing his strategy." Manchester, 370; Tugwell, 407.

CHAPTER NINE: CONTACT

Page 124: *1949 war crimes trial of Sadae Inoue*: Three kempei soldiers—Kazuo Nakamura, Chihiro Kokubo, and Yoshimori Nagatome—were prosecuted for murder and neglect of duty in January 1948. In March 1949, Inoue and his chief of staff, Tokuchi Tada, were prosecuted for "Violation of the Law and Customs of War." National Archive Record 1661897; Navy JAG Case Files 162658 and 168346.

Page 125: *"They said if they ever met up"*: Scannon Logs, Book 3, 49.

Page 126: *"I always have a very, very deep, deep level of skepticism"*: Interview with Bill Belcher, December 8, 2008.

Page 130: *"if you skydive a thousand jumps"*: Interview with Pat Scannon, August 18, 2011.

Page 132: *Nora's family had sufficient money*: The House of Esterházy, from which Scannon's mother is descended, is one of the leading noble families in Hungary.

Pages 133–34: *still illegal for a US soldier*: Biddiscombe, 611.

Page 134: *Whether or not that story*: The Scannon children have never been able to confirm the Göring story. Interview with Pat Scannon, June 10, 2011; interview with Harriet Scannon, July 12, 2012.

Page 134: *a staple of scholarly studies*: For example, Bobrow, Moore, Wiarda, and Bernard Harvey. Moore wrote, "The concept of military civic action was first developed fully by Harry Walterhouse in *A Time to Build*."

Page 135: *"There wasn't a lot of joy"*: Interview with Harriet Scannon, July 12, 2012.

CHAPTER TEN: WASTELAND

Page 139: *"Here I am at last"*: Letter from Ted Goulding to Carman Graziosi, July 31, 1944.

Page 139: *"We sure got dunked"*: Letter from Jimmie Doyle to Myrle Doyle, August 5, 1944.

Page 140: *"I have read everything in the paper"*: Letter from Jimmie Doyle to Myrle Doyle, August 2, 1944.

Page 140: *"Why, on a clear day"*: Philips, 4.

Page 140: *"Sorta got the blues in a way*: Letter from Jimmie Doyle to Myrle Doyle, July 12, 1944.

Page 140: *"Where is this farm of Tracy's?"*: Letters from Jimmie Doyle to Myrle Doyle, June 25, 1944; July 2, 1944; July 14, 1944.

Pages 140–41: *"Tell Gladys it's a good thing"*: Letters from Jimmie Doyle to Myrle Doyle, June 4, 1944; June 15, 1944; June 29, 1944.

Page 141: *"She keeps him in a state"*: Letter from Jimmie Doyle to Myrle Doyle, July 14, 1944.

Page 141: *"When he gets the blues"*: Letter from Jimmie Doyle to Myrle Doyle, July 14, 1944.

Page 142: *"Six months ago I got married"*: Letter from Johnny Moore to Mary Harvey, August 4, 1944.

Page 142: *the most intimate details of his life*: Some of the officers who volunteered for censor duty took more than a passing interest in the men's mail. Pilot David Zellmer, a dancer from the Martha Graham Dance Company in New York, became fascinated during his shifts as a censor by the letters from one enlisted man to the famous French pianist Robert Casadesus. Zellmer, 76.

Page 142: *"The officers that censor our mail"*: Letter from Ted Goulding to Carman Graziosi, August 6, 1944.

Page 142: *"You should have seen us bombing"*: Letter from Johnny Moore to Gilbert Harvey, August 9, 1944.

Page 142: *"I have shot down one Jap ship"*: Letter from Jimmie Doyle to Myrle Doyle, August 11, 1944.

Pages 142: *"Our pilot told us"*: Letter from Johnny Moore to Mary Harvey, August 11, 1944.

Page 142: *"Roosevelt and Leaders Map Plans"*: *New York Times*, August 11, 1944, A1.

Page 143: *some eight hundred languages*: Recent estimates put the number at 848. See www .ethnologue.com/country/PG.

Page 143: *sprinkled with Japanese holdouts*: On mainland New Guinea, holdouts continued to emerge until the mid-1950s; on the islands nearby, they stayed much longer. In 1974, a student named Norio Suzuki was trekking through the Philippine jungle when he came across one Japanese officer, Hiroo Onoda, who was still waiting for orders to leave his post; when Suzuki returned a few months later with Onoda's wartime commander, Onoda finally stood down. That same year, on Morotai Island just northwest of New Guinea, another holdout named Teruo Nakamura emerged after thirty years in the jungle. Trefalt, 77, 146, 160.

Page 144: *$666.66 a month*: Lindbergh, *Wartime Journals*, 621.

Page 144: *human test subject at the Mayo Clinic*: Lindbergh, *Wartime Journals*, 721.

Page 144: *a "loyal friend of Hitler"*: Berg, 436.

Page 145: *his mother, Evangeline, had been on a cruise ship*: Lindbergh, *Wartime Journals*, 873.

Pages 145–46: *"the largest and most modern office"*: June 18, 1942, report by Brigadier General R. J. Marshall, MacArthur Museum Brisbane.

Page 146: *his best guess was about 700 miles*: The extended range of the P-38 would lead to some controversy, as Air Force bomber units began to insist that fighters join them for long-range missions. For the September missions to Palau, the Long Rangers would not receive fighter coverage, but by October, the P-38s would play a crucial role in the unit's assault on Balikpapan. Lindbergh, *Wartime Journals*, 873; Berg, 452; and the writings of Pat Ranfranz, former historian of the 307th Bombardment Group, at charleslindbergh.com.

Page 146: *"MacArthur said it would be a gift from heaven"*: Lindbergh, *Wartime Journals*, 873.

Page 147: *"It banks frantically left"*: Ibid., 891.

Page 147: *"I think of Anne—of the children"*: Ibid., 892.

Page 148: *Lindbergh was to stop*: Ibid., 904.

Page 148: *"Wrecked planes lined"*: Ibid., 907.

Pages 148–49: *"Wakde resembles no island"*: Zellmer, 97.

Page 149: *"Wakde had recently been taken"*: Monthly History Report, 424th Squadron, 307th Bombardment Group, Captain Jack Vanderpoel commanding.

Page 149: *"hopped a landing barge for the mainland"*: Britt, 124.

Page 150: *"Johnny is making fun"*: Letter from Jimmie Doyle to Myrle Doyle, August 19, 1944.

Page 151: *went in the drink*: Sam Britt reports "a number of planes" hitting the water, but most veterans put the figure at one or two. Britt, 126.

Page 151: *"It was an ass-pucker"*: Interview with Al Jose, April 23, 2009.

CHAPTER ELEVEN: SECRET POLICE

Page 152: *"making the Palaus expendable"*: Peattie, 291.

Page 153: *"All residents of the Palau islands"*: Higuchi, 148.

Page 154: *"Bombers attacked. Barracks were burned"*: Journal of Aritsune Miyazaki, August 26, 1944. National Archives document 27432G.

Page 155: *"Morikawa, Roosevelt's spy"*: Higuchi, 151.

Page 155: *"how to cultivate tapioca"*: Higuchi, 153.

Page 156: *"near total abandonment of the Japanese"*: Peattie, 300.

Page 156: *little oversight from Sadae Inoue*: As Inoue's staff officer Toshihiko Yajima later put it, "The South Seas Kempei-tai at that time was not under the command of the Fourteenth Division and in the Palaus, therefore, the South Seas Kempei-tai was of equal status with the Fourteenth Division." Cross-examination of Toshihiko Yajima, March 30, 1949. National Archive Records, 1661897; Navy JAG Case File 168346.

Page 156: *"The unit commander liked to talk"*: Witness Statement of Keishiro Imaizumi, June 18, 1947, Guam War Crimes Trials, Evidence Files, Palau Case #3.

Page 157: *Born on a farm just west of Hiroshima*: Many of the Japanese soldiers were interviewed by reporters, doctors, and psychiatrists during the war crimes prosecution. I have drawn extensively on these interviews, and the men's own testimony at trial. Here, the information about Nakamura comes primarily from the account of his personal physician, and from Nakamura's own declaration at trial. Testimony of Chisato Ueno, Guam War Crimes Trials, January 14, 1948. Testimony of Kazuo Nakamura, Guam War Crimes Trials, January 26, 1948.

Page 157: *"chase us subordinates with his sword"*: Testimony of Kazuo Nakamura, Guam War Crimes Trials, January 26, 1948.

Page 158: *a sergeant from the southern tip of Japan*: Yoshimori Nagatome's petition to the court, Sugamo prison, December 25, 1947; Interview Report of Hoshio Yokoi, April 22, 1947; Witness Statement of Yoshimori Nagatome, April 23, 1947, Guam War Crimes Trials, Evidence Files, Palau Case #3.

Page 158: *"I always experienced loneliness"*: Personal Declaration of Chihiro Kokubo, Guam War Crimes Trials, January 26, 1948.

Page 158: *the crude and primitive conditions*: Kokubo recalled, "We had to move our headquarters in order to escape the devastating American bombings. In order to move into the jungle, we had to do hard work such as moving materials, building living quarters, making air raid shelters and other work, so we were all exhausted from this." Personal Declaration of Chihiro Kokubo, Guam War Crimes Trials, January 26, 1948.

Page 159: *"There is no kempei-tai in the whole world"*: Miyazaki added that the number of prisoners "is increasing by four or five daily," including those who stole food and clothing, and "uncooperative idlers." Speech by Aritsune Miyazaki to Korean workers on Babeldaob, May 9, 1945. Transcript printed May 9, 1945, in the *Victory Daily News*.

Page 159: *ten times as likely to be killed*: Fewer than 3 percent of American POWs died in Nazi captivity; roughly 30 percent of American POWs died in Japanese hands. Ferguson, 186.

Page 160: *"Tapatau had many specialists"*: Burdick and Moessner, 75.

Pages 160–61: *"every prisoner should receive a gift"*: Burdick and Moessner, 12.

Page 161: *"the Japanese mind"*: Iris Chang notoriously waded into this territory in *The Rape of Nanking*, a flawed work that nevertheless contains extraordinary revelations about the Japanese atrocities in that city. Chang, 54.

Page 161: *"the Japanese ordered Tang"*: Chang, 85.

Pages 161–62: *twelve thousand Americans*: Norman and Norman, 60.

Page 162: *A quarter of those men died*: Most prisoners on the Death Railway were British, Dutch, and Australian. Mortality figures are still in dispute, but I have used the most common estimates. For differing accounts, see Kratoska, 13.

Page 162: *"the present condition of affairs"*: Browne, 146.

Page 162: *"a Western wall of race and arms"*: Lindbergh, *Reader's Digest*, 65.

Page 162: *"Their desire is to exterminate the Jap"*: Lindbergh wrote these words while camped on the New Guinea satellite island of Owi. Across a three-mile strip of water, he could see the cliffs of Biak Island, where a handful of Japanese troops held back an overwhelming Allied assault for weeks. "If positions were reversed," Lindbergh wrote, "and our troops held out so courageously and well, their defense would be recorded as one of the most glorious examples of tenacity, bravery, and sacrifice in the history of our nation." Lindbergh, *Wartime Journals*, 879.

Chapter Twelve: Last Days

Page 165: *"Griping and grousing are prevalent"*: Monthly History Report for August 1944, 424th Squadron, 307th Bombardment Group, Captain Jack Vanderpoel commanding.

Page 165: *Vanderpoel led the unit's first mission*: This account draws on the 424th Squadron's mission report for August 23, 1944, but also the account Vanderpoel gave to Pat Scannon about the mission.

Page 166: *"Johnny and I went swimming"*: Letter from Jimmie Doyle to Myrle Doyle, August 23, 1944.

Page 166: *"Sis, if you can send me some camera film"*: Letter from Johnny Moore to Mary Harvey, August 23, 1944.

Page 166: *"dreadful looking"* . . . *"ugly ducklings"*: Elphick, 19.

Page 167: *"Bob, I was one of those lucky guys"*: Faith, 165.

Page 167: *Hope himself cracked wise in baggy fatigues*: This scene is drawn from several sources, including the memories and journals of airmen from the Long Rangers, film footage stored at the National Archives, photos and recollections in the Long Ranger keepsake volume *We'll Say Goodbye* (84), Hope's written account in his syndicated column, and the biography *Bob Hope: A Life in Comedy* (165).

Page 168: *"23 B-24s attacked"*: Journal of Aritsune Miyazaki, August 26, 1944. National Archives document 27432G.

Page 168: *wrapped inside the white handkerchief*: The story of Ikushima's remains was recounted by every man on the execution detail. At trial, Kokubo explained, "Much has been said about the ashes of my deceased friend. Such things are worshiped by the Japanese. I am just an ordinary person." Personal Declaration of Chihiro Kokubo, Guam War Crimes Trials, January 26, 1948; Witness Statement of Chihiro Kokubo, July 22, 1947; Witness Statement of Yoshimori Nagatome, November 13, 1947; Statement of Giichi Sano, December 11, 1947; Witness Statement of Genshiro Hayashi, January 12, 1948, Guam War Crimes Trials, Evidence Files, Palau Case #3.

Page 169: *"as big as a hat"*: Journal of William Edward Shivers, 372nd Bomb Squadron, 307th Bombardment Group. Courtesy of Pat Ranfranz, Missing Air Crew Project.

Page 169: *two of the Liberators collided*: According to the mission report, "35 miles from the target . . . as the squadron entered a frontal zone these two aircraft were seen to enter a cloud low and to the right. . . . On emerging from this cloud, one aircraft was seen to explode into two pieces and go down in flames. . . . Pilot saw the second ship impact of explosion and turn over on its back." Mission Report, 372nd Bomb Squadron, 307th Bombardment Group, August 25, 1944.

Page 169: *A third . . . simply disappeared*: According to a witness statement in the after-action report, the pilot "feathered all engines and nosed the ship down and disappeared into a cloud bank about 2,000 feet below us. This was the last we saw of Airplane #596." Missing Air Crew Report #8873, August 26, 1944.

Page 169: *"Watched tanks and boats shell"*: Journal of William Edward Shivers, 372nd Bomb Squadron, 307th Bombardment Group. Courtesy Pat Ranfranz, Missing Air Crew Project.

Page 169: *flying the long route to Yap*: Pilot David Zellmer of the 371st Squadron wrote, "All the while, one stares out at the vast, barren, blue-green sea, aching for the sight of a ship, even some floating debris, to dissemble the monochrome seascape." Zellmer, 68.

Page 169: *Lightning cracked and turbulence shook*: Mission Reports, 372nd Bomb Squadron, 424th Bomb Squadron, 307th Bombardment Group, August 28, 1944.

Page 170: *"How far below base"*: This scene drawn from multiple sources, including Mission Reports, 372nd Bomb Squadron, 424th Bomb Squadron, 307th Bombardment Group, August 28, 1944; Journal of Al Jose, 424th Bomb Squadron; Journal of William Edward Shivers, 372nd Bomb Squadron; Missing Air Crew Report #15302, August 29, 1944; Britt, 127.

Page 171: *"Commanding officer of 372nd"*: Journal of Al Jose, 424th Bomb Squadron.

Page 171: *"That boy still doesn't realize"*: Letter from Jimmie Doyle to Myrle Doyle, August 28, 1944.

Pages 171–72: *lost more than forty men*: The planes that collided on August 25 carried eleven men each, the Fifth group plane that disappeared the same day carried ten, and the Dixon crash on August 28 claimed eleven—for a total of forty-three casualties in four days. Two members of the Fifth crew may have survived the crash and been captured by the Japanese. The BentProp Project is investigating that loss.

Page 172: *"This war is beginning to get rough"*: Monthly History Report for August 1944, 307th Bombardment Group, Major Saul C. Weislow, adjutant.

Page 172: *"How is everyone at home?"*: Letter from Earl Yoh, August 31, 1944.

Pages 172–73: *"Sweet . . . my mind is nearly a blank tonight"*: Letter from Jimmie Doyle to Myrle Doyle, August 31, 1944.

Page 173: *They gathered at the airstrip*: This scene is drawn from dozens of sources, most notably the following: Mission Reports, 372nd Bomb Squadron, 424th Bomb Squadron, and 307th Bombardment Group (Consolidated), September 1, 1944; journal of Al Jose, 424th Bomb Squadron, September 1, 1944; journal of William Edward Shivers, 372nd Bomb Squadron, September 1, 1944; film footage of Wakde Island, September 1, 1944, National Archives; Missing Air Crew Report #8641, September 2, 1944.

Page 173: *He was scheduled to fly*: Interview with Cindy Campora, August 3, 2012.

Page 174: *two members of that crew, and the wife of a third*: They are Jack Pierce, Dick Johnson, and Jim Raysor's wife, Martha.

Page 174: *"He was bossy"*: Interview with Jack Pierce, August 6, 2012.

Page 174: *"He thought he was better than the rest"*: Interview with Martha Raysor, August 6, 2012.

Page 175: *Another pilot, Charles McRae, had been sidelined for weeks*: McRae's crew had been flying temporarily with an older pilot, Carl Appling, who was finishing up his tour. Interview with Greg Babinski, June 12, 2012.

Page 175: *Twice . . . he was forced to turn back*: Mission Reports, 424th Bomb Squadron, 307th Bombardment Group, July 3 and 10, 1944.

Page 176: *a close cousin*: Interview with Carolyn Arnett Rocchio, October 14, 2009.

Page 176: *their mama's pet*: These and many details about Jack Arnett come from his mother's keepsake journal, "A Book without an Ending."

Page 177: *"When we first got there"*: Interview with Al Jose, April 23, 2009.

Page 179: *"Palau is hell"*: Journal of William Edward Shivers, 372nd Bomb Squadron, 307th Bombardment Group. Courtesy Pat Ranfranz, Missing Air Crew Project.

CHAPTER THIRTEEN: BREAKTHROUGH

Page 180: *at least four others*: In addition to the original three, there were two B-24s that collided on August 25, one that disappeared the same day, and one that vanished on September 2.

Page 181: *"I want to express my sincere gratitude"*: Letter from Jim Jones to Pat Scannon, April 17, 2002.

Page 183: *"The bulb went off"*: Interview with Flip Colmer, April 25, 2009.

Page 185: *"What do you think these are?"*: Interview with Pat Scannon, December 4, 2008; interview with Flip Colmer, April 25, 2009.

Page 187: *"1100—Now on Pacific"*: Scannon Logs, Book 7, 4.

Page 187: *"'Maybe this guy is crazy'"*: Interview with Joe Maldangesang, February 23, 2009.

Pages 189–90: *"I was on the hill at Aimeliik"*: For this scene and several others, I have relied on footage provided by Dan O'Brien and Jennifer Powers of the BentStar Project.

Page 191: *"They found something!"*: Quote taken from BentStar footage, as noted above.

Page 191: *"I was not letting go!"*: Interview with Jennifer Powers, March 4, 2008.

Page 193: *"I finally got the answer"*: Journal of Reid Joyce, January 26, 2004.

Page 193: *"It was pure joy"*: Interview with Bill Belcher, December 8, 2008.

Page 195: *"What a lucky day!"*: BentStar footage.

CHAPTER FOURTEEN: FALLOUT

Page 197: *third-bloodiest week*: The only comparable periods were July 6 to 13, 1943, when the unit lost five planes, and July 13 to 19, 1944, when the unit lost six. Odenweller, 6.

Page 198: *"My father didn't talk much"*: Interview with Eric Vanderpoel, June 18, 2012.

Page 198: *"It is my regrettable duty"*: Letter from Jack Vanderpoel to Katherine Moore, September 28, 1944.

Page 198: *He promised himself:* Interview with Cindy Campora, August 3, 2012.

Page 199: *"I won't say she abandoned the baby":* Interview with Paul Graziosi, August 29, 2012.

Page 199: *travel aboard the* Titanic: Interview with Ted and Bev Goulding, August 28, 2008.

Page 200: *"I thought he had amnesia":* Interview with Diane Corrado, née Goulding, August 26, 2008.

Page 200: *"Everything is so uncertain":* Letter from Diane Goulding to Myrle Doyle, September 20, 1944.

Page 200: *"I got another letter from Diane":* Letter from Katherine Moore to Myrle Doyle, March 15, 1945.

Page 201: *"you did get more of Jimmie's things":* Letter from Katherine Moore to Myrle Doyle, March 15, 1945.

Page 201: *"Mama said she lost them both":* Interview with Melba Moore, July 15, 2008.

Page 201: *he made a detour over Palau:* Interview with Millie Arnett, September 30, 2009.

Page 202: *"That was his biggest regret":* Interview with Cindy Campora, August 3, 2012.

Page 202: *"It is doubtful that a more dangerous":* Britt, 138.

Page 202: *"This turn back . . . was made due to pilot illness":* Mission Report, 424th Bomb Squadron, 307th Bombardment Group, October 3, 1944.

Page 203: *"he lost his nerve":* Interview with Greg Babinski, June 12, 2012; also, notes taken by Babinski during interview with Jack Vanderpoel, August 19, 2004.

Page 203: *"He wore the same outfit":* Interview with Gary Coorssen, April 22, 2009.

Page 203: *"Always blue, always a Pontiac":* Interview with Helen Coorssen, April 23, 2009.

CHAPTER FIFTEEN: RECOVERY

Page 206: *"'I'm not reading what I'm reading'":* Interview with Nancy Doyle, March 17, 2008.

Page 215: *"brain surgery with a chain saw":* Interview with Eric Emery, March 14, 2008.

Page 215: *"Sailor of the Year":* The award had previously been given to SEALs and EOD bomb disposal technicians. Faram, 2.

Page 218: *"You go to these meetings":* Interview with Tommy Doyle, March 17, 2008.

Page 218: *"I probably had hundreds of dreams":* Interview with Paul Graziosi, August 29, 2012.

Page 218: *"It would play over and over":* Graziosi's written remembrances carry the title "1936 Oldsmobile" in honor of Ted's coupe.

Page 219: *"The darker the night, the brighter they shine":* Letter from Dessie Arnett to Myrle Doyle, September 10, 1945.

Page 219: *"She believed he was alive":* Interview with Carolyn Arnett Rocchio, October 14, 2009.

Pages 219–20: *"I received a letter from the War Department":* Letter from Diane Goulding to Myrle Doyle, September 20, 1944.

Page 220: *"No, no, that letter is yours":* Interview with Nancy Doyle, March 17, 2008.

CHAPTER SIXTEEN: TRAPPED

Page 223: *"Two guys bailed out"*: Journal of Al Jose, 424th Bomb Squadron, September 1, 1944.

Page 224: *"1st Lt. Arthur Schumaker"*: From Casualty Message No. 356093, PAC, December 22, 1945. The misspellings of Schumacher's and Vick's names originated with the Japanese, who first named the three men in a telegraph sent to Tokyo command on September 9, 1944. This telegraph was later surrendered in a memo from Vice Admiral Ito Kenzo to Brigadier General Ford Rogers, September 19, 1945.

Page 224: *the lead investigator simply closed the case*: The June 12, 1947, report found that "the fliers were captured and on 5 September 1944 were placed aboard the NANSHIN MARU for Davao. All efforts to trace the fliers from this point have met with negative results. No further investigation will be conducted by this office. The case is closed."

Pages 224–25: *"All the sea lanes were mined"*: Interview with Pat Scannon, June 10, 2011.

Page 226: *"place where the prisoners squatted down"*: Witness Statement of Genshiro Hayashi, January 12, 1948, Guam War Crimes Trials, Evidence Files, Palau Case #3.

Page 226: *"where we buried the bones"*: Witness Statement of Harukichi Iwamoto, December 2, 1947, Guam War Crimes Trials, Evidence Files, Palau Case #3.

Page 227: *"about 1100 on the first of September"*: Witness Statement of Toshio Watanabe, December 15, 1947, Guam War Crimes Trials, Evidence Files, Palau Case #3.

Page 228: *"sitting in a room at the end"*: Witness Statement of Hideo Ishizuka, January 19, 1948, Guam War Crimes Trials, Evidence Files, Palau Case #3.

Page 228: *"the prisoner said, 'Thank you'"*: Interview Report of Sekio Seki, January 29, 1948, Guam War Crimes Trials, Evidence Files, Palau Case #3.

Pages 228–29: *"If we are lucky enough to survive"*: Zellmer, 93.

Page 229: *"I learned about the organization"*: Testimony of Toshihiko Yajima, Guam War Crimes Trials, January 20, 1948, 44.

Page 229: *After three days of questioning*: The same day that Yajima called off questioning, the Long Rangers sent their final search plane to look for the missing crew. Pilot David Zellmer recorded in his journal, "No rafts, no floating oxygen bottles, no torn strips of aluminum, no oil slicks; only the blue-gray Philippine Sea from horizon to horizon and the pencil-line coast of Babeldaob in the distance. Could the men have been picked up by the Japanese? Would we ever know? We crept back to Wakde in the silence of our failure." Zellmer, 102.

Page 229: *on September 6*: The date is disputed by Japanese soldiers who were present. Some believe the air raid and execution took place on the fourth or fifth of September. I have gone with the sixth because it is the date recalled by Watanabe, whose memory was correct on so many other details. Witness Statement of Toshio Watanabe, December 15, 1947, Guam War Crimes Trials, Evidence Files, Palau Case #3.

Page 229: *"Suspend the investigation"*: Testimony of Toshihiko Yajima, Guam War Crimes Trials, January 20, 1948, 44.

Page 230: *"Miyazaki said to me"*: Witness Statement of Giichi Sano, December 11, 1947, Guam War Crimes Trials, Evidence Files, Palau Case #3.

Page 230: *Nakamura's health was declining*: As noted earlier, the description of Nakamura comes from his own testimony and that of his personal physician. Testimony of Chisato Ueno, Guam War Crimes Trials, January 14, 1948; testimony of Kazuo Nakamura, Guam War Crimes Trials, January 26, 1948.

Page 230: *"I was slowly beginning to recover"*: Witness Statement of Yoshimori Nagatome, November 13, 1947, Guam War Crimes Trials, Evidence Files, Palau Case #3.

Page 230: *"The prisoners were sitting"*: Testimony of Yoshimori Nagatome, Guam War Crimes Trials, January 25, 1948, 88.

Page 231: *"We came to a wide grassy field"*: Witness Statement of Sekio Seki, January 29, 1948, Guam War Crimes Trials, Evidence Files, Palau Case #3.

Page 231: *Schumacher fell*: There is some disagreement between Japanese soldiers about the sequence of the killings. I have gone with the most common account, which has Colonel Miyazaki killing Schumacher first, officer to officer, with a gun, before ordering the two beheadings.

Page 232: *"'This is for Ikushima'"*: Witness Statement of Chihiro Kokubo, July 22, 1947, Guam War Crimes Trials, Evidence Files, Palau Case #3.

Page 232: *"The depth of the wound"*: Witness Statement of Giichi Sano, December 11, 1947, Guam War Crimes Trials, Evidence Files, Palau Case #3.

Page 232: *"Bury the bodies"*: Witness Statement of Genshiro Hayashi, January 12, 1948, Guam War Crimes Trials, Evidence Files, Palau Case #3.

Page 233: *"Here's what I want to do"*: From observation. I was with Atherton and the Navy divers for this.

ACKNOWLEDGMENTS

This book began as an article for *GQ* magazine, where I spent many happy years as a writer. Under the guidance of Jim Nelson and Andy Ward, there seemed no subject too peculiar or provocative, and if there was any limit to the time and travel one could spend on a story, I would like to meet the reporter who found it. Certainly I tried. Most articles began with a simple question and ballooned wildly from there. In this case, I happened to read a news item about a US soldier whose remains were discovered on a construction site in Belgium, and, wondering what might happen to those remains, I suggested we poke around. Two weeks later, I was strapped to the sidewall of a KC-135 transport jet on military travel orders, at the start of a journey that would eventually cross sixty thousand miles and lead to this book. The notion that any part of that journey has been a "job" or "work" seems alien; with editors like Jim, Andy, and now Geoff Kloske at Riverhead, it is quite simply the most fun thing I can imagine doing, every single day. Even when it's cold, dark, heartbreaking, and involves eating bat soup.

So many people offered time and help that it's embarrassing to consider them all at once. My thanks go first to the families of the missing, who shared their painful, personal memories, even when my questions must have seemed spectacularly trivial, like the color of the drapes. I am especially grateful for the trust and patience of Tommy and Nancy Doyle; Ted and Bev Goulding; Diane Corrado; the Moore family, including Melba, Leta Boone, Tamara Newsom, and Charles Harvey; Millie Arnett and Carolyn Arnett Rocchio; Gary and Helen Coorssen; Dale and Bob Yoh; Leona Frederick; Arne Schumacher; and Richard Stinson.

Dozens of veterans of the 307th Bombardment Group tried to help me comprehend the war, the islands, the bombers, the bases, and the fragile tenor of the airman's life in a world that was often unimaginable even to them. I owe a special debt to Al Jose, who flew missions with the Big Stoop boys and vividly described their camp on Wakde and their final, fateful flight. Relatives of the 307th also shared crucial documents and details, including Jay Cosgrove, Dottie McGill, Martha Raysor, Jack Pierce, Cynthia Campora, Eric Vanderpoel, John Rodwick, and the president of the 307th reunion group, Jim Walsh.

Navy deep-sea divers are a special set. To a man, the members of the 2008 recovery mission devoted their personal time to help me understand the operation as it unfolded on the seafloor. Particular thanks to Master Divers Rod Atherton and Totch Mabry; Diving Medical Officer Andy Baldwin; and Warrant Officer Randy Duncan. Hooyah, gentlemen.

The photographer Tim Hetherington also joined the 2008 mission, taking some of the most beautiful images of Palau that I have ever seen, including the cover of this book. What those photos cannot capture is the overwhelming generosity Tim brought to his work, and the instant trust the men had in him. Tim was an extraordinary reporter, and I benefitted enormously from his insights and observations. I did not know him well or long; I wish I had.

The work of Pauline Boss is indispensable to anyone interested in the distinctive character of MIA grief, and Boss herself was an invaluable guide as I tried to grasp the enduring pain of families and the stories I kept hearing from them.

No American has done more to bring home missing service members than Johnie Webb. Over the past forty years, he has helped to build the Joint POW/MIA Accounting Command into one of the world's great humanitarian missions. With tens of thousands still missing, there is no shortage of work remaining, but all it takes is a connection with one family to appreciate how precious that work is. My thanks to Johnie and everyone at JPAC—George Mitroka, Rich Wills, Byron Johnson, Bill Belcher, Tom Holland, Chris McDermott, James Pokines, Robert Mann, Elias Kontanis, and Denise To—but most especially Eric Emery, without whom this book and its story would not have happened.

The National Archives in College Park, Maryland, contain two billion cubic feet of records. Trying to locate the ten thousand pages relevant to this story would have been impossible without the guidance of Rich Boylan and Katie Rasdorf of NARA and Cashwell LLC, respectively. Their early introduction to the file system and structure of the archive, from the top floor to the underground stacks, informed every visit I made.

Hunter Chaney at the Collings Foundation went far beyond any reasonable request by allowing me to climb into the nose turret of the last working B-24J and fly across open water for a glimpse of the world I was trying to describe. The foundation is a national treasure.

Countless writers nudged, nagged, nurtured, and inspired me throughout this process. Some, like Nathaniel Philbrick and Winston Groom, reminded me through their work that it was possible to write a complex history with story and character at the fore. I've tried to do justice to their example. Others, like Michael Paterniti and Philipp Meyer, took precious time from their own deadlines to read an advance copy of this book and offer generous thoughts. The great Mark Bowden materialized unexpectedly one day in my office while I was struggling with a passage to drink a few beers and offer writing wisdom I'll never forget. My friend Michael Downs gave me a late, careful, and invaluable read. Throughout, my friend and editor at the *New York Times Magazine*, Joel Lovell, has been a font of patience and good sense. And my friend Andy Ward came through, as ever, in the clutch—offering a secluded idyll to draft the final pages, for which I cannot possibly express enough thanks.

At its core, this is a story about family, and my own has been a wellspring of encouragement and support through months of travel and long nights writing. Jenny, Liam, Sylvie, I love you.

Every member of the BentProp Project contributed time and insight to this book, but Reid Joyce, Flip Colmer, Dan O'Brien, and Jennifer Powers deserve special mention. Reid is the wizard behind the BentProp team archive, which was a constant resource. Flip led me through the jungle and sea on a diet of

Spam, Oreos, and relentless good cheer. And Dan and Jennifer directed the touching documentary *Last Flight Home* about BentProp, sharing countless hours of their outtake footage so that I might witness these events in color. Their nonprofit foundation, BentStar, helps finance BentProp, and anyone interested in supporting this work should visit bentstarproject.org.

Finally, Pat Scannon. Words fail. I first heard the name whispered in the Palau night, and looking back, a whisper seems right. In twenty years of reporting, I have never encountered anyone like Pat, who spent hundreds of hours sharing the details of his story, while insisting at every turn that it wasn't his story at all, but part of something much larger and deeper that would only become clear to me with time. He was right, and it has. I am donating a portion of the proceeds from this book to support the ongoing search in Palau.

IMAGE CREDITS

Cover: Palau island. Photograph by Tim Hetherington.

Frontispiece: The Big Stoop crew, July 11, 1944 (back: Robert Stinson, Ted Goulding, Jimmie Doyle, Johnny Moore, Leland Price, Earl Yoh, Mario Campora; front: Norman Coorssen, Frank Arhar, Art Schumacher). Courtesy of Tommy and Nancy Doyle.

Maps: Drawn by Aaron Becker.

Prologue: Navy divers in Palau, 2008. Photograph by Christopher Perez, courtesy of JPAC.

Chapter One: Jimmie Doyle, 1943. Courtesy of Tommy and Nancy Doyle.

Chapter Two: Pat Scannon on a Corsair in Palau. Courtesy of Flip Colmer.

Chapter Three: The Big Stoop crew in B-24 training, Tonopah, Nevada, May 1944. Courtesy of Gary Coorssen.

Chapter Four: The Arnett map. Courtesy of the National Archives.

Chapter Five: Tent City, Los Negros Island. Courtesy of the National Archives.

Chapter Six: Jack Arnett, 1943. Courtesy of Carolyn Arnett Rocchio.

Chapter Seven: A POW/MIA flag. Courtesy of the National League of POW/MIA Families.

Chapter Eight: B-24 bombers on a mission over Palau. Courtesy of the National Archives.

Chapter Nine: A BentProp challenge coin. Courtesy of Pat Scannon.

Chapter Ten: Wakde Island. Courtesy of the National Archives.

Chapter Eleven: Kempei-tai commander Aritsune Miyazaki. Courtesy of the National Archives.

Chapter Twelve: Bob Hope on Wakde, August 25, 1944. Courtesy of the National Archives.

Chapter Thirteen: The white spots. Courtesy of the National Archives.

Chapter Fourteen: Johnny Moore's empty grave. Photograph by Wil Hylton.

Chapter Fifteen: A Navy diver prepares to splash. Photograph by Christopher Perez, courtesy of JPAC.

Chapter Sixteen: Scannon scours a cave for evidence. Courtesy of Katie Rasdorf.

Chapter Seventeen: The burial caisson at Arlington. Courtesy of Flip Colmer.